This book represents the most rigorous, social-scientific study to date demonstrating that neither urban environments themselves nor the change in modern societies from predominantly rural to urban "causes" crime. Focusing on Germany between 1871 and 1914, the period of its industrial revolution and emergence as a world power, this volume explores crime patterns, criminal justice institutions and practices, and popular and elite attitudes toward crime, criminals, and criminal justice authorities.

Criticizing as largely conservative and elitist in origin the notions that cities cause crime, the book demonstrates that the real roots of crime in German society are to be found in a mix of economic hardship, ethnic bias, and political repression – conditions that conscious political decisions, law, and legal officials either can help overcome or indeed can make even worse. In examining how the crime drama was played out in Imperial Germany, the book credits German law, judges, police, and populace for their technical expertise, high intellectual level, and orderly nature. It also indicts them for launching Germany on a dangerous path that would allow German judges and police in the mid–twentieth century to claim that they were acting only in the well-respected tradition of legal positivism.

Urbanization and Crime

Urbanization and Crime

GERMANY 1871–1914

ERIC A. JOHNSON
Central Michigan University

PUBLISHED BY THE PRESS SYNDICATE OF THE UNIVERSITY OF CAMBRIDGE
The Pitt Building, Trumpington Street, Cambridge, United Kingdom

CAMBRIDGE UNIVERSITY PRESS
The Edinburgh Building, Cambridge CB2 2RU, UK
40 West 20th Street, New York NY 10011–4211, USA
477 Williamstown Road, Port Melbourne, VIC 3207, Australia
Ruiz de Alarcón 13, 28014 Madrid, Spain
Dock House, The Waterfront, Cape Town 8001, South Africa

http://www.cambridge.org

© Cambridge University Press 1995

This book is in copyright. Subject to statutory exception
and to the provisions of relevant collective licensing agreements,
no reproduction of any part may take place without
the written permission of Cambridge University Press.

First published 1995
First paperback edition 2002

A catalogue record for this book is available from the British Library

Library of Congress Cataloguing in Publication data
Johnson, Eric A., 1956–
Urbanization and crime: Germany, 1871–1914 / Eric A. Johnson.
p.   cm.
Includes index.
ISBN 0 521 47017 X (hardback)
1. Crime – German – History – 19th century. 2. Crime prevention –
Germany – History – 19th century. 3. Crime justice,
Administration of – Germany – History – 19th century. 4. Urbanization –
Germany – History – 19th century. I. Title.
HV6973.J64   1995
364.943–dc20   94-45503 CIP

ISBN 0 521 47017 X hardback
ISBN 0 521 52700 7 paperback

For my mother,
Frances Elizabeth Barrett Johnson

Contents

Preface		page ix
Introduction		1
1	The Criminal Justice System: Safe Streets in a Well-organized Police State	15
	The Criminal Law and the Criminal Code	22
	The Police	30
	Courts, Criminal Procedure, Judges, and Attorneys	39
	Punishment	48
2	Popular Opinion: Crime as a "Foreign" Concept	53
	Newspapers and Crime	55
	A Comparison of Four Berlin Newspapers	61
	Crime in the Socialist Press	75
	Crime in the Conservative Press	78
	Crime in the Liberal Press	83
	Crime in Middle-Class Magazines	88
	Crime in German Literature	95
	Conservative and Moderate Writers	96
	Left-Liberal Writers	102
	Conclusion	106
3	Long-Term Trends: The Modernization of Crime and the Modernization of German Society?	109
	Modernization and Crime?	110
	Yearly Crime Trends Prior to Unification	116
	Yearly Crime Trends in Imperial Germany	120
	Trends in Violent Crime	126
	Trends in Property Crime	134
	Explanations of Yearly Crime Trends and Conclusions	137
4	Urban–Rural Differences, Ethnicity, and Hardship: Cities Are Not to Blame	145

vii

	Regions	147
	Urban–Rural Differences and Urbanization	158
	Hardship and Ethnicity	171
5	Criminals and Victims: The Crucial Importance of Gender	183
	PART I: CRIMINALS	184
	Gender	184
	Age	191
	Marital Status	198
	Religion	201
	Social Standing/Occupation	206
	PART II: VICTIMS	212
	Urbanization, Ethnicity, and Religion	217
	Age and Marital Status	223
	Means of Death	226
	Conclusion	226
6	Conclusion: Crime Rates, Crime Theories, and German Society	229
Index		239

Preface

It is fitting that I finish this book in one of Germany's greatest cities on a day of joy and celebration. For, despite some recent concerns about the reemergence of German nationalism, attacks on foreigners, and even rising rates of urban crime, I have always enjoyed myself fully and felt quite secure and very much at home in German cities. Their sensible organization, clean streets, ample parks, good transportation systems, and bountiful amusements have proven many times over, to this American at least, that cities can be wonderful places in which to live and work. My feeling of well-being in the German metropolis has resulted even more directly from the friendship, support, and hospitality shown to me and my family by many German people over the years, especially by our closest German friends, Rolf and Asja Hamacher, Karl-Heinz Reuband, Helmut and Lucia (Lambertini) Thome, and the Antoine family. Also receiving my gratitude in this regard are several colleagues and associates, such as Ralph Ponemereo, Harald Rohlinger, Willi Schröder, and Christiane Wever, at the Center for Historical Social Research and the Central Archive for Empirical Social Research of the University of Cologne, where much of this book has been written.

Many scholars and friends from other countries have done much to influence my thinking and improve my scholarship. Richard Evans of the University of London and Konrad Jarausch of the University of North Carolina have been inspirational in their exemplary work on German social history and have been particularly supportive of my own efforts over the past decade. I am also grateful to Pieter Spierenburg of the University of Rotterdam and Jan Sundin of the University of Linköping, from whom I have learned much on the subject of criminal justice history. My colleagues at Central Michigan University also merit my sincere thanks. Their generous and continued support of my research efforts, including their willingness to shoulder many teaching and administrative burdens during my several lengthy absences, as well as their helpful criticism of my work in departmental seminars, have done much to make this book possible. In particular, I wish to thank Tom Benjamin, Charles Ebel, John Haeger, Dave Macleod, Steve Scherer, and Jim Schmiechen. Many other people from other universities have read individual chapters or the entire manuscript along the way and also deserve my thanks. Tony DiIorio of the United States Holocaust Memorial Museum and Steve Hochstadt of Bates College long ago made important suggestions on the earliest drafts. Volker Berghahn of Brown University and Vernon Lidtke of Johns Hopkins University read the entire manuscript. Their painstaking and always constructive suggestions and advice not only helped me provide needed focus to this study but also alerted me to many mistakes I would otherwise have made. The book is a much better one for their efforts, although whatever mistakes and weaknesses that may remain are to be charged completely to my account.

A special word of appreciation also goes to Frank Smith of Cambridge University Press. He has been a very kind, responsive, and understanding editor.

Finally, five people, very close to me, have my deepest gratitude. John C. Johnson, my father, inspired me with an interest in scholarship and in German society. A downed American pilot and prisoner of war in Stalag Luft I, and later professor of physics, he had an enthusiastic intellectual curiosity and heartfelt fair-mindedness that have always been my foremost examples. Were he still alive, I know he would be happy to see this book finally in print. Signe Haas, my sister, shared his legacy and loss with me, and I am happy to share with her my joy over the publication of this book. Mary Johnson, my wife, has been by my side during the many years of this book's development and has patiently and lovingly supported me through thick and thin. She has thought and read through this book with me more times than either of us cares to remember. Benjamin Johnson, my son, let me use his bedroom to write much of the book and provided me with a kind of extra inspiration that perhaps only parents can understand. Frances Johnson, my mother, receives my deepest and final thanks. Without her love and nourishment I would never have written any book. This book is dedicated to her.

Cologne, Rosenmontag, February 14, 1994

Introduction

With recent headlines like TATORT GROSSSTADT (SCENE OF THE CRIME – THE BIG CITY), the German media, like the media in other western countries, frequently remind a fearful public that big cities cause crime.[1] Even though a considerable body of sociological theory has supported this near article of faith in the belief systems of contemporary Europeans and Americans and has been preached again and again in popular magazines, newspapers, and college textbooks in developed countries for more than a hundred years, its empirical foundations are less than secure. To be sure, crime and violence levels have increased significantly in the last decades of the twentieth century in major German cities such as Berlin, Cologne, and Frankfurt, just as they have in Amsterdam, Stockholm, Detroit, Washington, and many other large European and American cities.[2] But are these increases part of a consistent pattern of inexorably rising levels of urban violence and criminality, or are they likely to be of a temporary nature like other crime waves of the past? Is there something inherent in the nature of urban civilization that is particularly crime inducing? Have urban-crime levels always been higher than suburban and rural levels? To what extent are the cities themselves the causes of their own problems? What role has political bias against urban populations had in the genesis of urban crime? How different are contemporary Germans' fears of urban crime from those of people in other societies, and indeed from those of their own ancestors?

In the course of examining these questions in the context of four and a half decades of rapid urban growth and industrial expansion in Germany's

---

1   *Der Stern*, January 14, 1993.
2   For recent German homicide and other crime rates in large cities, see ibid. For recent Scandinavian and Dutch rates in a historical context, see Eva Österberg, "Criminality, Social Control, and the Early Modern State: Evidence and Interpretations in Scandinavian Historiography"; and Pieter Spierenburg, "Long-Term Trends in Homicide: Theoretical Reflections and Dutch Evidence, 15th–20th Centuries," in Eric A. Johnson and Eric H. Monkkonen, *Violent Crime in Town and Country since the Middle Ages* (University of Illinois Press, forthcoming).

first nation-state, this study contributes both to the sociological understanding of crime and urban development and to the historical understanding of modern German society and politics. Fundamentally arguing against "modernization"- and "urbanization"-based theories of crime causation, it systematically analyzes a mass of empirical quantitative and qualitative evidence that highlights the importance of societal attitudes and biases, political decision making, oppressed ethnic minorities, gender, demographic change, and raw economic hardship in the genesis of illegal behavior. In observing how the crime drama was acted out in Germany's rise to world-power status in the late nineteenth and early twentieth centuries, this study also contributes to the debate about the issue of continuity in modern German history.[3]

Indeed, many parallels between Germany's Second and Third Reich are noted. In both societies, urban-based populations, such as socialist and communist workers and Jews, were held in suspicion and subjected to often ruthless treatment by heavy-handed police and legal officials acting under the authority of specially created laws to control these populations. Bismarck's Anti-Socialist Laws of the 1880s and other laws meant to contain the rise of socialism in the Wilhelmian years (which will be shown to have accounted for nearly the entire increase in official crime rates in the period of the Second Reich) made Hitler's Reichstag Fire Decrees, which clamped down on any real or imaginary socialist and communist opposition, seem not all that extraordinary.[4] Deeply engrained biases against Poles, Lithuanians, and other slavic minorities – especially visible in newspaper and literary accounts of criminality in the Second Reich – endured from the nineteenth century into the middle of the twentieth century; these repressed

---

[3] For a useful discussion of the continuity debate, see Richard J. Evans, *Rethinking German History: Nineteenth Century Germany and the Origins of the Third Reich* (London, 1987), esp. chaps. 1–3. The continuity debate overlaps with the recent, heated struggle among German historians (*Historkerstreit*) about the uniqueness of the German fascist experience. For intelligent English-language treatments of this struggle, see Charles S. Maier, *The Unmasterable Past: History, Holocaust, and German National Identity* (Cambridge, Mass., 1988); and Richard J. Evans, "The New Nationalism and the Old History: Perspectives on the West German *Historikerstreit*," *Journal of Modern History* 59 (1987): 761–97.

[4] Compare Klaus Saul, *Staat, Industrie, Arbeiterbewegung im Wilhelminischen Reich 1903 bis 1914* (Hamburg, 1974); Hans-Ulrich Wehler, *Das Deutsche Kaiserreich 1871–1918* (Göttingen, 1980); Alf Lüdtke, ed., *"Sicherheit" und "Wohlfahrt": Polizei, Gesellschaft und Herrschaft im 19. und 20. Jahrhundert* (Frankfurt am Main, 1992); Ingo Müller, *Hitler's Justice: The Courts of the Third Reich* (Cambridge, Mass., 1991); Ralph Angermund, *Deutsche Richterschaft 1919–1945: Krisenerfahrung, Illusion, politische Rechtsprechung 1919–1945* (Frankfurt am Main, 1990); Lothar Gruchmann, *Justiz im Dritten Reich 1933–1940: Anpassung und Unterwerfung in der Ära Gürtner* (Munich, 1988); Detlev J. K. Peukert, *Die KPD im Widerstand: Verfolgung und Untergrundarbeit an Rhein und Ruhr 1933 bis 1945* (Wuppertal, 1980); and Dirk Blasius, *Geschichte der politischen Kriminalität in Deutschland 1800–1980: Eine Studie zu Justiz und Staatsverbrechen* (Frankfurt am Main, 1983).

peoples were incarcerated far beyond what their numbers would warrant in both Imperial and Nazi Germany.[5] Freedom for even the "normal" German citizenry was curtailed in both societies by militaristic and seemingly omnipresent police authorities,[6] by heavy press censorship, and by extensive and widely interpreted libel laws.[7] Despite this, most Germans in both societies accepted their plight and were usually willing to sacrifice liberty for order and prosperity – perhaps especially those from the middle and upper orders but also most men and women,[8] and even most workers as well. This perhaps helps explain the comparatively low rates of crime in Imperial Germany and the lack of meaningful resistance in Nazi Germany.

In sum, Imperial Germany's entrenched and threatened conservative elites, with their arch concerns for order and safety, oversaw the development of a technically advanced but overly positivistic legal and criminal justice system with highly trained judges, attorneys, and police who rather successfully contained crime. But, in so doing, they also promoted excessive fear of criminality and lawlessness, which they used to justify the repression of their working-class, socialist, and ethnic enemies (often resident in city settings) and to dampen demands for democracy and freedom. The proficient but authoritarian nature of German law and justice developed in the Second Reich launched Germany on a dangerous path that helped make it possible for German judges and police in the Third Reich to claim that they were acting only in the well-respected tradition of legal positivism of their ancestors when they used the full measure of their powers to destroy all

5 On the persecution of Poles in the Kaiserreich, see Hans-Ulrich Wehler, *Krisenherde des Kaiserreichs 1871–1918* (Göttingen, 1979), pp. 203–37; and C. Murphy, *A Polish Community in Wilhelmian Germany* (Boulder, Colo., 1983). On the persecution of eastern European, forced laborers in the Third Reich, see, for example, Ulrich Herbert, *Fremdarbeiter im Dritten Reich: Politik und Praxis des "Ausländer-Einsatzes" in der deutschen Kriegswirtschaft* (Berlin, 1985). For a discussion of the persecution of Poles in both periods, see C. Klessmann, *Polnische Bergarbeiter im Ruhrgebiet, 1870–1945: Soziale Integration und nationale Subkultur einer Minderheit in der deutschen Industriegesellschaft* (Göttingen, 1978).

6 Recent scholarship on the powerful Gestapo demonstrates, however, that the Gestapo was not as omnipotent, omnipresent, or as different from the police forces of Imperial and Weimar Germany as it was once thought. See Robert Gellately, *The Gestapo and German Society: Enforcing Racial Policy 1933–1945* (Oxford, 1990); and Klaus-Michael Mallmann and Gerhard Paul, "Allwissend, allmächtig, allgegenwärtig? Gestapo, Gesellschaft und Widerstand," *Zeitschrift für Geschichtswissenschaft*, 41 (1993): 984–99.

7 For the extensive prosecution of libel under the notorious "Heimtückegesetz" in the Third Reich, see Pieter Hüttenberger, "Heimtückefälle vor dem Sondergericht München 1933–1939," in Martin Broszat, et al., eds., *Bayern in der NS Zeit* (Munich, 1981), 4:435–526; and Angermund, *Deutsche Richterschaft*, pp. 133–57.

8 See, for example, Ute Frevert, *Women in German History: From Bourgeois Emancipation to Sexual Liberation* (Oxford, 1989); and Eric A. Johnson, "German Women and Nazi Terror: Their Role in the Process from Denunciation to Death," paper presented to the International Association for the History of Crime and Criminal Justice Convention, Paris, June 5, 1993.

potential opposition (again, especially from predominantly urban residents like communists, socialists, and Jews) and any measure of freedom.[9]

Having noted some of the continuities between nineteenth- and twentieth-century Germany in the arena of law, justice, and criminality, it is important to keep in mind that there were also significant disruptions over time, that there were also significant parallels between German society and other European societies, that the study of German history should not degenerate merely into a study of the roots of the twentieth-century fascist experience, and that this book is predominantly about crime in a rapidly urbanizing and industrializing Germany that had democratic as well as authoritarian strains. The British historians David Blackbourn and Geoff Eley have intelligently pointed out that the uniqueness of German society's development has often been overstated. Germans can hardly claim to have a monopoly on biases against city populations, foreigners, ethnic minorities, and Jews.[10] Only half of Europe had developed into democratic societies by the mid–twentieth century. The victory over authoritarian tendencies in even the most successful democracies required a struggle. The problems Germany faced during its industrial revolution and its aftermath, posed by rapid urban growth, industrial expansion, worker unrest, changing gender roles, and not always beloved minority populations, were not unlike those encountered by most European and North American societies.

In several ways, Bismarckian and Wilhelmian Germany provides an ideal society for the study of urbanization and crime. Without significant external distractions caused by foreign warfare and with little energy drawn away from its own problems by the demands of imperialist expansionism for most of its history, the potentially distorting impact of many possible intervening variables was absent in Imperial Germany. The pace and extent of German urbanization in the last several decades of the nineteenth century and the first decade and a half of the twentieth century were second to none.[11] With large cities like Berlin, Cologne, Hamburg, Munich, and many others in the industrialized Ruhr area growing by several times in a matter of decades, with scores of significant, moderate-sized industrial and metropolitan centers popping up out of former villages and small towns, with masses of former farmhands fleeing the land for the city throughout the country, and

9 In addition to the works cited in notes 4–7 above, see Michael Burleigh and Wolfgang Wippermann, *The Racial State: Germany 1933–1945* (Cambridge, 1991).
10 David Blackbourn and Geoff Eley, *The Peculiarities of German History* (Oxford, 1984). Andrew Lees, *Cities Perceived: Urban Society in European and American Thought, 1820–1940* (Manchester, 1985).
11 Hans Jürgen Teuteberg, ed., *Urbanisierung im 19. und 20. Jahrhundert* (Cologne, 1983); Andrew Lees and Lynn Lees, eds., *The Urbanization of European Society in the Nineteenth Century* (Lexington, Mass., 1976).

with strong biases on the part of many of the country's leaders against cities and urban populations, if ever a society had massive urban problems to contend with, and if ever a society should have had a strong correlation between urbanization and crime, that society would be Imperial Germany.

But Germany did not witness soaring urban crime rates. One could speculate on many reasons this did not happen: German workers' wages were the highest in Europe, and the disparities between rich and poor were not as great as in many other societies;[12] Bismarck's comprehensive social welfare system and Germany's attention to worker health and public hygiene protected its workers from the kind of economic destitution that often leads to criminality;[13] Germany was acknowledged as having the most advanced urban planning in the world;[14] with its history of being separated into many individual states with their own regional capitals, Germany did not have one dominant metropolis as England or France did and its urban growth was more diffuse, and possibly more manageable.[15] Whatever the reason, the demonstration, which follows in the body of this book, that neither urban growth nor the urban condition itself had a particularly powerful impact on most German crime rates is of real sociological and theoretical significance.

A final reason for arguing that Imperial Germany offers an excellent test case for studying urbanization and crime is that its statistical records are excellent.[16] The many quantitative analyses conducted in this book to determine the relationships between different types of crime rates and urbanization and other variables are made possible by the voluminous nature of German judicial statistics and census documents. Starting with the early 1880s, and following in each successive year (lasting until the mid-1930s, but the data for the period of Imperial Germany are much more extensive and trustworthy than those of the later periods), the justice ministry in Berlin painstakingly published a huge yearly volume of crime statistics, complete

---

12 Gerhard Bry, *Wages in Germany, 1871–1945* (Princeton, N.J., 1960).
13 In a review of two recent books on the German bourgeoisie, Noel Annan explains, for example, that whereas Germans in the nineteenth century were vaccinated against smallpox, 100,000 Frenchmen died of the disease because they were not. Noel Annan, "The Age of Aggression," *New York Review of Books*, January 13, 1994, p. 44. On the social and political ramifications of health issues in nineteenth-century Germany, see Richard J. Evans, *Death in Hamburg: Society and Politics during the Cholera Years, 1830–1910* (Oxford, 1987).
14 Anthony Sutcliffe, "Urban Planning in Europe and North America Before 1914: International Aspects of a Prophetic Movement," in Teuteberg, ed., *Urbanisierung*, pp. 441ff.
15 On the growth of German cities, see R. Hartog, *Stadterweiterungen im 19. Jahrhundert* (Stuttgart, 1962); and Jürgen Reulecke, *Geschichte der Urbanisierung in Deutschland* (Frankfurt am Main, 1985).
16 See my discussion in "Counting 'How It Really Was': Quantitative History in West Germany," *Historical Methods* 21 (1988): 61–79. The best guide to German criminal statistics is Helmut Graff, Die deutsche Kriminalstatistik: Geschichte und Gegenwart (Stuttgart, 1975). See also Herbert Reinke, "Die 'Liason' Strafrechts mit der Statistik: Zu den Anfängen kriminalstatistischer Erzählungen im 19. und 20. Jahrhundert, *Zeitschrift für Neuere Rechtsgeschichte* 12 (1990), 169–79.

with important commentary on how the statistics were generated and what the ministry officials saw as the reasons for the trends indicated. Entitled "Kriminalstatistik für das Jahr" (Criminal Statistics for the Year), these volumes are part of the main German governmental statistical series entitled *Statistik des Deutschen Reichs* (Statistics of the German Empire). Other yearly volumes in this series contain important and equally massive information on population movements, economic trends, and so on, with a special population census volume (*Volkszählung*) appearing every five years and an occupational census volume (*Berufszählung*) appearing more irregularly. In addition to these sources, the Prussian government, also centered in Berlin, had its own major statistical series running through all of these years, entitled *Preussische Statistik* (Prussian Statistics). This is particularly useful for locating homicide statistics based on judicial investigations instead of the less reliable conviction statistics offered in the "Kriminalstatistik" volumes. Finally, there are many other published volumes of statistics for German communities, individual cities, and states in addition to Prussia that this study has often used to advantage.[17]

Besides the sheer volume of the statistical information available, the German statistics permit many analyses that are not possible for other countries during the same or even other periods. This is because Germany had a uniform criminal code and criminal procedure, and a uniform way of compiling statistical data for most of the period under study. It is also because the judicial statistics for the different types of communities (such as counties) usually coincide neatly with the necessary demographic statistics. This enables one to correlate the crime variables (for example, yearly murder rates) with reliable population-density or other types of figures over hundreds of communities at different points in time. This is not possible in most other societies, the United States and Britain serving as good examples. Hence criminal justice historians in those and many other societies have often had to limit themselves to considerations of individual counties or states.

Although Michel Foucault and others have managed to help move the study of crime and deviance away from the periphery and toward the center of social and historical investigation in France, Britain, the United States, Scandinavia, Holland, and several other societies, neither crime in particular nor social history in general has been afforded much attention in Germany

---

17 There is no comprehensive index for the *Statistik des deutschen Reichs* series, and it can be difficult to locate the other smaller series of national and local governmental statistics. For a guide to these sources, one should consult the index (*Quellennachweis*) included in the individual yearly volumes of the German statistical yearbook (*Statistisches Jahrbuch für das deutsche Reich*).

until very recently.[18] This comparative lack of social-historical investigation in German history can perhaps be partially explained by the disruption caused by and the importance attached to Nazism, the two world wars, and the postwar division of Germany into two weakened, externally controlled states. It can also be attributed to Germany's strongly entrenched historicist tradition, which considers only the study of politics, war, and ideas to be proper subjects for the historian. Since the mid-1960s, however, the historicist straitjacket has been loosened, owing much to the pathbreaking efforts of the Hamburg historian Fritz Fischer, to the "Bielefeld school" of social historians surrounding Hans-Ulrich Wehler and Jürgen Kocka, and to several British and American historians such as David Blackbourn, Richard Evans, Konrad Jarausch, and Michael Kater.[19] Because of their work, the study of the masses' role in politics and the masses' activities for their own sake have finally become more central in the German historical debate, just as in other countries.

With only few exceptions, however – most notably in the scholarship of the English historian Richard Evans and the German historian Dirk Blasius – have crime and justice issues been treated in any detail.[20] The only time they have received much attention is, in fact, where everything in modern German history receives attention – the Nazi period. And even in this period most of the attention has been of very recent vintage, and most has been on criminally prosecuted political dissent against the Nazi Regime and on the role of the police and the courts in propping up the Third Reich's leadership.[21] Very little empirical work has been done on normal criminal

18 Foucault's most significant work on crime is *Discipline and Punish: The Birth of the Prison* (New York, 1979). For a discussion of social history in several national contexts, see Georg G. Iggers, *New Directions in European Historiography* (Middletown, Conn., 1984).
19 For useful discussions, see Jürgen Kocka, *Sozialgeschichte: Begriff, Entwicklung, Probleme* (Göttingen, 1986); Richard J. Evans, *Rethinking German History*; and Georg G. Iggers, *The German Conception of History: The National Tradition of Historical Thought from Herder to the Present* (Middletown, Conn., 1983).
20 Richard J. Evans, ed., *The German Underworld: Deviants and Outcasts in German History* (London, 1988); Evans, "In Pursuit of the *Untertanengeist*: Crime, Law and Social Order in German History," in his *Rethinking German History*, pp. 156–87; Evans, *Rituals of Retribution: Capital Punishment in Germany since 1600* (forthcoming); Dirk Blasius, *Bürgerliche Gesellschaft und Kriminalität: Zur Sozialgeschichte Preussens im Vormärz* (Göttingen, 1975); Blasius, *Kriminalität und Alltag: Zur Konfliktgeschichte des Alltagslebens im 19. Jahrhundert* (Göttingen, 1978); Blasius, "Kriminologie und Geschichtswissenschaft: Bilanz und Perspektiven interdisziplinärer Forschung," *Geschichte und Gesellschaft* 14 (1988): 136–49.
21 For an important discussion of some of the newest of this literature in addition to that cited in notes 4, 6, and 7 above, see Robert Gellately, "Situating the 'SS-State' in a Social-Historical Context: Recent Histories of the SS, the Police, and the Courts in the Third Reich," *Journal of Modern History* 64 (1992): 338–65.

and justice behavior in German history, whether in the Nazi or any other period.

Proceeding into somewhat uncharted territory, this book is one of the first in German history to employ both quantitative and qualitative empirical data and methodologies to treat criminal justice issues. As suggested previously, special emphasis is placed on sorting out the relationships among societal modernization, urbanization, and crime. Although the argument of this book is that these factors are less important in causing crime than other factors such as political repression, bias against ethnic minorities, and socioeconomic hardship, which should be seen as the real culprits, there are many reasons one would expect cities and their growth to cause crime. As arguments positing that cities and the modernization process cause crime have a long history and have been argued by some of the greatest minds of the last two centuries, and because they continue to appear in textbook treatments and to influence government policy in many countries, they need to be confronted directly. To state them chronologically goes something like this:

1. *The Conservative Political Argument.* With the industrial revolution and the massive urban expansion of the nineteenth century came an economic and political battle for the control of society. Conservative leaders with a base of power in the countryside, like the Junkers of eastern Prussia, fought to protect their values of honor and status against an increasingly powerful bourgeoisie and working class, both interested in economic well-being and political enfranchisement and power. To convince the rest of society that it should continue to follow their lead, the conservatives, often in league with the heads of important institutions, like the churches, attempted to brand the rapidly growing cities – homes of their political enemies, such as workers, socialists, Jews, and liberals – as being dens of iniquity, full of crime and violence, and devoid of honor, virtue, and other qualities society needs in its leadership.[22] If conservatives could get society to accept this view, not only would they keep their political power, they would also not have to pay to remedy the problems of the cities. They argued that it was the cities themselves, not the poverty of or the discrimination against the people in them, that caused the problems. In Germany and elsewhere, the conservatives' anti-urban bias was often adopted by business, financial, and other elites who found it convenient to accept an argument that would not oblige them to share their wealth and power to solve social problems.

---

22 See Lees, *Cities Perceived;* and the discussion on the conservative press in Chapter 2.

2. *The Marxist Argument.* The view that cities cause crime was strengthened in the nineteenth century by the most hostile enemy of the existing conservative and liberal elites – the Marxist-socialist movement. Although Marx himself and most of his followers, including the leaders of established social-democratic parties such as that of the SPD in Germany, were not as direct in their criticism of the cities as the conservatives, especially as they wanted to convince people that confirmed socialists were law-abiding citizens, the Marxists added their share to the negative view of cities by harping on their miserable conditions, which they argued were brought on inevitably by bourgeois capitalism.23

3. *The Classical Sociological Argument.* Toward the end of the nineteenth century, the discipline of sociology was founded and crime was one of its central issues. Noting the massive growth of city populations and the huge changes and problems this implied, scholars like Durkheim and Tönnies gave intellectual and academic credence to the argument that cities cause crime.24 Whereas Durkheim and Tönnies pointed to the change in society from rural to urban, from "community to society," as causing anomie and normlessness that resulted in crime, suicide, and other social ills, others argued that it was more the state of city living that caused the problems. The congested metropolis provided an environment where people did not know or care about their neighbors, where thieves found much to steal and easy escape routes, where gangs festered, and where a general attitude of lawlessness prevailed.25

4. *The American Sociological Argument.* Starting in the 1920s with the celebrated "Chicago School," American sociologists turned to empiricism to test theories of social behavior such as criminality. Using the most advanced mathematical and methodological tools available to them, they graphed city populations on maps and eventually became adept at studying huge numbers of people with the aid of modern computers. What they usually found was that inner-city populations were more crime infested than suburban or rural populations. Sometimes with propagandistic zeal, they argued that this was because of the fact that cities are centers of social disorganization, which leads to crime. As explained by Gareth Stedman

---

23 See the discussion of the socialist press in Chapter 2.
24 Emile Durkheim, *Suicide: A Study in Sociology* (London, 1952); Durkheim, *The Division of Labor in Society* (New York, 1964); Ferdinand Tönnies, *Gemeinschaft und Gesellschaft* (Leipzig, 1887).
25 The leading work on crime in Germany prior to the First World War is Gustav Aschaffenburg's *Crime and Its Repression* (Montclair, N.J., 1968). First published in 1913, Aschaffenburg's work was influential outside of Germany as well. Many German sociologists are still sympathetic to the classical Durheimian perspective. See, for example, Helmut Thome, "Modernization and Crime: What Is the Explanation?" paper presented to the Social Science History Association Annual Convention, Baltimore, Maryland, November 4, 1993.

Jones, the twentieth-century urban sociologists found that cities are marked by

> the substitution of primary contacts for secondary ones, the weakening of bonds of kinship, the decline of the social significance of the family, the undermining of the traditional basis of social solidarity and the erosion of traditional methods of social control. . . . Class divisions become geographical divisions. Social contrasts become more dramatic and abrupt. The neighborhood loses its significance; people can live in close physical proximity but at great social distance; the place of the church is taken by the press.[26]

With this type of argument, but with more advanced techniques, the American "Chicago School" of urban sociologists basically tested and modified the theories of the classical sociologists by using American empirical data. But that was the problem. American society had its own special historical development, in which cities frequently became swollen magnets for poor, oppressed African Americans and impoverished immigrant groups that might have turned to crime in any setting. What was true for the development of American cities was not necessarily true for other societies that they did not study but that they assumed followed the American model.[27]

5. *The Recent European Historical-Cultural Argument.* In the 1970s, several European and American scholars, influenced by the Annales tradition of studying mass behavior over the long term and aware of the advantages offered by modern computer technology for the analysis of large amounts of social data, began to test empirically the relationships between crime rates and various socioeconomic indicators in several urbanizing and modernizing societies.[28] Their statistical studies often found that neither Durkheimian notions of anomie, caused supposedly by rapid urban growth, nor simplistic urban–rural dichotomies explained patterns in European crime rates in the nineteenth century. Nevertheless, they were still hesitant to drop

---

26 Gareth Stedman Jones, "The Threat of Outcast London," in Mike Fitzgerald, Gregor McLennan, and Jennie Pawson, eds., *Crime and Society: Readings in History and Theory* (London, 1990), p. 174.
27 The leaders of this school were Robert Park, E. W. Burgess, and Clifford Shaw. Of their most important works on the subject are Park and Burgess, *The City* (Chicago, 1925); Park and Burgess, *The Urban Community* (1927); Shaw, *Delinquency Areas* (Chicago, 1929); and Shaw and H. D. McKay, *Juvenile Delinquency in Urban Areas* (Chicago, 1942).
28 Ted Robert Gurr, Peter N. Grabowsky, and Robert C. Hula, *The Politics of Crime and Conflict: A Comparative Study of Four Cities* (London, 1977); Eric H. Monkkonen, *The Dangerous Class: Crime and Poverty in Columbus, Ohio, 1860–1885* (Cambridge, Mass., 1975); Abdul Q. Lodhi and Charles Tilly, "Urbanization, Crime, and Collective Violence in 19th-Century France," *American Sociological Review* 79 (1973): 296–318; Howard Zehr, *Crime and the Development of Modern Society: Patterns of Criminality in Nineteenth-Century France and Germany* (London, 1976); Vincent E. McHale and Eric A. Johnson, "Urbanization, Industrialization and Crime in Imperial Germany, Parts I and II," *Social Science History* 1 (1976 and 1977): 45–78 and 210–47.

all modernization notions. Some, like Howard Zehr, who studied crime trends in nineteenth-century France and Germany, helped develop a new kind of modernization theory that resembled a popular French argument called "de la violence au vol" (from violence to theft). This posits that any declines in observable rates of violence following the growth of urban settlement are simply replaced by (and in effect caused by) increases in theft and other property crimes that generally occur with the growth of cities.[29] Whereas it is not entirely clear, to me at least, who first developed this explanation for the progression of crime trends over time, its currency was certainly increased by the endorsement it got from the French social philosopher Michel Foucault's studies of imprisonment and incarceration, which had become enormously popular by the late 1970s and early 1980s.[30]

Although several scholars of an empirical bent are beginning to question some of Foucault's arguments,[31] his theoretical work has had enormous influence on criminal justice studies in the past decade. Above all, he should be credited for helping to set a scholarly agenda for crime studies that is historically and culturally sensitive. Critical of modern, western society, Foucault attributes any long-term changes in crime patterns to changes in enforcement and punishment practices attributable to fundamental changes in mentality that accompanied the rise of the bourgeois, capitalist-dominated state in modern urban society. In his view, society's changing response to crime and criminals is far more significant than, and indeed accounts for, changing crime trends. With the change from preindustrial rural society to industrial urban society, an ever more jealous and powerful state, dominated by an acquisitive, materialist, bourgeois elite, develops a monopoly over the means of violence, places ever more emphasis on punishing property offenders, and hides its vengeful nature by substituting the (Foucault thinks) far crueler punishment of the mind for the punishment of the body, through mass incarceration. Neither crime in general nor violent crime in particular really declines over time. Any perceptible reductions in the rates of violent offenses stem from modern capitalist society's greater

---

[29] Zehr's work is discussed in considerable detail in Chapter 3. See also the discussions of his and others' work on this issue in Eric H. Monkkonen, "The Quantitative Historical Study of Crime and Criminal Justice," in David Inciardi and Charles Faupel, eds., *History and Crime: Implications for Criminal Justice Policy* (Beverly Hills, Calif., 1980), pp. 53–73; and in Louise I. Shelley, *Crime and Modernization: The Impact of Urbanization and Industrialization on Crime* (Carbondale, Ill., 1981).

[30] Foucault, *Discipline and Punish,* and *Madness and Civilization: A History of Insanity in the Age of Reason* (New York, 1965).

[31] Pieter Spierenburg, *The Spectacle of Suffering: Executions and the Evolution of Repression from a Preindustrial Metropolis to the European Experience* (Cambridge, 1984); Spierenburg, *The Prison Experience: Disciplinary Institutions and Their Inmates in Early Modern Europe* (New Brunswick, N.J., 1991); and Evans, *Rituals of Retribution.*

concern for prosecuting property offenders (which leads to perceived increases in theft rates) and from the state's depriving individual citizens of the potential for carrying out violence. Finally, the true level of violence in modern western society has often increased, according to Foucault, with the murderous barbarity of the state-sponsored, hidden-away-from-the-public, mass violence of Hitler's concentration camps providing the ultimate example.

The importance of mentality and of historically and culturally sensitive treatments of crime trends over time has also been underscored of late by the revival of the emigré German sociologist Norbert Elias's thinking on societal modernization. Like Foucault more of a theorist than an empiricist, but far more optimistic, Elias has also been associated with the "from violence to theft" argument for explaining crime trends. Although Elias hardly mentioned crime directly in his famous two-volume study "Over the Process of Civilization," his reasoning has become extremely influential in European criminal justice history circles.[32] Unlike Foucault, however, Elias saw the state's rise and the change in mentality associated with the passage from preindustrial rural to industrial urban society as leading to a more civilized society with lower rates of violent crime and a question mark about rates of property crime. Using Elias as a guide, several scholars have recently argued that the rise of the modern state helped reduce levels of violence over time.[33] Increasingly rational inhabitants of urban society turned to a benevolent state that offered a rational means of settling disputes. Replacing the atavistic, eye-for-an-eye and tooth-for-a-tooth means of seeking retribution that engendered soaring rates of violent crime in medieval and early-modern society, the sober laws and courtrooms provided by the modern state enabled the citizenry to lay down their arms. Finally, the old preoccupation with preserving one's honor in feudal society that helped inflate levels of violence was eventually replaced by a new preoccupation with material acquisition that some argue led logically to higher levels of theft and property crimes in capitalist society.

In the past couple of decades, then, the long-held view that urban growth and change and the city itself cause crime has begun to give way in scholarly circles, if not in the general public. Although important differences of opin-

---

32 Norbert Elias, *Über den Prozess der Zivilisation*, 2 vols. (Munich, 1969; orig. published 1939). For a recent discussion of the importance of his work for the history of crime and criminal justice, see Pieter Spierenburg, "Elias and the History of Crime and Criminal Justice," paper presented to the Social Science History Association Annual Convention, Baltimore, Maryland, November 4, 1993.
33 See the essays on England, Holland, and Sweden by J. A. Sharpe, Pieter Spierenburg, Eva Österberg, and Jan Sundin, in Johnson and Monkkonen, eds., *Violent Crime in Town and Country*.

ion still separate Foucault followers, Elias adherents, and other students of criminal justice history, there is evidence that scholars are moving toward some level of consensus.[34] This has been achieved by careful, culturally sensitive, empirical investigations, undertaken by many individual scholars working in a variety of national and temporal contexts.

34 In the attempt to move toward consensus, the European-based International Association for the History of Crime and Criminal Justice (IAHCCJ) and the American-based "crime network" of the Social Science History Association (SSHA) have held several recent specialized conferences and promoted several individual panel sessions on this theme (e.g., IAHCCJ conference, Stockholm, July 6, 1990; and SSHA panels on "crime and modernization over the long term," New Orleans, November 1, 1991; and on "Modernization, Norbert Elias, the 'Civilizing Process' and Criminal Justice/Legal History" (Baltimore, November 4, 1993).

1

The Criminal Justice System: Safe Streets in a Well-organized Police State

Ray Stannard Baker, an American traveler to Germany at the turn of the century, exclaimed: "From the moment of landing on German soil, the American begins to feel a certain spirit of repression which seems to pervade the land."[1] Intellectually and visibly struck by the omnipresent guiding and rather militaristic hand of the German government – erect, militarily dressed, and heavily armed policemen on nearly every corner; statues and sculptures honoring and commemorating German leaders and soldiers on the rooftops of city buildings, in public parks, at important and sometimes unimportant intersections; and uniformed soldiers constantly on drill or parade – Baker concluded that he never before knew "what it really means to be governed,"[2] and that he agreed with the sarcastic remark of a German socialist who had said: "It takes half of all the Germans to control the other half."[3]

---

1 Ray Stannard Baker, *Seen in Germany* (New York, 1901), p. 4. Baker was known as a muckraking American journalist. For a good general introduction and a fine bibliography on the subject of crime and justice in German history, see Richard J. Evans, "In Pursuit of the *Untertanengeist*: Crime, Law and Social Order in German History," in his *Rethinking German History: Nineteenth-Century Germany and the Origins of the Third Reich* (London, 1987), pp. 156–87. See also Evans's introductory essay in his edited volume, *The German Underworld: Deviants and Outcasts in German History* (London, 1988), pp. 1–27; Heinz Reif's introductory essay in his edited volume, *Räuber, Volk und Obrigkeit. Studien zur Geschichte der Kriminalität in Deutschland seit dem 18. Jahrhundert* (Frankfurt am Main, 1984, pp. 7–16; and Klaus Saul, *Staat, Industrie, Arbeiter-bewegung im Kaiserreich. Zur Innen- und Sozialpolitik des Wilhelminischen Deutschland 1903–1914* (Düsseldorf, 1974), esp. pp. 188–210.
2 Baker, *Seen in Germany*, p. 3.
3 Ibid., p. 7. After having been in Germany for about a week and observing "Germany's immense army, her cloud of officials, great and small, and her omniscient policemen," Baker explained, "You have been in Germany a week, more or less, when the policeman calls." Other foreigners traveling in Germany had similar impressions. Henry Vizetelly, a British traveler to Berlin in the 1870s, wrote that upon his arrival at the Berlin train station he noticed immediately that nearly everyone was official-looking and wearing some kind of uniform. For example, he described the *Groschkenbesteller*, from whom he had to hire a cab from the train station to his lodgings, as "a military-looking individual who from his towering stature might have been a direct descendant from one of Friedrich Wilhelm the First's gigantic guards." Henry Vizetelly, *Berlin: Under the New Empire* (New York, 1968: originally published in 1879), 1:13.

Most vexing of all to Baker were the ever-visible signs posting the comprehensive government and police regulations that seemed to deal with nearly all forms of human behavior, prescribing what was allowed and more often proscribing what was *verboten*. Feeling the "wild west in me slowly suffocating," he eventually came to amuse himself by making a curious game of trying to discover what was not yet forbidden but, no doubt, soon would be. One of his odder discoveries concerned the hitherto unregulated automobile buses of Berlin, which "tooted up and down the streets like so many steam locomotives, running at a rate of speed much greater than that of the ordinary trams." These buses rapidly caused a great stir, as they "did such a flourishing business that the other tram companies, which had long been compelled by stringent laws to limit the speed of their cars, made complaint to the police." A "great searching of the statute books" revealed that "every sort of vehicle from a wheelbarrow up was mentioned and regulated, but there was not a word about the automobile bus. Consequently there was nothing to do but to let it pursue its wild career until such time as a law could be devised and passed." This turned out to be a matter necessitating some serious deliberation by the government, so that by the time a law entered the books, the automobile company had nearly driven its competitors out of business. Apparently, a similar scenario took place when the bicycle was introduced. Although, by Baker's time, it had been "regulated out of all comfort," bicycle riders had previously "demoralized the police" for several months, having a glorious time tipping over pedestrians and riding how, when, and where they pleased.[4]

Baker's observations help illustrate some of the cardinal features of prewar Germany's criminal justice system. In Imperial Germany, as in all societies, crime was what the state defined it to be and what the state's agents prosecuted or punished. Baker's remarks make it clear that the German government and its agents staunchly enforced a system of laws that regulated civic activity more comprehensively than was comfortable for an American witness. But even if the German system deserved criticism for being overbearing and even repressive, it had some positive features. Hence Baker found much to praise as well as to condemn. He found that the alert watchfulness of the German authorities made German cities "safer for strangers, perhaps, than any other in the world." Also, he explained that the "close police supervision in the matter of garbage disposal, street litter, sewage, and so on, has been a factor in giving Germany a well-deserved reputation for clean,

---

4 Baker, *Seen in Germany,* pp. 5–6.

healthy cities." Finally, even if the German system might have discomfited foreigners, Baker did not think that it did this to Germans: "For every pfennig that the German pays in taxes, he expects and receives a pfennig's worth of government. He enjoys being looked after, and if he fails to hear the whirring of the wheels of public administration, he feels that something has gone wrong."[5]

Indeed, the criminal justice system as well as the entire governmental structure of the Kaiserreich has had a fair measure of admirers, both inside and outside of Germany, at least until the last few decades, and it remains a heated, contested issue whether or not the Kaiserreich and its system of government and laws represented what is best in Germany or what set the stage for the future mockery of law and justice in Hitler's Third Reich.[6] However, before the recent historiographical debate on the continuity or discontinuity of modern German history elicited in the last several decades by the works of Fritz Fischer, Hans-Ulrich Wehler, and others, the specific issues of law and justice had been largely overlooked,[7] and the criminal justice system of Bismarck and the Kaisers, with the possible exception of its police officials, was looked upon rather positively, except by left-wing contemporaries. For example, two respected law professors, one an American and the other an expatriate German, writing in 1944 in the *Michigan Law Review* about the German tradition of criminal law and criminal justice, described the system as being "smooth-working and efficient," with justice "simple, cheap and speedy" and also "certain and even-handed."[8] But speaking for those on the Left who experienced the system firsthand, was August Bebel, the leader of the German Social Democratic Party, who, at the Congress of the Second International in Amsterdam in 1904, probably

---

5 Ibid., p. 8. It is doubtful that this stereotypical viewpoint was shared by German workers, however, as Richard Evans makes clear in his edited volume on Hamburg workers' attitudes, *Kneipengespräche im Kaiserreich. Stimmungsberichte der Hamburger Politischen Polizei 1892–1914* (Hamburg, 1989).

6 See, for example, Ingo Müller, *Hitler's Justice: The Courts of the Third Reich* (Cambridge, Mass., 1991); and Ralph Angermund, *Deutsche Richterschaft 1919–1945. Krisenerfahrung, Illusion, politische Rechtsprechung* (Frankfurt am Main, 1990).

7 On the continuity debate, see Evans, *Rethinking German History*, esp. pp. 23–92. Until the last decade, social-historical work on crime and justice in nineteenth-century Germany, as Heinz Reif explained in 1984, "rested alone on the works of Dirk Blasius" (Reif, *Räuber, Volk und Obrigkeit*, p. 8). Whereas this is a bit of an overstatement, Blasius has certainly been a leading figure in this area. Most significant, perhaps, of Blasius's works on the topic are *Bürgerlichegesellschaft und Kriminalität. Zur Sozialgeschichte Preussens im Vormärz* (Göttingen, 1976); *Kriminalität und Alltag. Zur Konfliktgeschichte des Alltagslebens im 19. Jahrhundert* (Göttingen, 1978); and "Kriminologie und Geschichtswissenschaft. Bilanz und Perspektiven interdisziplinärer Forschung," *Gesellschaft und Geschichte* 14 (1988): 136–49.

8 Burke Shartel and Hans Julius Wolff, "Civil Justice in Germany," *Michigan Law Review*, 42 (1944): 864.

mouthed the sentiments of many Germans when he said, "Certainly Germany is a reactionary, feudal, police state, the worst governed country in Europe except for Turkey and Russia."[9]

For those who believe that a good government is an efficient administration, and thus that a good criminal justice system should be highly rationalized, uniformly administered, technically advanced, and staffed by highly trained officials who adhere strictly to the letter of the law and also are not swayed by the vagaries of public opinion or fettered by constitutional safeguards of individual liberty, Imperial Germany's criminal justice system merits praise. Modeled on the Roman system of statute law, the German system arguably defined crime less directly as "what the courts decide[d]" than do Anglo-American societies, where case, precedent, the relative skills of prosecutors and defenders, the mood and biases of judges and juries, and the differing and often overlapping laws of different localities weigh heavily in judicial determinations and frequently make the law and criminal justice ambiguous and arbitrary.[10] Although there were, to be sure, capricious and biased judges, prosecutors, and policemen, as well as several laws and ordinances that were certainly unfair and biased (especially against the lower orders) in the Kaiserreich, what was considered to be crime in Germany was conceived and administered rather consistently and uniformly in comparison to many other societies. The criminal law was clearly written and precisely defined in the *Strafgesetzbuch* (Criminal Code), which applied uniformly throughout Germany from 1872 on. With the passing of the *Strafprozessordnung* (Code of Criminal Procedure) in 1879, the criminal law was also adjudicated uniformly throughout the Reich by a criminal procedure that called for a hierarchical court system with strictly defined boundaries and a heavy reliance on the scientific testimony of court-appointed, expert witnesses, and that made the acquittal of the accused or the throwing out of the case on minor technicalities an uncommon occurrence.[11] The people who made, safeguarded, and administered the law in Imperial Germany were arguably the best trained in the world. Virtually all police officers from the rank of lieutenant up, all attorneys, all judges, and all

---

9   Cited in Barbara Tuchman, *The Proud Tower: A Portrait of the World Before the War: 1890–1914* (New York, 1967), p. 511.
10 See, for example, E. J. Cohn and W. Zdzieblo, *Manual of German Law*, vol. 1 (London, 1968), esp. pp. 3–56. For the vagaries of American criminal justice, see Samuel Walker, *Popular Justice: A History of American Criminal Justice* (New York, 1980).
11 Franz Exner, "Development of the Administration of Criminal Justice in Germany," *Journal of Criminal Law and Criminology* 23 (1933): 248–59. Werner Gentz, "The Problem of Punishment in Germany," *Journal of Criminal Law and Criminology* 22 (1932): 873–94. Fritz Ostler, *Die deutschen Rechtsanwälte 1871–1971* (Essen, 1971), pp. 34–51. Michael John, *Politics and the Law in Late Nineteenth-Century Germany: The Origins of the Civil Code* (Oxford, 1989).

government bureaucrats held university degrees, had passed arduous governmental examinations, had interned for lengthy periods, and were expected to adhere to the highest moral and ethical standards, as the government maintained special, stringent laws to guarantee the high personal standards of its officials.[12]

Despite their high personal and professional standards, their expertise, and their slavish adherence to the letter of the law, the agents of the German criminal justice system were also agents of the German government, and, as such, they acted to uphold the values of a society that was far from democratic, egalitarian, fair, and just. In the words of Samuel Walker: "The administration of justice mirrors the distribution of political power in society. Those with power have never hesitated to use the criminal justice system to serve their own interests at the expense of the less powerful: racial and ethnic minorities, political dissidents, and those pursuing alternative cultures and lifestyles."[13] Considering that Walker's focus is on the history of the American criminal justice system, a system that the common masses have had a sizable amount of participation in and control over, a system that he labels "Popular Justice" – and not on the more authoritarian German criminal justice system, one should hardly expect the far from popularly controlled German system to have acted less strenuously to protect the values of its political elite. In German society political power was firmly in the grasp of a narrow stratum of propertied individuals who certainly did not hesitate to mobilize the machinery of justice against Poles, socialists, liberals, Catholics, and all others who aspired to break their hold over them.[14]

---

12   On the training, education, and standards of criminal justice officials, see Ostler, *Die deutsche Rechtsanwälte;* Konrad H. Jarausch, *The Unfree Professions: German Lawyers, Teachers and Engineers 1900–1950* (New York, 1990); Hannes Siegkrist, "Public Office or Free Profession? German Attorneys in the Nineteenth and Early Twentieth Centuries," in Geoffrey Cocks and Konrad H. Jarausch, eds., *German Professions 1800–1950* (New York, 1990), pp. 46–65; Frederick F. Blachly and Miriam E. Oatman, *The Government and Administration of Germany* (Baltimore, 1928); Erich Döhring, *Geschichte der deutschen Rechtspflege seit 1500* (Berlin, 1953), especially chaps. 2–4 and 7; R. C. K. Ensor, *Courts and Judges in France, England and Germany* (London, 1933), pp. 52–79 and 125–41; Raymond B. Fosdick, *European Police Systems* (New York, 1915); Franz Laufer, *Unser Polizeiwesen* (Stuttgart, 1905); Paul Riege, *Die preussische Polizei: Kurze Darstellung ihrer Entwicklung und heutigen Form* (Berlin, 1932); Burke Shartel and Hans Julius Wolff, "German Lawyers – Training and Functions," *Michigan Law Review* 42 (1943): 521–27; Hans E. Stille, "Legal Education and Practice in Germany," *American Bar Association Journal* 16 (1930): 246–50; and Louis O. Bergh, "The Training of Lawyers in Germany," *American Bar Association Journal* 15 (1929): 47–48.
13   Walker, *Popular Justice,* p. 6.
14   See, for example, Saul, *Staat, Industrie, Arbeiterbewegung,* p. 189ff.; Alf Lüdtke, *"Gemeinwohl," Polizei und "Festungspraxis." Staatliche Gewaltsamkeit und innere Verwaltung in Preussen, 1815–1850* (Göttingen, 1982), pp. 349ff.; Wolfram Siemann, *"Deutschlands Ruhe, Sicherheit und Ordnung." Die Anfänge der politischen Polizei 1806–1866* (Tübingen, 1985); Christoph Klessmann, *Polnische Bergarbeiter im Ruhrgebiet 1870–1945. Soziale Integration und nationale Subkultur einer Minderheit in der deutschen Industriegesellschaft* (Göttingen, 1978); Richard Charles Murphy, *Guestworkers in the German*

With a constitution that did not even mention fundamental individual rights, that provided for a crippled and only partially elected legislature, and that guaranteed the leadership position of the semifeudal state of Prussia,[15] political power in Germany was largely the preserve of Prussia's hereditary and appointed officials. That their historic devotion to extremely conservative principles would be maintained in Imperial Germany was made clear during Robert von Puttkamer's reactionary regime as Prussian minister of the interior between 1881 and 1888. Puttkamer made adherence to such principles an actual prerequisite for holding office, and although his successors were acclaimed to be more moderate, arch-conservatives remained the mainstays of Prussian officialdom.[16] Best represented and most characteristic of all Prussian officials were the Junker aristocrats from east Elbia who were known to be "conservative to the bones."[17] Although they held nearly one-third of all ministry presidencies in Prussia during the entire Imperial German period, it was perhaps at the local level, typically as *Landräte*, that the Junkers' reactionary influence on German government and criminal justice was most sorely felt.

Whereas it might not quite be true that "in the last analysis Prussia is ruled by the *Landrat*,"[18] as one contemporary observer claimed, the *Landrat* certainly held tremendous power at the local level and richly deserved the reputation of being the "administrative backbone" of the Prussian government. The *Landrat* held a kind of double stranglehold over local government: he served as administrative head of the *Kreis* (circle or county), which was the most important administrative district of the state, and presided over local self-government as chairman of the *Kreistag* (county assembly). It was

---

Reich: *A Polish Community in Wilhelmian Germany* (Boulder, Colo., 1983); and Alex Hall, *Scandal, Sensation and Social Democracy: The SPD Press and Wilhelmine Germany, 1890–1914* (Cambridge, 1977).

15 This is laid out best, perhaps, in Hans-Ulrich Wehler's *Das deutsche Kaiserreich 1871–1914* (Göttingen, 1973).
16 Muncy, *The Junker in the Prussian Administration under Wilhelm II, 1888–1914* (New York, 1970), p. 109; Gordon A. Craig, *Germany 1866–1945* (New York, 1978), pp. 157–64; Jane Caplan, *Government Without Administration: State and Civil Service in Weimar and Nazi Germany* (Oxford, 1988), pp. 1–13; H.-J. Henning, *Die deutsche Beamtenschaft im 19. Jahrhundert* (Stuttgart, 1984); Margaret L. Anderson and Kenneth D. Barkin, "The Myth of the Puttkamer Purge and the Reality of the Kaiserreich: Some Reflections on the Historiography of Imperial Germany," *Journal of Modern History* 54 (1982): 268–84.
17 Muncy, *The Junker in the Prussian Administration*, p. 110.
18 Quoted in ibid., p. 180. In pp. 175–96, Muncy provides figures that showed that prior to 1914 roughly 60 percent of all *Landräte* were either Junkers or other nobles in Prussia. In East Elbia over 50 percent of the *Landräte* were Junkers. Other figures that demonstrate the domination of the Junkers and other nobles in the German administration are provided by Alex Hall in his *Scandal, Sensation and Social Democracy*, p. 45. In Prussia in 1914, three-fifths of all trainees for public administration were from the nobility and nobles constituted 92 percent of all *Oberpräsidenten*, 64 percent of *Regierungspräsidenten*, 57 percent of *Landräte*, and 68 percent of *Polizeipräsidenten*.

assured that he would fundamentally serve state and not local or popular interests, as he was appointed by and responsible to the central state government (the Prussian government). *Landräte* usually had very close ties to the military, the landowning classes, and the Conservative Party; almost all were reserve officers, 40 percent or more of them owned estates while still in office, and many held positions as Conservative party representatives to the Prussian House of Deputies. As the *Landräte* normally were tied, then, to very conservative political and economic interests, and as they had tremendous power at all levels of government and administration, not least of which was the control over local police forces in all but the major cities, and as their consent was needed to hold any popular gathering, many a socialist, Polish, or liberal voice remained mute or was quickly silenced.[19] In sum, conservative political interests held steadfast in Imperial Germany despite the changing outcomes of Reichstag or even local elections. As one obviously atypical official lamented in 1910: "How is it possible for us to have liberal government? . . . We are in an iron cage of conservative administration and self government."[20]

Junker control over local administration and police was by no means the only guarantee that the administration of justice would follow conservative political interests. As we shall explore in greater depth later on, the training and supervision of all personnel and machinery involved in criminal justice were of perhaps equal importance. Nearly the entire system and its officials, with the only significant exceptions coming from the ranks of often liberal-minded but usually quite weak defense attorneys, had a conservative and almost military cast. Police patrolmen had all served long terms as soldiers, and police officers had almost always been military officers; and the police as a whole were granted rather wide latitude to search, conduct surveillance, and even punish. Although justices and attorneys were usually the social inferiors of the higher administrators, and the latter often held bourgeois

---

19 See the discussion on this point by Paul Riege who was himself a police major in Berlin (Riege, *Die preussische Polizei*), pp. 21–4. For earlier works not yet cited on this, see Karl Frohme, *Politische Polizei und Justiz im monarchischen Deutschland* (Hamburg, 1926), pp. 73ff.; and A. Bertold, *Volksjustiz oder Klassenjustiz?* (Hamburg, 1895). The SPD satirical journal, *Der wahre Jakob*, often satirized the ridiculous lengths or depths to which the police would go to keep up their repressive surveillance of SPD activities. For example, the front cover of the September 26, 1899, issue was a cartoon depicting a group of men dressed in deep-sea diving suits and sitting on the seabed in apparently animated conversation. Next to them was an old man of the sea (*Aegir*) wearing a spiked helmet, holding a notebook in hand, and standing at attention. Under the cartoon ran an inscription explaining that the *Aegir* had been asked by the police to provide the necessary surveillance and reports of the meeting of the deep-sea divers on the seabed. See also Dirk Blasius, *Geschichte der politischen Kriminalität in Deutschland 1800–1980* (Frankfurt am Main, 1984), esp. pp. 55–68; and J. Wagner, *Politischer Terrorismus und Strafrecht im deutschen Kaiserreich von 1871* (Hamburg, 1981).

20 Quoted in Muncy, *The Junker in the Prussian Administration*, p. 110.

sentiments, the judges nearly always and the attorneys often cast their lot and passed their judgments in favor of the political Right.[21] It has become a common complaint to fault Weimar for failing to unseat the old German judiciary, police, and administration, and few would now disagree that "the courts, in fact, aided and abetted the process of erosion of democracy in Weimar."[22] Evidence of the right-wing leanings of German justices is provided by an examination of the sentences meted out to political murderers in Weimar. Although right-wing extremists carried out 354 assassinations as opposed to only 22 by left-wing radicals, ten from the Left were sentenced to death and not one from the Right, who received only an average of four months in prison.[23]

To provide a fuller understanding of the way in which crime was handled, and to some extent generated, in the last decades of the nineteenth and the first decade and a half of the twentieth century, the following sections examine the criminal justice system in the approximate sequence by which a wrongdoer would pass through it – by discussing its criminal law, its police, its court and criminal procedure, its judges and attorneys, and finally its punishment practices.

THE CRIMINAL LAW AND THE CRIMINAL CODE

"The letter of the law is adhered to in Germany perhaps more than in any other country," explained an American commentator in 1910. "The first question the judge asks himself is, 'What does the code say?' For the law – criminal, civil, and commercial – has been codified, and crimes and illegalities with their respective punishments, are laid down in black and white with absolute precision, but giving a maximum and minimum within which the court must limit itself."[24] Indeed, the criminal law of Imperial Germany was fully codified, highly precise, and uniformly applied throughout the Reich with confidence and rigor. Moreover, the confidence the authorities placed in the law code was not misplaced. It was so highly respected elsewhere that it formed the basis for the criminal codes of many other countries, such as Austria, Switzerland, and later Poland;[25] and compared to the

---

21 On the status and mentality of lawyers and judges in Imperial Germany, see Jarausch, *The Unfree Professions*, pp. 9–24.
22 Cohn and Zdzieblo, *Manual of German Law*, p. 28. See also, Angermund, *Deutsche Richterschaft 1919–1945*, and Ingo Müller, *Hitler's Justice*.
23 Cohn and Zdzieblo, *Manual of German Law*, pp. 27–8.
24 Robert M. Berry, *Germany of the Germans* (New York, 1910), p. 104.
25 On the similarities of German law with law in other countries on the Continent, see Carl Ludwig von Bar, *A History of Continental Criminal Law*, trans. Thomas S. Bell (New York, 1968).

systems of criminal law used in many other societies, even more democratic ones like England, France, or the United States, it was a model of efficiency and, in some respects, of moderation. Finally, it passed the test of time, although many modern observers would not consider this to be a necessarily positive fact. Although from the date of its adoption, January 1, 1872, the German Criminal Code (*Reichstrafgesetzbuch*) was to be the continued source of much scholarly and political debate, and was amended and appended by legislation on a number of occasions, it survived the Reich itself, remaining materially in force throughout the years of the Weimar Republic, and indeed even later.[26]

Even though prior to unification there was no universally accepted criminal code in effect throughout the German lands, and the system of statutory rather than case law that Imperial Germany employed did not recognize the binding power of historical precedent, the *Reichstrafgesetzbuch* certainly had historical antecedents. Beginning in 1532 with the passing of the *Carolina* (*Constitutio Criminalis Carolina*), which replaced the mainly unwritten feudal laws and practices that employed such awful practices as ordeals and feuds to determine guilt or innocence, German law had a lengthy history of being molded by academic scholarship, of being codified, and, at least after the new criminal code was passed in Prussia in 1851, of becoming less obviously and publicly sadistic. (In Germany and elsewhere in Europe, as Foucault and his followers have argued, the decline of bodily punishment and public spectacles of torture, punishment, and execution were replaced by a new form of private, spiritual and mental torture, out of sight of the citizenry, during the great "lock-up" of the nineteenth century, and, as Richard Evans has argued, this may have helped to make possible the rather clandestine, behind-closed-doors execution excesses of the Third Reich.)[27]

---

26 For evidence that the law changed very little, compare the two English-language translations of the German criminal law published by Geoffrey Drage in 1885 and by R. H. Gage and A. J. Waters in 1917. Drage, *The Criminal Code of the German Empire* (London, 1885); Gage and Waters, *Imperial German Criminal Code: Translated into English* (Johannesburg, 1917). The latter includes all amendments to the criminal law up to June 1912. For the minimal changes made in Weimar, see Exner, "Development of the Administration of Criminal Justice in Germany," and for the changes made by Hitler, see Friedrich Honig, "Recent Changes in German Criminal Law," *Journal of Criminal Law and Criminology*, 26 (1936): 857–61; and Ostler, *Die deutschen Rechtsanwälte*, pp. 241–49.

27 Richard J. Evans, "Öffentlichkeit und Autorität. Zur Geschichte der Hinrichtungen in Deutschland vom Allgemeinen Landrecht bis zum Dritten Reich," in Reif, ed., *Räuber, Volk und Obrigkeit*, p. 245. Michel Foucault, *Discipline and Punish: The Birth of the Prison* (New York, 1979). Pieter Spierenburg, *The Spectacle of Suffering. Executions and the Evolution of Repression: From a Preindustrial Metropolis to the European Experience* (Cambridge, 1984). For discussions of the historical development of German criminal law, see Eberhard Schmidt, *Einführung in die Geschichte der deutschen Strafrechtspflege* (Göttingen, 1965); C. von Schwerin, *Deutsche Rechtsgeschichte* (Leipzig, 1915); Bar, *A History of Continental Criminal Law*; and for a brief but useful summary, Drage, *The Criminal Code of the German Empire*, pp. 1–20.

Bavaria was the first German land to adopt a "liberal" and "modern" system of law and punishment. The new Bavarian code of 1813 was "epoch making in the development of liberal theory, and formed the basis of modern criminal law until the rise of Fascism."[28] Resembling closely the French *Code Penal* of 1810, it separated law and morality, attempted to provide a precise formulation of facts, gave the judge only narrow latitude in fixing the punishment within well-defined maximum and minimum sentences, and concentrated on the criminal act instead of on the wrongdoer, as punishment was to be in proportion to the damage inflicted. Furthermore, "all these achievements were theoretically applicable to every citizen."[29]

Even though the Bavarian Code became the model for many of the new codes passed in other German states, the criminal law practiced everywhere in Germany in the first half of the nineteenth century was certainly no model of moderation. Although, in lands following the Bavarian code, punishments were supposed to fit the crime, the punishments for many crimes still were unquestionably severe. For example, the stealing of a plum from a tree or a turnip from the field was punished by a penalty of three years' imprisonment. Elsewhere torture was still used to exact confessions and to punish wrongdoers and capital punishment was practiced rather widely for many offenses.[30]

In Prussia these developments were little felt before the second half of the nineteenth century, as the Prussian *Landrecht* of 1794 obtained until the Prussian Criminal Code of 1851 was passed. This code was very similar to the code adopted in 1872 for all of Germany, and it marked an advance in German legal development comparable to that made by the Bavarian Code of 1813.[31] Patterned after the Bavarian Code and the French *Code Penal*, it made attempts to make punishments equal to the severity of the crime: It prohibited corporal punishment, restricted the death penalty to murder, high treason, grave cases of manslaughter, and crimes endangering the gen-

28 Georg Rusche and Otto Kirchheimer, *Punishment and Social Structure* (New York, 1968), p. 100.
29 Ibid. Rusche and Kirchheimer, however, qualify this statement by arguing that at least in the first half of the nineteenth century there were still serious class differences in the punishment that German citizens received. The upper classes usually got lighter sentences than the lower classes and also had the privilege of separate confinement. See pp. 100–4.
30 Capital punishment came under attack throughout Germany in the first half of the nineteenth century and by 1850 many states had eliminated the death penalty altogether (e.g., Thuringia, Saxony-Weimar, Saxony-Meiningen, Coburg, Gotha, Anhalt-Dessen, and Schwarzburg-Rudolfstadt). But elsewhere it was still used for a wide variety of cases that might even include robbery, extortion, arson, and sometimes perjury, as well as, of course, murder, manslaughter, and high treason. See Bar, *A History of Continental Criminal Law*, pp. 344–6; Evans, "Öffentlichkeit und Autorität"; and Theodor Berger, *Die konstante Repression. Zur Geschichte des Strafvollzugs in Preussen nach 1850* (Frankfurt am Main, 1971).
31 Bar, *A History of Continental Criminal Law*, pp. 349–52.

eral public; and mandated that all death sentences were to be carried out within prison walls and thus were not to be the occasion of sadistic public spectacles as was still the case in many other countries.³² On the whole, it was more temperate than the French code in that its punishments were usually more lenient, exile and transportation were not employed, and capital punishment was used less often.³³

The Imperial German Criminal Code, which came into force for all states of the empire on January 1, 1872, retained most of the basic features of the Prussian Criminal Code of 1851. Operating on the principle of *nulla poena sine lege* (no law, no punishment),³⁴ the German criminal law was statute law which was decided upon by the legislators, not case law decided upon by citing precedent. Thus it attempted "to form a coherent, systematic general doctrine applicable to the largest number of imaginable cases."³⁵ The code's 370 sections mentioned virtually all imaginable criminal deeds, leaving only very minor infractions for the separate states to rule on themselves, such as small offenses related to taxation, fishing, hunting, the maintenance of roads, curfews, and public park regulations. In no case could punishment exceed two years' imprisonment for the laws that were not part of the general criminal code. Although the majority of the sections of the code were concerned with felonies (*Verbrechen*), punished by from five years' hard labor to death, and misdemeanors (*Vergehen*) or minor felonies punished by fines greater than 150 marks or up to five years imprisonment, the code itself also ruled on a large number of contraventions, delinquencies, or minor offenses (*Übertretungen*), for which punishment was usually limited to a maximum of 150 marks or short jail terms of up to six weeks.³⁶ However, these minor infractions were usually ruled upon differently by the separate states, and

---

32 For a literary treatment of the spectacle of capital punishment in Victorian England, see Michael Crichton's *The Great Train Robbery* (Boston, 1975).
33 H. S. Sanford, *Penal Codes in Europe* (Washington, D.C., 1854), pp. 58–60. Sanford's book also includes an English-language translation of much of the Prussian Penal Code of 1851. See also Lüdtke, "*Gemeinwohl," Polizei* und "*Festungspraxis.*"
34 C. Friedel, *Die polizeiliche Strafverfügung: Hilfsbuch bei Ausübung des polizeilichen Strafrechts für Polizei Behörden und Beamte* (Berlin, 1905), p. 28.
35 Cohn and Zdzieblo, *Manual of German Law*, p. 20.
36 These three different categories of criminal offenses correspond closely to the three categories delineated in the French penal code – *crimes, delits, contraventions*. The German categories are not easily translatable into English, as some English writers translate *Vergehen* as "small felonies," whereas others translate it as "misdemeanors," and *Übertretungen* is variously translated as "small offenses," "contraventions," "misdemeanors," or "minor offenses." In general, I shall stick to the German words themselves, as this will lead to the least possible confusion. On the criminal statistics, see Helmut Graff, *Die deutsche Kriminalstatistik: Geschichte und Gegenwart* (Stuttgart, 1975); and Herbert Reinke, "Statistics, Administration, and Concepts of Crime: Remarks on the Development of Criminal Statistics in Nineteenth-Century Germany," *Historical Social Research/Historische Sozialforschung* 37(1986): 39–49.

local police authorities were additionally empowered to levy ordinances (*Polizeiverordnungen*) to guarantee public safety and security.

Although some might argue that, on face value, the criminal law of Imperial Germany appeared to be quite moderate, at least in comparison with other western countries in the same period, including France, England, and the United States,[37] in some subtle ways the criminal law opened the Pandora's box to capricious, overbearing, and freedom-denying applications by the authorities, and sometimes even by the citizens themselves. Two particularly important examples of this are the comprehensive and nitpicking nature of the police ordinances and laws dealing with minor infractions, and the extensive application of libel laws by both officials and citizens. As they had frequently done to harass the socialists during the period of Bismarck's antisocialist legislation between 1878 and 1890, the police, the local authorities, and indeed the state enacted and enforced an ever-growing number of police ordinances and laws against minor infractions after Bismarck was gone, thereby proving to working-class Germans their contention that the state was becoming ever more unfair and authoritarian by using the law in discriminatory, *Klassenjustiz* fashion to keep the lower orders in check. Typical examples of these were national laws passed with increasing frequency after 1890 regulating work and workers' activities, which added to a growing multitude of meddlesome local laws, combined with a spate of old laws such as those dealing with the unauthorized wearing of official insignia, uniforms, and decorations; the unauthorized playing of a game of chance in a public street or resort; the placing of an object on a public road, street, or waterway obstructing traffic; and even the driving of a sleigh or sledge without a fixed pole or bells.[38]

Perhaps even more injurious to both the social-democratic enemies of the state and to the cause of freedom in general were the broadly defined libel laws. Used frequently by the authorities to silence the criticism of social-

37 Samuel Walker argues that the criminal law in nineteenth-century England and the United States was becoming less lenient. He points out that whereas other nineteenth-century European societies were becoming more enlightened in their criminal codes, England was becoming "more barbaric," as after 1800 England increased the number of capital crimes to nearly two hundred different offenses (Walker, *Popular Justice*). On England, see also J. J. Tobias, *Urban Crime in Victorian England* (New York, 1972), esp. pp. 199–223.
38 For other examples, see Evans, *Kneipengespräche*, pp. 205ff. Klaus Saul explains that after the end of the antisocialist laws, the "justice and administrative authorities, in close cooperation, used all possible means . . . to inhibit the socialists' expansion. According to reports of the SPD executive leadership, between 1890 and 1912, party members were sentenced for 'political' infractions to 164 years and two months in penitentiaries, 1,244 in jails, and 557,481 marks of fines" (Saul, *Staat, Industrie, Arbeiterbewegung in Kaiserreich*, p. 189). See also the Weimar government's own official discussion of the growth of political repression in this period in *Kriminalstatistik für das Jahr 1927*, in the series *Statistik des deutschen Reichs* 370 (1928): 32–4, 57.

democratic newspaper editors (discussed more fully in the following chapter), they were also employed rather widely by individual citizens to defend their reputations and to get back at their own private rivals and enemies. Although comparative scholarship on other countries' usage of libel laws in the same period needs to be undertaken to substantiate the claim, the widely used practice of employing the criminal and not merely the civil law in libel (*Beleidigung*) cases in the Kaiserreich enabled the Gestapo, Sondergericht (special court) judges, and other authorities of Hitler's Third Reich to maintain that they were acting "legally" and in accord with past practices in using libel laws (most typically to prohibit supposed "malicious gossip") to silence their former communist and socialist enemies and any other possible sources of antifascist public opinion such as church leaders.[39]

Although any assessment of the criminal law needs to keep these antidemocratic and repressive features in mind, there were some relatively moderate and humane features to it. This is especially true in the nature of its punishments. Only a small number of very grave offenses carried a penalty of life imprisonment; only two (premeditated murder and attempted murder of the Kaiser or ruler of a federal state) carried the death sentence;[40] and the maximum for all other offenses was not to exceed fifteen years' imprison-

[39] On libel laws in Imperial Germany, especially as they applied to newspaper reporting, see Ellis Paxon Oberholtzer, *Die Beziehungen zwischen dem Staat und der Zeitungspresse im Deutschen Reichs* (Berlin, 1965), pp. 102ff.; and Hall, *Scandal, Sensation and Social Democracy*, pp. 71ff. Special courts (*Sondergerichte*) were established at the beginning of the Third Reich to provide legality for the persecution of the Nazis' political enemies. On the same day the law was passed establishing the Special Courts, March 21, 1933, a law was passed giving these courts authority to try people for malicious attacks against the Nazi government. Known as the *Heimtückegesetz*, this law was substantially broadened and replaced by a new "law against malicious gossip" on December 20, 1934. Although it is impossible to state with certainty how many people were arrested, sentenced, or simply sent to concentration camps on the legal basis of this law during the Third Reich, certainly the number was over 100,000 and maybe several times that, and clearly it was the most common official ground for political arrest. For an intelligent discussion of the *Heimtücke* law and the special courts, see Angermund, *Deutsche Richterschaft* pp. 133ff. For quantitative estimates of its application, see Rheinhard Mann, *Protest und Kontrolle im Dritten Reich. Nationalsozialistische Herrschaft im Alltag einer rheinischen Grossstadt* (Frankfurt, 1987); Peter Hüttenberger, "Heimtückefälle vor dem Sondergericht München 1933–1939," in M. Broszat, E. Fröhlich, and F. Wiesemann, eds., *Bayern in der NS-Zeit* (Munich 1979), 4:435–526; and Robert Gellately, *The Gestapo and German Society: Enforcing Racial Policy 1933–1945* (London, 1990). For an excellent overview of the newest research on the topic, see Gellately's review essay "Situating the 'SS-State' in a Social Historical Context: Recent Histories of the SS, the Police, and the Courts in the Third Reich," *Journal of Modern History* 64 (1992), 338–65.

[40] The death sentence was almost abolished on March 1, 1870, when the Reichstag voted on its abolition and the abolitionists won by a vote of 118 to 81. Only a vigorous defense of capital punishment by Bismarck convinced the upper house to vote for it, but only for two offenses, premeditated murder and attempted murder of the Kaiser. Finally the Reichstag acceded to the wishes of Bismarck and the upper house, but the debate over the complete abolition of capital punishment reappeared again and again throughout the years of Imperial Germany. For a discussion of the rising critique against capital punishment, see Evans, "Öffentlichkeit und Autorität," esp. pp. 237ff.

ment, because the German authorities believed that a person was no use to society after a longer term.

Other examples of the code's moderation pertain to its treatment of youth, its relatively mild treatment of morals offenses, and the absence of any mention of the crime of wood theft. Crime could not be imputed to anyone under twelve years old and was to be doubted for those between twelve and eighteen. Youths between twelve and eighteen could be prosecuted, but the judge was obligated to determine if they had acted with intent; if intent was not found, they would be given a much lighter sentence. Finally, youths were to be sentenced to shorter terms than adults, and they had to be set free by the age of twenty; thenceforth they were to be treated as if they had been acquitted and not condemned.[41]

Whereas many contemporary societies were very squeamish concerning morals offenses, the Germans apparently were not. Adultery was punished only when it caused a separation between husband and wife and the sentence was imprisonment with labor of up to six months. Abortion was punished by imprisonment with hard labor of from six months to five years, depending upon the existence of extenuating circumstances. Rape and incest were punished by a maximum of ten years' hard labor. Sodomy, defined as unnatural acts between men or between men and beasts, was punished by an unspecified though usually brief prison term. Infanticide, which frequently was punished harshly in the eighteenth century, was punished by a maximum sentence of three years' imprisonment without hard labor; in Imperial Germany the authorities took a much more lenient view of the trying circumstances unwed mothers are usually in when they murder their illegitimate child in its first few days of existence.

As to the matter of wood theft, the unauthorized gathering of fallen wood on someone else's property, the makers of the new code decided not to mention it in the code and thus it became another minor matter for the individual states. This was a very significant step in the direction of increased moderation, for wood theft had been far and away the most common offense, averaging about 500,000 convictions per year at mid-century. Various commentators assure us that the severe punishments previously handed out for this offense so outraged the lower classes that they often led people to commit more serious offenses, such as resisting arrest, assault on police and court officials, and even arson. Because no mention of this offense was made in the *Reichstrafgesetzbuch,* it was, in a sense, decriminalized, as the punishment the states were permitted to set could only be very mild. This

---

41 Drage, *The Criminal Code of the German Empire,* p. 40.

serves as an example not only of the moderation of the German authorities but also of their wisdom, especially as several scholars have maintained that the severe prosecution of wood theft in the first half of the nineteenth century contributed greatly to the revolutionary class consciousness of the lower classes.[42]

Indeed, the government of Imperial Germany could boast of having a rational and quite effective criminal law that, on the surface, appeared moderate and equitable. All persons were theoretically considered equal under the law, and all punishments were supposed to be graded as to the severity of the offense in disregard to the status of the offender. Criminal offenses and their punishments were well defined and clearly indicated; punishments were comparatively modest. There was little question as to the jurisdiction of a particular court or the applicability of a particular law, and there were few loopholes.[43]

Beneath this surface, however, the criminal law of Imperial Germany was paternalistic, supportive of authoritarian rule, and not infrequently conducive to capricious applications. Not only might one be wary of the overbearing attempt to regulate so much of human activity, but one might also be alarmed that the criminal law was rather more concerned with protecting society in general than the rights of individuals.[44] For example, the code punished criminal negligence more often and rather more severely than codes in more democratic societies that placed the utmost stress on criminal intent and not on the result of one's activity, no matter how harmful.[45] In sum, the criminal law most certainly was used throughout the nearly fifty years of the Second Reich to enforce conformity, to combat ideological criticism, and to "destroy the opponents of the political group in power," as an American policeman observed shortly before the First World War.[46] To this end were the numerous sections (80–145) in the criminal code dealing with offenses against authorities and public order, the extensive libel laws, the local police ordinances, and the various additions to the criminal law

---

42 See Dirk Blasius, *Kriminalität und Alltag;* and Peter Linebaugh, "Karl Marx, the Theft of Wood, and Working Class Composition: A Contribution to the Current Debate," *Crime and Social Justice: Issues in Criminology* 6 (1976): 5–16.

43 Until well after the Second World War, Germany's criminal law had enjoyed a generally positive reputation abroad. For an example as late as 1944, see Burke Shartel and Hans Julius Wolff, "Civil Justice in Germany."

44 See Franz Exner, "Development of the Administration of Criminal Justice in Germany," *Journal of Criminal Law and Criminology* (1933), 250ff.

45 See Drage's commentary on intent and negligence in German law in his *The Criminal Code of the German Empire,* pp. 56–64. Although criminal negligence could lead to several years' imprisonment, in general crimes involving negligence without proven intent were punished far less severely than crimes involving proven intent.

46 Quoted in Fosdick, *European Police Systems,* p. 18.

regulating workers and work practices that were legislated with increasing frequency throughout the entire period. But to learn of the truly repressive features of the German criminal justice system, perhaps one should look less at the criminal law itself and more closely at the people, institutions, and processes that carried out the law.

THE POLICE

August Bebel's charge that the Kaiserreich was a "police state" deserves some credence. Speaking just before the First World War, Karl Weidlich, a scholar of German and European police activities and a German judge, explained: "While the constitutional struggles of the last hundred years in Germany and Austria have not left police powers unaltered, it is scarcely an exaggeration to say that in spirit and procedure they still represent the constitutional absolutism of the 18th century."[47] Indeed, the most frequent word observers have used to describe the German police is "militaristic." Militaristic in organization, militaristic in training, militaristic in dress and demeanor, and militaristic in outlook, the German police were also like the German military in that they were removed from the civilian population, immune from popular opinion and popular control, and often endowed with an "arrogance hardly to be tolerated in democratic countries."[48]

Highly trained, well staffed, well armed, and highly regimented, the officers and men of the police no less than the members of the German army and navy avidly and efficiently carried out their duties. Furthermore, they were given wide latitude and powers. Without warrant the police could barge into saloons or other lower-class haunts, round up several people, and carry them off to headquarters. There they often subjected their captives to third-degree tactics to extort confessions and information, all of which sometimes led them to find reasons to convict people who had never been arrested for any particular criminal activity in the first place. Whereas such tactics possibly proved advantageous in detecting criminals, the brutality and bias the police displayed in carrying out, in Alf Lüdtke's words, "a permanent and offensive 'police war'" in the Kaiserreich against social democrats and Catholic and Polish *Reichsfeinde* (enemies of the Reich), "makes one wonder if crime was retarded or possibly increased as a consequence."[49]

47 Ibid., p. 79.
48 Morris Plescowe, "The Organization for the Enforcement of the Criminal Law in France, Germany and England," *Journal of Criminal Law and Criminology* 27 (1936): 317.
49 Lüdtke, "*Gemeinwohl,*" *Polizei und* "*Festungspraxis,*" p. 350. In his book on the police in the first half of the nineteenth century, Lüdtke argues that German police were much more militaristic and

Although there was no uniform system of police administration in Imperial Germany, the police force faithfully served as "the right arm of the ruling classes, responsible to the Crown or the higher authorities rather than to the people."⁵⁰ Most states followed the lead of Prussia, where, since the foundation of the *Gendarmerie* in 1820 and the Berlin *Schutzmannschaft* in 1848 as the first rural and municipal police forces in Germany, "The police is [was] always under the the authority of the state, no matter if its powers were to be applied at the state or the local level."⁵¹ Certainly public opinion and interests mattered little to the German police, who were organized thoroughly on a military model, often selected from the military itself and sometimes still members of it, overseen by state-appointed officials, and paid and pensioned by the state treasury.

With few exceptions, only three types of police forces existed and all were under direct or indirect state control.⁵² In most large cities the police were called *Staatliche Beamtenkorper* (state police).⁵³ The commissioners of these forces (usually called *Polizeipräsidenten*) were picked by and responsible to the minister of the interior and were most typically career state bureaucrats or military officers who did not come from the cities they served. The forces themselves were organized on a military model, with a clear separation between officers and men of the ranks. The highest-ranking officers were

antidemocratic than police in France, England, and the United States (p. 335), that they took a "Sonderweg" (pp. 339–47), and that their militarism and overbearing nature increased in Imperial Germany (p. 349). Dirk Blasius argues in his *Kriminalität und Alltag* that police brutality and the unfair criminal justice system caused increased criminality in the first half of the nineteenth century. See also Klaus Saul, "Der Staat und die 'Mächte des Umsturzes.' Ein Beitrag zu den Methoden antisozialistischen Repression und Agitation vom Scheitern des Sozialistengesetzes bis zur Jahrhundertwende," *Archiv für Sozialgeschichte* 12 (1972): 293–350; Saul, *Staat, Industrie, Arbeiterbewegung*, pp. 189ff; Ralph Jessen, *Polizei im Industriegebiet: Modernisierung und Herrschaftspraxis im westfälischen Industriegebiet 1848–1914* (Göttingen, 1991); Albrecht Funk, *Polizei und Rechtsstaat. Die Entwicklung des staatlichen Gewaltsmonopols in Preussen 1848–1914* (Frankfurt am Main, 1986); Alf Lüdtke, ed., *"Sicherheit" und "Wohlfahrt." Polizei, Gesellschaft und Herrschaft im 19. und 20. Jahrhundert* (Frankfurt am Main, 1992), and Robert Harnischmacker and Arved Semerak, *Deutsche Polizeigeschichte* (Stuttgart, 1986), pp. 56–71.

50 Fosdick, *European Police Systems*, p. 200.
51 Riege, *Die preussische Polizei*, p. 12.
52 Exceptions to this were in Württemberg where all municipal forces were locally controlled, and in Saxony and Bavaria where only the leading cities of Dresden and Munich were under the state's direct jurisdiction whereas other communities were under local direction. See Laufer, *Unser Polizeiwesen*, pp. 14–73, and especially pp. 60–71, where Laufer provides examples of the organization, size, and functions of the police forces in four different sized communities. On the organization and functions of the Berlin force, see Frank J. Thomason, "Uniformed Police in the City of Berlin under the Empire," in Emilio C. Viano and Jeffrey H. Reiman, eds., *The Police in Society* (Lexington, Mass., 1976), pp. 105–19. For the Cologne force, see Paul Lauing, *Die Geschichte der Kölner Polizei* (Cologne, 1926). For Düsseldorf, see Elaine Govka Spencer, "State Power and Local Interests in Prussian Cities: Police in the Düsseldorf District, 1848–1914," *Central European History* 19 (1986): 293–313.
53 In Alsace-Lorraine and in Posen, the state police were the only police authorities.

known as *Polizeiobersten,* whose rank corresponded to a military colonel and who commanded several police majors (*Polizeimajore*). Under the police majors came the lower police officers, most police lieutenants who typically headed individual *Reviere,* or police precincts. All of the officers came from different social standings and had far more academic and technical training than did the men of the ranks. The common patrolmen (*Schutzmänner*) corresponded closely in function, title, and status to the enlisted men and noncommissioned officers in the military from which they usually came.

The rural *Gendarmerie* were, if anything, even more militaristic and highly controlled than the municipal authorities. They were overseen by the state-appointed and often feudalistic *Landräte,* whose power commanded such fear locally that "when people tell their children that the Pope is not allowed to marry, then they ask if the *Landrat* has forbidden it."[54] Heavily armed and mounted on horseback, the typical *Gendarm* had served nine years in the military (usually having attained the rank of *Unteroffizier,* or corporal) and in most cases was still considered an active member of it, his time in service with the *Gendarmerie* counting as service toward his military pension.

The only major exception to the rule of state control of the police was provided by the Communal Police (*kommunalen Polizeiexecutivbeamten*) of the smaller cities and towns. Although these bodies were usually under the immediate direction of the local mayors and not the state officials, too much should not be made of this exception. Various factors worked to make the Communal Police more of a nominal than a real exception. Usually they were underfunded and undermanned, and had to work closely with the *Gendarmerie* to keep law and order. Also, they were "so hedged about by state regulations that little was left to the discretion of local authorities."[55] In their organization and personnel they aped the other police bodies in exuding a militaristic cast and, in Prussia at least, they were also overseen by the *Landräte.* All of this adds up to mean that they too were responsible to state and not to local authorities.[56]

If the police shared some of the negative features of the military and the bureaucracy in that they were removed from popular, democratic control, they also shared some positive features, as in their professional standards and expertise. From the police commissioners of the major cities down to the

---

54 This was by an unnamed *Landrat* quoted in Muncy, *The Junker in the German Administration,* p. 180. On the police powers of the *Landräte,* see also Riege, *Die preussische Polizei,* pp. 21–24.
55 Fosdick, *European Police Systems,* p. 69.
56 Paul Riege, a police major in Berlin who himself had written a book on the communal police, argues that this was the case: "Indeed the communal police is not responsible to the community assemblies, rather it is responsible to the state government alone." Riege, *Die preussische Polizei,* p. 12.

common patrolmen on the beat, policemen were thought to be generally honest, hard-working, well trained, and educated for whatever position they held.[57]

Police commissioners and police officers usually came from a high social standing and were, of course, the best trained, but they were also obligated to conform to the most stringent standards of integrity and discipline so as to set an example for their men and to guarantee the respect of the police force in general. The commissioners had university degrees in law and had followed the rigid Prussian administrative training course, which included several years as administrative interns and the passing of several difficult examinations before appointment.[58] Their position as police commissioner was considered to be very high up in the administrative hierarchy, for they were usually promoted from the position of *Landrat* or *Regierungspräsident* (head of larger government districts), and many were of aristocratic background. They were never promoted from the lower ranks, and few had been police officers before taking their commission. Although charges of corruption surrounded some of the police commissioners during their terms of office, like von Richthofen, who served from 1885 to 1895, this was true of nearly every society: but, in general, they were thought to hold to high personal standards, and none of the ten police commissioners of the city of Berlin from 1848 to 1919 had ever been removed from office for any reason, and very few had ever been removed elsewhere (though this, of course, may simply highlight the difficulty of prosecuting the police). Nevertheless, this fact so impressed an American police expert that when he asked around about the methods used for removing corrupt commissioners, he found that "in several of the German cities the police authorities, when questioned on this matter by the writer, were obliged to consult their law books to find out how such action could be taken."[59]

Officers in German police departments may not have come from quite such illustrious backgrounds as the police commissioners they served, but they usually came from a higher social background than the men in the ranks

---

57 Richard Evans documents how German workers, however, frequently complained about police corruption and brutality, even if they accepted that the police were needed in society: see his *Kneipengespräche*, 206, 211–12.
58 See the discussion of German legal training in the following section.
59 Fosdick, *European Police Systems*, p. 170. From the time of the formation of the Berlin force, all police commissioners were of aristocratic background. Of them, three died while in office, three retired honorably, and the rest were promoted to higher positions in government service. The Berlin police commissioners were: von Hinckeldy, 1848–56; von Zedlitz-Neukirch, 1856–61; von Bermuth, 1862–67; von Wurmb, 1867–72; von Madri, 1872–85; von Richthofen, 1885–95; von Windheim, 1895–1903; von Borries, 1903–8; von Stubenrauch, 1908–9; and von Jagow, 1909–14.

and they certainly had much more training and education. Most police officers were selected from the ranks of military officers or from the university where they had studied law. They had to be at least five feet seven inches tall; they had to have passed through the gymnasium or its equivalent; they had to have served in the military at one point or another; and they had to have proof of solid character. Before they could be appointed to the force at the rank of lieutenant, they had to follow an eighteen-month training course. During this period they were unsalaried (thus they usually came from backgrounds of some considerable means), and they had to spend six months in precinct stations, five in a detective bureau, and the rest with various administrative sections. After they were appointed, which was usually between the ages of twenty-four and thirty, they were to continue their training by attending regular lectures and special courses useful to their work.

The normal recruit for the lower ranks of the police force was older, shorter, less educated, less well trained, and from a lower social station than the officers. He only had to be five feet six inches tall; he did not have to possess a high school degree, though he had to be literate; he only needed six weeks of formal police training; and he had to be less than thirty-five years old (in Berlin in 1914, the average was thirty-one). Almost all police departments, however, stipulated that their recruits had to have served at least five years in the military, which was thought to be the best training the normal policeman could have, and to have attained the rank of *Unteroffizier* (corporal). In Berlin, the police recruits had to have served at least six years in the army, and, after 1907, nine years. Although the normal German policeman was expected to continue his training by taking specialized courses periodically and could not be promoted without doing so, there was not a great deal of incentive for him to try very hard to improve himself. He could not be promoted to the officer ranks because he did not have the necessary education; furthermore he was too old. The best he could do was be promoted to the rank of police sergeant or to the detective force, which was also normally considered a promotion.[60]

Certainly German policemen did, like policemen everywhere, make frequent complaints about being overburdened and subjected to lack of funds and equipment, but in comparison with policemen in other societies they were as well equipped as they were well trained.[61] They possessed the most advanced chemical, physical, and photographic means and devices for estab-

---

60 On the training and backgrounds of the police officers and men, see Fosdick, *European Police Systems*, pp. 182–252, and Funk, *Polizei und Rechtsstaat*.
61 Laufer, *Unser Polizeiwesen*, pp. 93–4.

lishing identification and detecting criminals, and they had the best technical aids, such as elaborate criminal indexes and registers, of perhaps any society of their period. The German police forces also had incredibly large numbers of policemen in comparison to other societies.[62]

Complaining German policemen were not simply whiners, however, for they were expected to perform many duties not required of police elsewhere. Whereas police in England or the United States only had to worry about conducting traffic, maintaining order, and apprehending criminals, German police were charged with numerous administrative functions and were usually divided into many separate departments to handle such diverse matters as the regulation of theaters, public toilets and sewage removal, and the overseeing of poor relief, building codes, fire prevention, manufacturing and mining, game and hunting laws, and civilian registration. The Berlin police force in 1914, for example, had twelve different departments, of which only two – the uniformed force (*Schutzmannschaft*) and the detective force (*Kriminalabteilung*) – dealt with functions handled by municipal police forces in English and Scottish cities.[63]

These exceptional administrative duties may have been a heavy burden for the German police, but they may also have facilitated their task of law enforcement. Because they were so intimately involved with so much of civilian behavior, and because they were given a truly wide scope in matters of surveillance, search, and seizure, the German police gained the reputation of being omnipresent and omniscient. Real substance to this reputation was provided by the police's role in the German system of civilian registration (*Meldewesensystem*). According to this system, the police kept a record of the movements of all persons in German territory. In all communities, large and small, all persons had to report their arrivals, departures, and changes of dwelling to the police within twenty-four hours. This was true not only for people making permanent moves but also for people visiting friends or taking lodgings in a hotel or guest house for the purposes of tourism or business. In the words of a British traveler: "So complete is the surveillance

---

62 Fosdick, *European Police Systems*, chaps. 3 and 8. The municipal police forces were expanding at a very rapid rate in the years of Imperial Germany. In 1880 the Berlin force, the nation's largest, employed 5,286 people; by 1908 it had grown to 9,414 employees. Hamburg had the second largest force, which in 1908 numbered 4,300 employees. (These figures are from Hall, *Scandal, Sensation and Social Democracy*, p. 44.) On the growth and development of the Berlin force and for some discussion of the growth and development of some of the other municipal forces, see Willy Feigel, *Die Entwicklung des Königlichen Polizei-Präsidiums zu Berlin in der Zeit von 1809 bis 1909* (Berlin 1909).

63 Laufer, *Unser Polizeiwesen*, pp. 13–73; Fosdick, *European Police Systems*, pp. 20–1, and 111–13; Dawson, *The Evolution of Modern Germany* (New York, n.d.), pp. 290–92; and Walther von Hippel, *Handbuch der Polizeiverwaltung* (Berlin, 1910), pp. 113–50.

exercised over the inhabitants of a German town that . . . it is possible, at a few moments' notice, to learn the exact whereabouts of any resident."[64] Not only did the *Meldewesen* records track the simple comings and goings of German citizens and foreigners on German soil, but also these records contained voluminous information pertaining to people's occupational history, material wealth, and social standing. This information made it possible for the police to make a quick check of anyone who might have had a criminal record, was wanted elsewhere for a criminal offense, or simply seemed suspicious. Most societies were justifiably hesitant to adopt such a system because of its authoritarian implications, but it probably did help the German police detect criminals, and it may even have helped to deter criminal activity. At least, this was the opinion of one American tourist: "The labeling and cataloguing of the population enables the police to watch the criminal classes and to keep them in subjection to an extent quite astonishing."[65]

Two other aspects of the police's powers of surveillance worth mentioning were the *Razzia* system and the police's responsibility for overseeing public meetings and demonstrations. The *Razzia* system allowed them to keep close tabs on and even to make frequent raids on lodging houses, cafés, and restaurants frequented by suspicious persons. Without a warrant, the police could simply gather up the patrons, shake them down, and detain them at police headquarters for as long as twenty-four hours without charging them with an offense, while at the same time making checks of their records to see if any of them was wanted for a criminal offense anywhere in the Reich. "Thus on the evening of July 19, 1913, the Berlin police raided the Jungfernheide, an amusement park of questionable character in North Berlin. Over 300 persons who could give no satisfactory account of themselves were taken to police headquarters. Sixty of these were found to be criminals for whom the police had for some time been searching."[66] The police not only kept a watchful eye on persons suspected of criminal wrongdoing but also intervened frequently in everyday public meetings and demonstrations. The police's permission was necessary for any such activity to be held, and the police usually posted one or more constables on duty at the meeting or demonstration itself. Particularly if the activity was being held for political purposes, and especially if it involved socialists or Poles, the police often acted in an obstructionist fashion. They could not only deny the

64 Dawson, *The Evolution of Modern Germany*, p. 290.
65 Baker, *Seen in Germany*, p. 8.
66 Fosdick, *European Police Systems*, p. 358.

group permission to meet or close down the meeting at will, they could also harass the attenders so much as to make it impossible to conduct any business. For example, they could require Polish citizens to speak German even though "not one in fifty of those present may know any but their native language."67

The police's power was made even more ominous in that they were endowed with legislative and judicial powers not entrusted to policemen in most other societies. Although the last section of the criminal code specified numerous trifling contraventions, some of which have already been mentioned, these were just a small fraction of the huge list of activities that were *verboten*. In all communities the police had the right to post their own particular list of activities they wanted circumscribed. Often these ordinances and regulations (*Polizeiverordnungen* and *Polizeiliche Strafverfügungen*) seemed exceedingly trivial. For example, the Berlin police regulated the color of automobiles, the length of hatpins, and the methods of purchasing fish and fowl. In Stuttgart, a customer could not fall asleep in a restaurant, children could not slide on slippery sidewalks, and drivers could not snap their whips while guiding their horses in the street. Although the offenses themselves may have seemed trifling, the failure to obey these police regulations often resulted in severe punishment. Punished as *Übertretungen*, trivial violations of police ordinances could result in a fine of up to sixty marks or imprisonment of up to fourteen days.

Not only did the police have the power to make certain laws, in some cases they had the power to pass sentence on lawbreakers as well. The majority of these cases were handled without a semblance of judicial procedure. What happened was that the police officer filed a report to his superior officer. The superior officer, without hearing from the defendant, then determined the penalty and notified the defendant of the punishment. Although the defendant had the right to appeal to the *Amtsgericht* (district court), this usually did not happen, because if the defendant appealed and lost, he or she was immediately imprisoned until the case was decided and had to pay the fees for lawyers and court costs. Certainly, these legislative and judicial powers of the police were quite exceptional, as Imperial Germany convicted about ten times as many citizens for such minor offenses as did England at the time. In the words of a German judge: "Police judgments are showering over us like hail-stones. A German citizen who has not had at least one such punishment must be looked for with a lantern."68

67 Dawson, *The Evolution of Modern Germany*, p. 293.
68 Quoted in Fosdick, *European Police Systems*, p. 35. Stuttgart, a city of about 300,000 in the immediate prewar years, had circa 40,000 police penalties imposed each year. This would be equal to about

Clearly the awesome powers of the police, their efficiency, and their solid training must have contributed to making life difficult for criminals and would-be criminals. But the powers and also the methods of the police greatly contributed to making many honest citizens uncomfortable as well, and the police themselves were aware of the very bad image they had with the public. Writing in 1905, one policeman categorized police-citizen relations as being "without understanding, mistrustful, and hostile."[69] He blamed society for not devoting enough money for good law enforcement. One suspects, however, that more money would not have improved police-citizen relations; rather, more money would have made the police all the more meddlesome and disliked. How would more money, no doubt much of which would have been spent on more weaponry, have made the pistol-toting, saber-rattling, "armed as if for war" patrolman seem less brutal and threatening? How would it have made German citizens more comfortable with the boastful comment of the police lieutenant who said, "I can search my neighbor's house and lock him up for twenty-four hours, although he may be innocent as a lamb"?[70] It certainly would not have made most Poles happy to find even more policemen stationed at their meetings. Nor would it have made most social democrats any more comfortable with the police officers who considered their party to be a modern Pied Piper (*ein moderner Rattenfänger*) for all kinds of undesirables and malcontents.[71] And most people would not have enjoyed the more vigorous enforcement of petty police regulations it would have permitted. A few more real criminals might have been caught and punished, but the greatest effect of more financing would have been to make this authoritarian right arm of the German government all the more authoritarian.

98,000 in Manchester, England, but in 1911 Manchester's police only imposed 14,000 police penalties, most of which were for drunkenness, which the Germans seldom punished. On these issues, see also Laufer, *Unser Polizeiwesen*, pp. 71–91; C. Friedel, *Die polizeiliche Strafverfügung;* and for a comparison with the police practices employed in the United States and England, see Julius Hatschek, "Das Polizeirecht in der Vereinigten Staaten: Auf der Grundlage des englischen und im Vergleiche zum preussischen Rechte," *Archiv für Sozialwissenschaft und Sozialpolitik* 31 (1910): 67–101, and 32 (1911): 433–95.

69 Laufer, *Unser Polizeiwesen*, p. 92.
70 Quoted in Fosdick, *European Police Systems*, p. 312.
71 Laufer, *Unser Polizeiwesen*, p. 117. In some ways, however, the Social Democrats may have drawn strength from the perception that they were persecuted by the police and other criminal justice authorities. In his *Scandal, Sensation and Social Democracy*, p. 73, Alex Hall quotes Hans Delbrück in 1903 as saying: "One of the sources from which the tremendous power of Social Democracy draws its strength . . . is the sense that we in Germany do not live in a system of equality before the law. It is the concept of 'Klassenjustiz' which awakens a most passionate form of hate."

COURTS, CRIMINAL PROCEDURE, JUDGES, AND ATTORNEYS

Given the horrendous record of German courts and their officials during the National Socialist period, it seems rather incredible that an English legal scholar could seriously argue in a book published in 1933 comparing courts and judges in England, France, and Germany, that the "German judicial system has, in its turn, some serious claims to be regarded as the best in Europe."[72] At the time of Hitler's takeover, however, few would have predicted that the Nazi manipulation of the legal system in the years that followed would be so easy, so complete, and so heinous. As we have already seen, there were, to be sure, ample grounds for criticizing the overly positivistic criminal code that attempted to regulate and often to proscribe so much of normal human behavior – the freedom-of-speech-denying libel laws and perhaps above all the militaristic and overbearing police force – but there were, at the time, some reasons why one could have expected better of German judges, attorneys, courts, and criminal procedure given their background, organization, and nature in the Weimar Republic and in the Kaiserreich.

The Englishman's praise was based on the following: German judges, attorneys, and court officials were highly educated, rigorously trained, and usually quite efficient in the exercise of their duties; the courts were organized in a clear hierarchy without overlapping jurisdictions and were plentiful enough to handle their caseloads; the uniform and scientific criminal procedure, in theory at least, treated all individuals equally and was employed quickly to establish the facts of the case, to apply the criminal code, and to determine guilt or innocence; German court fees were relatively inexpensive because little time was wasted in the process of establishing precedents, as precedents were of less importance than in Anglo-American law; cases were seldom thrown out because of legal loopholes or because of minor procedural matters; there was little room for grandstand plays or emotional pleas by defense attorneys attempting to secure an acquittal based on sympathy or ignorance; the judge determining sentence could choose only between quite narrow minimum and maximum sentences, which were graduated according to the severity of the deed and were clearly laid down in the criminal code; and the whole system of justice was set up by an admittedly flawed but, until 1933, not fully undemocratic society.[73]

72 R. C. K. Ensor, *Courts and Judges*, p. 52.
73 For a comparison between the German and the American systems, in which the author argues that he favored the German because the American system was so overly concerned with guaranteeing

Despite these praiseworthy aspects, and in addition to the problems associated with the police and the law itself, there were many reasons why an Englishman, or anyone else committed to the cause of democratic freedom and justice, should have found fault with the pre-Hitlerian German criminal justice system and its officials: particularly, its lack of respect for personal freedom and human weakness; the underlying conservatism of its judges and prosecutors; both their, and arguably wide sections of the German populace's, overdetermined respect for and narrow interpretation of the letter of the law, no matter who made it or for what purposes; and their penchant for cracking down on ethnic minorities and the political Left while overlooking the misdeeds of miscreants on the political Right.[74]

Indeed, though they might have fought crime and criminals efficiently, by carrying on a tradition of valuing the protection of society over the individual rights and liberties of its citizens, German courts and their officials in the late nineteenth and early twentieth century inadvertently helped to make the transmogrification of justice by the Gestapo, *Sondergerichte,* and *Volksgericht* of the Third Reich possible. Certainly the German courts in the time of Bismarck and the kaisers did not share the fundamental philosophy of criminal procedure prevailing in Anglo-American societies, whereby the protection of the innocent is more important than the conviction of the guilty. Rather, the inverse was applied: German courts preferred to risk the conviction of a few innocent people so as to assure the conviction of all who were guilty.

The odds were heavily stacked against the accused. The defendant was not granted the right to be presumed innocent until proven guilty beyond a reasonable doubt; actually, the defendant was presumed guilty until proven innocent. The defense attorney had very limited powers, and, in that the defense attorney was a salaried state employee, the defendant could not be sure if the defense attorney's allegiance was more to his client or to the state. Only in serious felony offenses did the defendant have the right to trial by a jury of his peers. And, finally, the defendant had but one appeal, and this was possible only for questions of law, not fact. Like the criminal law and the police, the courts, criminal procedure, judges, and attorneys acted efficiently

---

individual rights that it was prone to loopholes and that the American court proceedings were like a "contest in which the skill of the participants is much to be admired but the trial is not directed primarily to ascertain the truth," see H. R. Limburg, "Law Enforcement in Germany and in the United States – The Underlying Philosophy and Methods," *Virginia Law Review* 16 (1930): 659–88; quotation on p. 667.

74 On Weimar courts and their judges' harshness toward the Left and leniency toward the Right, see Angermund, *Deutsche Richterschaft 1919–1945,* pp. 19–44, and Müller, *Hitler's Justice,* pp. 10–24.

and uniformly, but they also acted paternalistically to uphold the values of an authoritarian society.[75]

The uniform organization of German courts and the criminal procedure they followed came into effect on October 1, 1879, as a result of the passing of the Code of Judicial Organization (*Gerichtsverfassungsgesetz*), which followed the Code of Criminal Procedure (*Strafprozessordnung*), passed on January 27, 1877. With some exceptions, court and criminal procedure thenceforth followed the procedures used in France and remained in effect throughout the remaining years of the Reich and into the Weimar period. Perhaps the most distinguishing features of the court system were the very limited use of jury trials and the widespread use of the court of lay assessors (*Schöffengericht*). A jury court (*Schwurgericht*) was only used in extremely serious felony offenses such as murder, manslaughter, arson, perjury, and rape. It was called periodically (similar to the courts of assizes in France) to hear such cases and was composed of three professional judges and twelve jurymen. The judges were to decide on all points of law and on sentencing; the jurors were to rule on the facts of the case and to determine guilt or innocence. Most offenses, however, were heard before a court of lay assessors. This could be made up either of a single judge and two lay assessors, as occurred in most simple misdemeanors (*Vergehen*) and minor offenses (*Übertretungen*), or of three judges and two lay assessors, for serious misdemeanors and minor felonies. The lay assessors were appointed from the citizenry by local authorities, and they assisted the judges in determining all matters, including questions of guilt and sentencing. The lay assessors were no doubt greatly influenced by the judges, especially as the judges voted with them in determining guilt; but they did help provide the defendant with some of the advantages of a jury trial in that their major role was to "contribute . . . elements of local knowledge, human sympathy, or representative public opinion."[76]

The hierarchy of courts was divided into four different levels. The court of first instance for most minor offenses and small misdemeanors was the district court (*Amtsgericht*). There was roughly one of these for each *Kreis* (in 1910 there were 1,944 in all of Germany), and they were presided over by a single judge, but in large cities the *Amtsgericht* was usually divided into several departments, each headed by a single judge. The judge would act alone in deciding only very minor offenses such as theft from the forest or field. Although the public prosecutor had the right to have more serious cases

---

75 On the weakness of defense attorneys, see Jarausch, *The Unfree Professions;* and Siegkrist, "Public Office or Free Profession?"
76 Ensor, *Courts and Judges*, p. 69.

tried in this way, usually the judge was assisted by two lay assessors, thus making a *Schöffengericht*. Together the judge and the two lay assessors would try all minor offenses and most simple misdemeanors.

Acting as a court of appeal for the *Amtsgericht* and as a court of first instance for most serious misdemeanors and felonies was the superior court (*Landgericht*). In 1910 there were 176 of these, and they usually presided over the territory of ten to twelve district courts. There were three different types of courts used in different matters at this level, two types of courts of lay assessors and a jury court. A *Schöffengericht* of one judge and two lay assessors heard appeals from the district courts when the judge acted alone; a *Schöffengericht* of three judges and two lay assessors heard appeals from the *Schöffengericht* of a district court and also acted as the court of first instance for serious misdemeanors and minor felonies; and a jury court was assembled to hear major felonies.

The final two levels of courts were the superior provincial court of appeals (*Oberlandesgericht*) and the Imperial Supreme Court (*Reichsgericht*). Both courts acted primarily as courts of appeal, but the Imperial Supreme Court had original jurisdiction in cases of treason. The twenty-eight Superior Provincial Courts were each made up of between ten and fifteen chambers, each containing three judges. They heard appeals from the superior provincial courts. The Imperial Supreme Court sitting in Leipzig had twelve separate chambers, eight for civil matters and four for criminal, each with five judges. Both types of appeals courts acted as courts of appeal for cases tried by jury courts and for cases involving thorny applications of federal laws. But the decisions of neither of these courts were binding as precedents for the lower courts, for German judges were to "formulate their own decisions according to their best knowledge and conscience" and were "not bound by precedents but solely by the code."[77] Nonetheless, the decisions of the superior provincial courts and the Imperial Supreme Court were kept in mind by lower court judges, who did not want their own decisions overturned by appeal.[78]

The Code of Criminal Procedure, followed by all German courts since 1879, paralleled closely the procedure used in French criminal proceedings established by their code of Criminal Examination in 1808. Although one must take exception to the limited rights it gave the defendant and the

---

[77] Hans E. Stille, "Legal Education and Practice in Germany," 249.
[78] For brief explanations of the hierarchy of German courts and their functions, see Detlev Vagts, introduction to Ingo Müller's *Hitler's Justice*, pp. ix–xviii; and Kenneth F. Ledford, "Conflicts within the Legal Profession: Simultaneous Admission and the German Bar, 1903–1927," in Cocks and Jarausch, eds., *German Professions*, pp. 253–4.

defense counsel, it compares not altogether unfavorably with the procedure used in many other countries at the time. Clearly, the orderly and thorough procedure used was much unlike the gamelike atmosphere of the American courtroom, where "the defense and prosecuting attorneys resembled players, the defendant the ball, and the judge the umpire who occasionally yelled foul."[79] As the German procedure was also quite informal (compared to the American), its goal being "to ascertain, as far as possible, the objective truth, on the basis of an oral hearing and by way of a free valuation of the evidence little hampered by formal rules of evidence,"[80] it in some ways compared favorably with American court procedure, which was often "twisted by adroit criminal lawyers, and full of delays, mistrials, hung juries, and dismissed cases."[81] Most trials, in fact, were concluded quickly, usually in one session, with, unfortunately for the defendant, a verdict of guilty.[82]

One of the reasons the defendant was usually found guilty was that much work had been completed before the trial itself to make sure that only cases sound in fact and with strong evidence against the accused would ever make it to court. Following French practice, the German system featured a public prosecutor's office whose duty it was to gather evidence against the accused, initiate the criminal proceedings, and present the evidence in a preliminary hearing. Once it was learned that a violation of the criminal code had occurred, the prosecutor's office would immediately start gathering evidence. The state attorney assigned to the case did not need to wait for a formal complaint from an injured party except in cases of adultery, defamation, and simple assault, as the state itself was considered an injured party with any violation of the code. The state attorney's investigation was quite informal. He did not even need to inform the person under suspicion or the person bringing charges that the investigation was under way. Once he had gathered enough evidence from all available sources – police, public bodies, private persons, and so on – to warrant solid grounds to bring formal court action he would then file an indictment (*Anklageschrift*) listing the charges and evidence against the accused and ask for the opening of a preliminary judicial examination (*Voruntersuchung*).

The preliminary examination was required in all cases to be heard before a *Schöffengericht* or *Schwurgericht;* it could be waived in favor of a summary trial only in very minor cases and upon the request of the defendant. Its purpose was to determine if there was a solid evidentiary base warranting full judicial

---

79 Limburg, "Law Enforcement in Germany and in the United States," p. 667.
80 Hans Julius Wolff, "Criminal Justice in Germany: II," *Michigan Law Review* 43 (1944): 163.
81 Norman Tressholmes's introduction to A. Esmein, *A History of Continental Criminal Procedure*, p. xi.
82 See the discussion of acquittal rates in Chapter 3.

proceedings in a formal trial and to guarantee the individual rights of the accused. Usually it was a brief proceeding conducted by a single judge, but it was also overseen by an independent tribunal, as would be any trial to follow. While the preliminary examination was under way, accused persons were usually set free, unless they were without domicile, were foreigners, or were deemed likely to flee or to destroy evidence or if they refused to give information about themselves. Although defendants had the right to defense counsel and one would be appointed for them if necessary, their defense attorney played a very limited role in the examination. The defense counsel could not examine the evidence against his client; he could not ask for acquittal if his client had admitted guilt to him, which was unlikely anyway, as he could not speak to his client unless they were in the presence of a court official; he did not have the right to ask questions of witnesses; he could not even take part in the interrogation of his client. Once the preliminary examination had been completed, and if the judge determined there were sufficient grounds to proceed to a full trial, the judge would then file an "Order to Hold for Trial" (*Eröffnungsbeschluss*), the defendant would be taken into custody, and soon afterward the formal trial would begin.[83]

Whereas the preliminary examination was held in private, the trial itself was open to the public, unless it would endanger public order or endanger someone's life. Evidence and testimony had to be presented orally, and it was to proceed without interruption. By far the most important role was played by the judge. He decided which witnesses would be introduced, when they would be introduced, what evidence was permissible, and when it would be introduced (little if any evidence was inadmissible, however, as all sorts of evidence was permitted, even hearsay). Furthermore, it was the judge's duty to call expert witnesses (all of whom, as court-appointed officials, could not act in a biased fashion to support either prosecution or defense); the judge did almost all of the questioning of the defendant; and the judge led the questioning of all other witnesses. Finally, the judge either acted alone in minor cases, or along with the lay assessors (*Schöffengericht*) when guilt or innocence was to be decided. "No objections or continual interruptions by counsel" were permitted as they played "quite a subsidiary part in the trial."[84] But the judge was supposed to allow the defense and prosecuting attorneys, the lay judges, and even the defendant to ask questions freely of

---

83 Wolff, "Criminal Justice in Germany: I," 1085–8; and Esmein, *A History of Continental Criminal Procedure*, pp. 599–606.
84 Limburg, "Law Enforcement in Germany and in the United States," p. 667. See also Raimund Kusserow, ed., *Richter in Deutschland* (Hamburg, 1982).

witnesses. Should the judge not like the tone or direction of their questions, however, he could withdraw this privilege.

Defendants had the right and duty of attendance and the trial usually could not proceed in their absence, though they could be asked to leave the courtroom for short periods if their presence would inhibit witnesses from divulging evidence. After the charges against them were read, they were the first to be heard. They were encouraged to tell their own story in their own way; they did not testify under formal oath; and they had the right to remain silent when asked questions, though silence could be held against them. After their testimony the other evidence and witnesses would be heard. All other witnesses, however, testified under oath and were to confine themselves to facts and not opinions. The trial ended with the final arguments of the prosecutor, the defense counsel, and lastly the defendant. Depending on the type of court employed, the judge and the lay judges or jurors then retired to chambers and decided the verdict, which would be guilty if a two-thirds majority of them agreed. After a decision was reached, everyone would return to the courtroom, where the judge would announce the verdict and, if acquittal had not been agreed upon, pronounce sentence.[85]

As the procedure followed in criminal cases placed prime emphasis on the provisions of the criminal code and virtually none on precedents set by verdicts delivered by civilian juries; as juries were used so sparingly in general; as the presiding judge had so much authority in all aspects of a criminal proceeding, even involving himself in the final decision of guilt or innocence; as all judges and attorneys were state-appointed officials and not elected or popularly selected; as expert witnesses were also state employees and were picked by the presiding judge and not employed by the competing parties in a criminal case; and as the state considered itself an injured party in all criminal cases, and, through its own public prosecutor, took prime responsibility in initiating almost all criminal proceedings, criminal justice in Imperial Germany was much more a state than a civilian or popular affair.

All this having been said, few societies at the time could boast that "every court of justice, high or low, is presided over by a trained judge, and every trained judge belongs to the same order."[86] Indeed, German judges and attorneys had to undergo an educational and training process that made their peers in most other countries look like unschooled amateurs.[87] After com-

---

85 Wolff, "Criminal Justice in Germany: II," 155–73; and Limburg, "Law Enforcement in Germany and in the United States," 667–87.
86 Ensor, *Courts and Judges*, p. 54.
87 The British traveler to Berlin in the 1870s, Henry Vizetelly, who was certainly not uncritical of Germany, was extremely impressed by the high academic standards of all German officials, even of

pleting high school studies and passing the *Abitur* exam, a prospective German judge or lawyer had to study law for at least three years at a university where he was trained by professors of great scholarly eminence.[88] Upon the successful completion of university legal studies, he was allowed to take the *Referendarexamen,* the first major state examination he would have to pass. Both oral and written in content, it took a few weeks to complete and was administered by university professors, judges of higher courts, and lawyers of high reputation. After this, he would spend a period of four years as a legal apprentice, during which time he was unpaid. The apprenticeship was divided into periods of time spent with various types of courts, a public prosecutor's office, and an attorney selected by the apprentice. During this period the apprentice was to apply the knowledge learned at the university to practical cases, and to continue his theoretical work by attending practical courses in which legal questions were discussed with other apprentices and judges. At the end of this apprenticeship he took the final major state examination (*Assessorexamen*), which qualified him for admission to the bar. This exam stressed the practical aspects of the law and criminal procedure more than the earlier examination had, and was held in the Ministry of Justice before a commission of three persons, usually including a judge, a barrister, and a high ministry official. It was very difficult – about half failed on first try and only one reexamination was allowed. Once this training was completed, usually the most successful would be selected to become judges and the less successful would become attorneys. If he were to become the former, he usually had to serve an additional several years as a poorly paid assistant judge who sat in on judicial proceedings but could not act independently.[89]

Although judges were rather highly respected and usually came from the propertied bourgeoisie, they were too poorly paid and their training was

---

common bureaucrats, whose studies were far less extensive than those of legal officials. Comparing German officials to those of his own country, he wrote: "To qualify themselves for posts that with us are occupied by men of humble birth and rudimentary education, men of the higher middle classes in Prussia go through a course of education that would fit them for an M.A. degree in any of our universities. About twelve years of hard study, and a standard of intellectual culture that would class him in the honors list of our Alma Mater, qualify a young Prussian with official aspiration for – let us say – a sortership in the Post Office, or a copying clerkship in the State Department." Vizetelly, *Berlin: Under the New Empire,* 1:95.

88 Shartel and Wolff, "German Lawyers – Training and Functions," pp. 521–3. All law professors had to hold doctorate degrees and had to have written a second thesis to admit them to teaching known as the *Habilitationsschrift*. These professors were extremely well respected in Germany and in the world, and were often called in by the courts to offer expert opinions. Shartel and Wolff assert that "there is no country in the world where the scholar, and particularly the legal scholar, enjoys the prestige which he enjoys in Germany."

89 For a fuller discussion of the training of attorneys and judges, see Jarausch, *The Unfree Professions.*

usually too onerous to attract men of the highest social classes. Judges were paid between four and eight thousand marks, making them roughly on a par with military captains or majors, and prosecutors and other attorneys made less.[90] Even though this was about the same pay that a *Landrat* or a lower member of one of the state ministries received, Junkers and other aristocrats in Germany usually preferred the latter positions because they did not call for quite such rigorous training and were considered more socially acceptable. Although 6 percent of all judges in Germany were of noble background; only a handful of provincial court judges in eastern Prussia were Junkers and no Junkers were judges in other parts of Prussia; and whereas Junkers made up one-third to one-fourth of all ministry presidents in Prussia and 10 percent of all ministry officials, no Junker was ever minister of justice during Imperial Germany, and only one of sixty-eight officials of the Ministry of Justice in 1914 was a Junker.[91] On the other hand, very few members of the lower classes were lawyers or attorneys, and almost no Social Democrats ever became judges.[92] Lower-class individuals could hardly afford the expensive university training and unpaid apprenticeship, and no doubt their lower social background would not help them get admitted to the bar even if they could afford it.

Most judges and attorneys, then, came from the middle to upper-middle rungs of the social ladder, with the judges usually from a higher rung than the attorneys, and most Germans had good reason to consider the legal profession a solidly bourgeois enclave.[93] But being bourgeois in Imperial Germany did not necessarily imply being liberal. In the first half of the nineteenth century most judges and attorneys were reputed to be liberal-minded, and many were even left-liberal. But over time their liberal spirit, particularly on the part of judges, receded. In the Frankfurt Parliament of 1848, 16 percent of the deputies were of the legal profession but in the

---

90 Erich Döhring, *Geschichte der deutschen Rechtspflege*, pp. 86–8; and Muncy, *The Junkers in the Prussian Administration*, pp. 87–96.
91 Döhring, *Geschichte der deutschen Rechtspflege*, pp. 74–5; and Muncy, *The Junkers in the Prussian Administration*, pp. 201–7.
92 Saul, *Staat, Industrie und Arbeiterbewegung*, p. 111; and Hall, *Scandal, Sensation and Social Democracy*, p. 47. Hall reports that the lay judges and jurors also were very unlikely to come from the lower classes. He found that out of 5,070 lay judges and jurors before 1907, only one was of working-class origin – a chimney-sweep's apprentice.
93 Jarausch, *The Unfree Professions*, p. 11. One indication of the bourgeois nature of the legal profession is that it attracted so many Jews. Peter Gay, in his *Freud, Jews and Other Germans: Masters and Victims in Modernist Culture* (Oxford, 1978), pp. 96–114, explains that, in 1907 14 percent of all German attorneys were Jewish, whereas Jews made up only about 1 percent of the general population. Jews, of course, were also heavily represented in the other "free professions," such as medicine, where they made up 6 percent of all medical doctors, and higher education, where they made up 12 percent of the *Privatdozenten* but only 3 percent of the full professors.

Reichstag of Imperial Germany only about 12 percent of the deputies were professional lawyers or judges. As Konrad Jarausch explains in his recent book comparing German lawyers, engineers, and teachers in the first half of the twentieth century, "the self-image of German attorneys was self-consciously liberal," but German attorneys, like other members of the German bourgeoisie in the Kaiserreich, "wavered between the illustrious legacy of liberalism and a rising tide of 'academic illiberalism.'"[94] And as Ingo Müller, the author of a recent controversial book on the courts of the Third Reich, argues, the requirement that judges had to have independent means (in force until 1911) and the judge's lengthy traineeship, which under Bismarck was often as long as twenty years, "offered ample opportunity to observe the candidates, to remove those elements associated with the opposition, and to suppress every liberal tendency. The only candidates who survived this ceaseless scrutiny were those who were loyal and compliant to a particularly high degree – those who, in other words, accepted the social and political order unconditionally."[95]

Hence, even though legal officials were well trained and the legal system was organized and administered efficiently, given this tradition of the unconditional acceptance of the letter of the law and of the authorities who made the law, the conservatism and great power of the judges, the weakness of the more moderate defense attorneys, the limited rights of the defendants, the relative absence of verdicts pronounced by a jury of one's peers, and the exclusion of most lower-class Germans from the legal professions – when added to the other authoritarian aspects of the criminal justice system – the compliance of the legal system and even the complicity of many of its officials after 1933 becomes more understandable.

PUNISHMENT

One might argue that the trend in punishment practices begun in the second half of the nineteenth century played a transitional role between the barbarous public execution ceremonies of the eighteenth century and the out-of-sight, out-of-mind secretive tortures and mass executions of the Nazi period.[96] But in this aspect of the criminal justice system, at least, it is not at all clear that Germany under Bismarck and the kaisers followed a developmental path that was very different from many other modernizing societies

---

94 Jarausch, *The Unfree Professions*, pp. 11, 24. See also Jarausch, *Students, Society and Politics in Imperial Germany: The Rise of Academic Illiberalism* (Princeton, N.J., 1982).
95 Müller, *Hitler's Justice*, p. 6.
96 Evans, "Öffentlichkeit und Autorität," p. 246.

in the nineteenth century. The evolution of punishment in Germany underwent, as Richard Evans explains, "the same long-term changes as Foucault for France, Ignatieff for England and Rothman for America have pointed out. Bodily punishment was gradually ended, and around the middle of the century – except in the case of the punishment for minor offenses carried out in the jails – was no longer used in Prussia."[97] Workers in Hamburg and other German cities as late as the mid-1890s frequently complained about the conditions in the jails and even about the continued usage of torture techniques such as the Spanish Bock, *Prügelmachine,* and food deprivation,[98] but by the late nineteenth century these were more the exception than the rule in the German penal system.

The "welcome whipping ceremonies" with which entering prisoners were always greeted up to mid-century were no longer allowed, prisoners no longer were forced to walk on wooden treadmills or to wear leg irons and wooden hobbles,[99] and "after 1851 a unified prison system was developed which increasingly concentrated on the prisoner's isolation and 'improvement' and no longer just on his punishment."[100] But it is debatable, as Evans, Foucault, and others have explained, whether this "enlightened" trend away from mere societal retribution and toward the rehabilitation of the criminal was as humane as its proponents boasted. Capital punishment declined in the late nineteenth century from .03 percent of all convictions in 1882 to .01 percent in 1913,[101] but it was replaced by confinement in jails and prisons that were intended to "strike fear even into the hearts of the starving"[102] and that arguably mentally brutalized the prisoners as much as the old torture ordeals had brutalized them physically. "Thousands of cells were built, in which the prisoners were isolated from the outside world. It was believed by this to check all evil and prepare the way for good influences . . . but, still, stupid, shattered, weak men came out."[103] Certainly few were improved by the prison experience as most had very slim chances of fitting back into society and finding meaningful employment with the label of *vorbestraft* (previously punished) affixed to them for eternity.[104]

97 Ibid., p. 236.
98 Evans, *Kneipengespräche,* pp. 205–21.
99 Bar, *History of Continental Criminal Law,* pp. 328–49; William Harbut Dawson, *The Vagrancy Problem* (London, 1910), pp. 51ff.
100 Evans, "Öffentlichkeit und Autorität," p. 236.
101 Rusche and Kirchheimer, *Punishment and Social Structure,* pp. 145–8. On the general trends in punishment, see Rupert Rabl, *Strafzumessungspraxis und Kriminalitätsbewegung* (Leipzig, 1936); and Franz Exner, *Studien über die Strafzumessungspraxis der deutschen Gerichte* (Leipzig, 1931).
102 Rusche and Kirchheimer, p. 134.
103 Werner Gentz, "The Problem of Punishment in Germany," *Journal of Criminal Law and Criminology* 22 (1932), 876.
104 For examples of Hamburg workers' views on this, see Evans, *Kneipengespräche,* pp. 207, 216–23.

Questions of humanity and enlightenment aside, the main goal of punishment was to deter criminality and, insofar as it served to maintain the existing power structure, to protect society.[105] To this end, the ultimate power to determine the length and severity of the sentence was entrusted to the presiding judge at the criminal trial, whose allegiance and conservatism were assured, and little was left to the discretion of the prison administration. The judge was supposed to place more weight on the criminal deed than on the circumstances of the criminal, the severity of the sentence was supposed to fit the severity of the deed, and the judge was supposed not to inflict a sentence that was not within the narrow minimum and maximum range set by the criminal code. Although the judge was expected to take the social and economic status of the offender into consideration as well as the amount of malice intended in the criminal act, this often heightened the problem of discriminatory justice in the Kaiserreich. Alex Hall explains in a book on German social democracy that "the sad truth was that purely extraneous considerations – the clothes a man happened to wear or the political convictions he held – continued to impress the courts of law much more than concrete legal evidence," and that if a worker brought complaint against a public servant, for example, the prosecutor and the judge were likely to turn the matter around so as to prosecute the worker for defamation of character.[106]

Once in the jail or prison, most convicts served out their prescribed terms, though parole was sometimes granted if the prisoner had displayed good behavior and had served at least three-quarters of his term. In making comparisons with other societies at the time and with German society in the past, however, one can point to some improvements in the conditions inside the penal institutions. Prisoners were usually given clean clothes and bedding, provided with some measure of light and space, and adequately fed. In most cases, with the exception of the penitentiaries where they were to work at hard labor, the prisoners could decide for themselves if they wanted to work, and if they did, were remunerated for their efforts. They could be punished for bad behavior by having their cells darkened, their wages taken away for some weeks, their books taken away for some months, or by being denied the right to work, but their physical, if not their mental, health was not to be jeopardized. A prisoner's life expectancy was roughly on a par with the average worker in the population, and cases of tuberculosis and other diseases related to poor diet and bad health were rare. This compares favor-

---

105 This argument has been attributed to Foucault in recent years, but Rusche and Kirchheimer perhaps argued it first, in their *Punishment and Social Structure*.
106 Hall, *Scandal, Sensation and Social Democracy*, p. 73.

ably with the first half of the nineteenth century, when between 60 and 80 percent of prison deaths were caused by tuberculosis and the life expectancy of a thirty-year-old prisoner in a Prussian prison at mid-century was the same as a sixty-year-old outside prison.[107]

On the whole, the consistent, unified, efficient, and scientific nature of the penal system was in step with the rest of the criminal justice system, and to a large degree with the society itself. Workers, Poles, Social Democrats, and other outsiders constantly complained of the brutal and class-based justice under which they suffered. Some of the propertied listened to them: Some editors of the bourgeois newspapers like the *Berliner Tageblatt,* even after the turn of the century, continued to deplore the immorality of the already greatly decreased practice of capital punishment, and some leading criminal justice scholars like Gustav Aschaffenburg continued to argue that crime could only be deterred by social and economic improvements, not by punishment.[108] Some improvements were undeniably made in several aspects of the system. But the basic system remained intact. Highly educated, conservative judges ruled with an unquestioning spirit on a body of narrowly defined laws that were the products of a technically advanced but authoritarian society. Well-equipped and militaristic policemen saw that the laws were obeyed. Unempowered, though reasonably compensated and well-intended, defense attorneys, like the educated middle classes from which they came, did little to defend clients, who usually came from the lower orders of society, and who were more subjects than citizens. There were complaints. But there was a strong sense of law and order.

107 Rusche and Kirchheimer, p. 109.
108 Evans, "Öffentlichkeit und Autorität," pp. 237–8. Gustav Aschaffenburg, *Crime and Its Repression* (Boston, 1913).

2

Popular Opinion: Crime as a "Foreign" Concept

Imperial Germany was an orderly society with a powerful elite, a highly trained and efficient corps of officials, and a well-defined system of law. It was also a society undergoing tremendous economic and social change. How did the society respond to these changes? Did the fantastic growth of cities and industry lead to a huge upsurge in urban crime and violence? After all, it spurred, among other things, a massive migration from countryside to town, a huge growth of the working class, a clamoring for reform, and sometimes a call to revolution – which clearly led to the government's increasing manipulation of the law and justice system to control its citizens and any revolutionary impulses. Were the thieves, robbers, and murderers the same people whom the government labeled and prosecuted for violating its overbearing political strictures? Who were their victims? What caused crime?

There are at least two logical ways to go about answering these questions. One is to examine the statistics of crime; another is to examine what contemporary German citizens thought and said. There are problems with each approach. Statistics are governmental and administrative artifacts subject to bias, and this is especially true in the case of crime statistics. Furthermore, the notorious "dark figure" in crime statistics of unreported and thus unrecorded acts makes statistical investigations of criminal activity tricky.

If there are problems with the statistical approach, there are also problems with a more qualitative approach. Can one really trust what contemporaries said about their problems? Not only could no one person or group of persons be so well informed as to know what the truth was, all people's interpretations of the truth were biased by their ideological, religious, social, and ethnic backgrounds. So which contemporaries' viewpoints should one consult: those of the government, those of intellectuals, those of criminals themselves? And where should one look to find their opinions: in governmental reports, in novels, plays, and short stories, in daily newspapers and popular magazines? How does one measure such opinions?

Still, given the problems inherent in each type of approach, there are many things one can learn from using them both, particularly in combination. Statistics, for all their faults, if used judiciously, are the most direct indicators of social behavior. Biases that affect their construction can be understood and can themselves be used as sources of information. And German society had some of the best-kept, detailed criminal and social statistics in the world.[1] The values and attitudes of contemporaries, though less directly measurable, provide a necessary context for the evaluation of the statistics and can themselves be useful indicators of criminal trends. Furthermore, when statistics and popular attitudes overlap and point in the same direction, conclusions are strengthened.

As J. J. Tobias demonstrated for nineteenth-century England and Louis Chevalier for nineteenth-century France, a useful way of uncovering what people thought about crime in their urbanizing and industrializing societies was to consult what Dickens, Thackeray, Balzac, Hugo, Sue, Zola, and other great literary minds had to say on the subject.[2] Whereas realist and naturalist portraits of crime and justice were popular with nineteenth-century audiences, and their authors were well known to the well-read inhabitants of the Kaiserreich,[3] few German writers of note took up these themes.[4] Hence, instead of trying to take the lead from the comparatively small number of German literary works on the topic, as one might do by discussing the handful of respected German novelists and playwrights like Suder-

[1] See my discussion in "Counting 'How It Really Was': Quantitative History in West Germany," *Historical Methods* 21 (1988), 61–79; " Herbert Reinke, "Die 'Liaison' des Strafrechts mit der Statistik – zu den Anfängen kriminalstatistischer Zählungen im 18. und 19. Jahrhundert," *Zeitschrift für Neuere Rechtsgeschichte* 12 (1990), 169–79; H. Graff, *Die deutsche Kriminalstatistik – Geschichte und Gegenwart* (Stuttgart, 1975); James J. Sheehan, "Quantification in the Study of Modern German Social and Political History," in Val R. Lorwin and Jacob M. Price, eds., *The Dimensions of the Past: Materials, Problems, and Opportunities for Quantitative Work in History* (New Haven, Conn., 1972), pp. 301–2; and Georg von Mayr, *Moralstatistk mit Einschluss der Kriminalstatistik* (Tübingen, 1917).
[2] J. J. Tobias, *Urban Crime in Victorian England* (New York, 1972); Louis Chevalier, *Laboring Classes and Dangerous Classes: In Paris during the First Half of the Nineteenth Century* (Princeton, N.J., 1981).
[3] On Germans' reading habits generally, see Rolf Engelsing, *Analphabetentum und Lektüre. Zur Sozialgeschichte des Lesens in Deutschland zwischen feudaler und industrieller Gesellschaft* (Stuttgart, 1973). On the popularity of Dickens and his influence on nineteenth-century German authors, see Emil Doernenburg and Wilhelm Fehse, *Raabe und Dickens. Ein Beitrag zur Erkenntnis der geistigen Gestalt Wilhelm Raabes* (Magdeburg, 1921). On p. 3 they explain: "It is remarkable how quickly he conquered the hearts of the German people. . . . When Copperfield appeared in 1849, every new monthly installment was looked forward to impatiently by man, woman, and child, and it was so important to us at the time that throughout Germany more was disputed over David and Agnes than over Radowitz and Manteuffel."
[4] Jörg Schönert, "Kriminalgeschichte in der deutschen Literatur zwischen 1770 und 1890. Zur Entwicklung des Genres in sozialgeschichtlicher Perpektive," *Geschichte und Gesellschaft* 9 (1983), 49–68. In 1910, in the introduction to one of the most famous collections of famous criminal cases in the Kaiserreich, a German justice authority explained that such collections were necessary because German literature on the subject was "so pitiful. . . . Our literature . . . leaves the researcher in the lurch." Erich Sello, in Hugo Friedländer, *Interessante Kriminal-Prozesse* (Berlin, 1910), 1: iv.

mann, Fontane, Hauptmann, Kretzer, and Rabbe who occasionally addressed these issues, we might more profitably turn first to popular newspapers and magazines and come back to them later.

NEWSPAPERS AND CRIME

In an age before television, radio, and modern motion pictures, popular newspapers took pride of place in informing and molding public opinion and providing popular topics of discussion. As continues to be the case today, crime stories were of exceptional interest to average citizens. Richard Evans explains in his study of Hamburg workers' pub talk that "in the pub people discussed not just everyday problems, religion and politics, but very frequently the newest newspaper crime accounts . . . whose function as popular dramas stimulating discussion have been taken over today by television series."[5] Newspapers were of equal interest and importance to other classes as well. In fact, they were so important, that to understand popular opinion in the second half of the nineteenth century, one might not want to go any further than the newspapers alone. In the words of a German contemporary in 1866, "What one refers to as popular opinion is in many cases simply a result of the daily press."[6] Many modern scholars share this view. Rolf Engelsing, the author of several important works on German reading habits and literary and journalistic literature, compared the influence of the German newspapers with that of the church and discerned that the newspapers were far more influential in molding public opinion.[7] Although a common joke in turn-of-the-century Germany indicated that the *Speisezettel* (Menu) was the preferred reading material of German citizens,[8] late-nineteenth- and early-twentieth-century Germans certainly had a healthy appetite for daily newspapers.

By the time the Reich was founded, there was hardly an educated family that did not get a daily newspaper,[9] and by the turn of the century over a

---

5 Richard J. Evans, *Kneipengespräche im Kaiserreich. Stimmungsberichte der Hamburger Politischen Polizei 1892–1914* (Hamburg, 1989), p. 182.
6 Rudolf Schenda, *Volk Ohne Buch. Studien zur Sozialgeschichte der populären Lesestoffe 1770–1910* (Frankfurt am Main, 1970), p. 488.
7 Rolf Engelsing, *Massenpublikum und Journalistentum im 19. Jahrhundert in Nordwestdeutschland* (Berlin, 1966), pp. 130–1.
8 When a Viennese was asked what his favorite reading material was, he responded, "Der Speisezettel." Schenda, *Volk Ohne Buch*, p. 461.
9 Rolf Engelsing, *Analphabetentum und Lektüre*, p. 135. At this time, most educated families also read magazines regularly, but few owned any books. About all that most educated families owned were schoolbooks, a cookbook, and books given as Christmas and birthday presents. Uneducated families, of course, owned even less.

third of all Germans held a subscription to at least one daily paper.[10] As only a very narrow stratum composed mainly of educated middle-class Germans regularly garnished their literary diets with novels, plays, short stories, or popular magazines,[11] the newspaper was the prime source of news and knowledge for most Germans. It may even have been of equal importance to the educated bourgeoisie as well. In 1908, the author of a study of German reading habits explained: "There are newspaper readers who never take a book in hand, and to this group belongs a large part of the middle class. For the German philistine, the newspaper is an equally important requisite as the beer glass."[12]

The contents of the newspapers also resembled the contents of the beer glasses: often they were heavy, but their taste varied considerably; usually they were produced and consumed locally, but they were of such high quality that their consumers felt little need for national brands. According to an article in *Vorwärts*, the leading organ of the Social Democratic Party, there were, in 1910, 3,929 newspapers in Germany. This compared to 2,067 in Italy and 1,350 in France.[13] Of these the majority were tied either directly or indirectly to one or another German political party: Only 1,344 described themselves as "non-party-political," but often these were in fact closely tied to one of the political parties. Of the rest, there were 710 semiofficial *Amtsblätter*, 495 Catholic Center Party papers, 388 Progressive, 378 Nationalist, 303 Conservative, 192 National Liberal, 100 Social Democratic, and 17 either Polish, Danish, or Guelph. Most newspapers were regional, with Berlin, which alone had 36 full daily papers in 1895 and 56 in 1918,

10 Schenda, *Volk Ohne Buch*, p. 452. Schenda cites figures showing that newspaper readership grew exponentially over the nineteenth century. Between 1840 and 1910, the number of newspaper readers grew nine times, from 4 percent of the general population to 36 percent.
11 Engelsing, *Analphabetentum und Lektüre*, p. 124. Between 1900 and 1913, the readership of the extremely popular magazine *Die Gartenlaube* comprised 20 percent salesmen and self-employed persons, 3 percent factory owners and directors, 10 percent academics and higher officials, 14 percent middle-level officials, 7 percent lower-level sales and bank employees, and 6 percent workers.
12 Rudolf von Gottschall, "Die Lektüre des heutigen Lesepublikums," *Deutsche Revue. Eine Monatsschrift* 23 (1908): 157. Engelsing, in *Analphabetentum und Lektüre*, p. 136, cites the *Sozialpolitiker* Lammers, who declared in 1880 that it was "amazing, how even the most educated people generally content themselves with the newspaper alone, added to perhaps by only the most essential occupational literature."
13 Alex Hall, *Scandal, Sensation and Social Democracy: The SPD Press and Wilhemine Germany 1890–1914* (Cambridge, 1977), pp. 29–30. Others give some different figures than Hall cites, but the overall impression that Germany had a true wealth of newspapers is the same. For example, Robert M. Berry, a Britisher who wrote a generalist's account of German society shortly before World War I, explained in his chapter on "The Press and Its Influence" that in 1910 there were 7,748 papers in Germany, of which 4,336 were dailies and the rest weeklies or monthlies. See his *Germany of the Germans* (New York, 1910), pp. 202–7. For a detailed discussion of the relationship between the press and the political parties, see Kurt Koszyk, *Deutsche Presse im 19. Jahrhundert* (Berlin, 1966), pp. 127–210.

acting as the center and having its newspapers quickly copied by others.[14] In 1885 there were only 5 papers in all of Germany that had a circulation of more than 40,000, and only 9 between 10,000 and 40,000. In 1900 ony 3.5 percent of all daily papers had a circulation of more than 15,000.[15]

The ideological and political message of the different newspapers varied greatly, but high intellectual quality and a sober style characterized most. This was true even for newspapers as disparate as the conservative *Die Kreuzzeitung* (the popular name for the *Neue Preußische Zeitung*), and for the socialist *Vorwärts*.[16] An average daily newspaper would have long editorials on current political, economic, and foreign policy matters. It usually would have about half a page devoted to a serialized novel, such as one by a foreign author like Zola or Dickens or a German author like Fontane. In the Sunday *Beilage* (supplements) there would usually be long scholarly and scientific articles on all kinds of subjects. In addition, the normal daily paper would contain theater and book reviews, stock reports, and lengthy columns of local society notes, such as who was visiting in which hotel, who was getting married, and who had died. There were, in short, a sea of words undiluted by any pictures (only the advertisements had drawings, and maps appeared only infrequently), and with little on cooking or fashion, only a very brief sports section, and very little use of bold type or italics. German newspapers informed, they seldom entertained.

Although crime stories were of great interest to Germans, on the surface they seemed conspicuous by their absence. One could read months of any paper and not find one mention of crime on the huge front page. In the Sunday supplements one found very little as well. Between 1870 and 1903 there were only 25 articles in the Sunday *Beilage* of the prestigious liberal paper, the *Vossische Zeitung*, on any subject relating to crime, law, or criminal justice. There were, on the other hand, 33 on Beethoven, hundreds on Berlin, hundreds on Friedrich the Great, 21 on Bismarck, hundreds on religion, and about 100 on Poles.[17] To a foreigner's eyes, at least, the scanty

---

14   Koszyk, *Deutsche Presse*, pp. 159ff; H. Diez, *Das Zeitungswesen* (Leipzig, 1919), p. 53. On Berlin newspapers in general, see Peter de Mendelssohn, *Zeitungsstadt Berlin* (Berlin, 1959), and Gerhard Masur, *Imperial Berlin* (New York, 1970), pp. 123–51.
15   Hall, *Scandal, Sensation and Social Democracy*, p. 36.
16   In his *Image of a People: The Germans and Their Creative Writing under and since Bismarck* (New York, 1964), p. 91, Derek Van Abbe argues that the press in Germany played a more active role "in the popularisation of serious literature than it does in English-speaking countries . . . in Germany the literary standards of the newspapers, provincial as well as metropolitan, has remained high. In the case of the left-wing journalists, one might call these standards even snobbishly 'literary.'"
17   These figures were compiled by working through the index of Heinrich H. Houben's *Die Sonntagsbeilage der Vossischen Zeitung, 1858–1913* (Berlin, 1914). Of the twenty-five articles relating to crime and criminal justice, there were two on *Kriminalität*, four on *Verbrechen*, eight on *Polizei*, and thirteen on *Strafrecht*.

news of crime and criminal justice that did appear in the newspapers seemed either to have been written in the driest prose by some literal-minded German scholar (as in the case of most of the articles in the Sunday supplements) or to be contained in brief matter-of-fact reports of just completed criminal court cases that the newspaper editors tucked away in some remote corner of the paper.

The prominent American policeman Raymond Fosdick, who came to Germany shortly before World War I to research a book on European police forces, was immediately struck by the lack of attention German newspapers paid to crime. In his resulting book he explains that even the gravest and most bizarre criminal cases merited only a few lines in the back of the paper. Even stories of police corruption, which were certainly rare in all but the socialist papers, failed to stir up much attention. Hence, a case involving three plainclothesmen from the Berlin force, who in 1913 had been brought to trial on the charge that they had been living off the earnings of prostitutes they supervised, only received twelve lines on the back page of the *Berliner Tageblatt,* a leading progressive paper.[18]

Although it will soon be argued that Fosdick's impressions were only partially correct, it is worthwhile to show why crime seemed to be reported so blandly and inconspicuously. Fosdick himself offered some explanations. To begin with, the police made it very difficult for newspaper journalists to gain information about crime. Fosdick reports that in the twelve years prior to World War I the Berlin police department never issued a comprehensive report of their activities, and this was apparently the rule, not the exception, as the Dresden force had not issued one since 1897. He also points out that the combined newspaper interests in Berlin could place only one journalist at police headquarters, and this journalist had to have official police approval. "Whatever news he is given is written out in a form acceptable to the police, and is printed in the various newspapers exactly as it was sent out, very much as legal notices are published in American or English journals. The same practice applies in Dresden."[19]

But Fosdick's explanations tell only part of the story. Even if the newspapers learned whom the police suspected of a crime or who the leading witnesses involved in the case were, they could not reveal their names to the public. In fact, other than reporting in the most general terms that a crime of a certain type had been committed in some locality, the newspapers could not provide any more details of the case at all until an official *Anklageschrift*

---

18 Fosdick, *European Police Systems,* p. 77.
19 Ibid., p. 78.

(indictment) had been filed by the public prosecutor or the case "had been placed in the public domain or the case had been decided in court."[20] A final regulation inhibiting the reporting of criminal news, and all other news as well, was that before a paper released its contents to its readers it had to file a copy with the police. The police would then inspect it to make sure that all the rules had been obeyed. Failing to comply with any of these regulations could result in stiff fines or even prison terms for the editors and journalists.[21] And, worse yet, if it was determined that the newspaper's contents had offended the emperor or ruler of a state, if they incited acts of class hatred, or if they urged disobedience to the law, the newspaper could be confiscated indefinitely without judicial decree.

The combined weight of all these strict regulations ensured that very little "scooping" was done by any paper and that the crime news that did appear in papers was all of the same stifled genre. But one more inhibiting factor still remains: the nearly all-encompassing libel laws. These laws were not defined very precisely in the criminal code; rather, a great amount of discretion was left to the individual judge to determine if someone or something had been criminally libeled or offended, and the law was applied so broadly that it even applied to dead people.[22] Newspaper editors were so worried about being convicted for libel (and they should have been, as in the first six months of 1913 alone, 104 Social Democratic journalists were convicted of libel, resulting in 40 years of imprisonment and 11,000 marks in fines) that virtually all papers resorted to the practice of designating one expendable person as the responsible editor (*Verantwortliche Redakteur*). Sometimes, as Alex Hall claims was the case for some socialist papers, this person was virtually a bum off the street.[23]

Despite all the official and legalistic restraints, German newspapers did report crime stories regularly, and with a purpose. Fosdick was correct in saying that these stories were usually very bland in style and that they were usually placed in rather inconspicuous places, at least to the untrained eye. It was also true that all newspapers had access to the very same news, so there was virtually no chance that one would print a story unknown to any other.

20 Ellis Paxson Oberholtzer, *Die Beziehungen zwischen dem Staat und der Zeitungspresse im Deutschen Reich* (Berlin, 1985), p. 102.
21 Ibid., p. 105. Oberholtzer explains that a "fine of as much as one thousand marks, or jail for up to six months" could result.
22 On all of this, see ibid., pp. 35–65. On the criminal libeling of a dead person, see p. 60.
23 Hall, *Scandal, Sensation and Social Democracy*, pp. 71ff. On the criminal liability of the editor, publisher, printer, etc., see Oberholtzer, *Die Bezeihungen*, pp. 105–23. For how the socialists and other newspapers dealt with censorship during the time of the antisocialist laws, 1878–90, see Friedrich Apitzsch, "Die deutsche Tagespresse unter dem Einfluss des Sozialistengesetzes" (diss., University of Leipzig, 1928).

But the newspaper editors could choose which stories they wanted to print, and many of them chose very different ones; and the stories a particular newspaper finally chose to print usually fitted into a clear pattern, a pattern that expressed the ideological preconceptions of the party the newspaper was tied to and that molded the views of crime and criminal justice of their readership. For example, a newspaper had the choice of picking crime stories that dealt with random violence or poverty-induced theft; it could report cases that resulted in convictions or acquittals; it could report stories in which the rich were the victims and the poor the criminals, or the poor were the victims and the rich the criminals. And even though editors were usually compelled to use the official statements of the police and court officials, they still had the possibility of altering the meaning by the clever use of headlines, italics, selective quotation, or a deftly placed or misplaced comma or exclamation point.

Every newspaper made purposeful use of these options. By the turn of the century most of them reported the majority of their crime news in a section of the paper called "court news" (*Gerichtszeitung*) or "from the courtroom" (*Aus dem Gerichtssaal*) or some other similar title. In some papers these columns appeared daily, in others semiweekly. Usually the column would describe the goings-on in from two to four separate court cases in anywhere from a few lines to a few paragraphs in length. Other crime news could be found in two other regular columns of most papers. In a column devoted to local news (usually called *Lokales*), one could find shorter articles, often no more than a sentence or two, devoted to the reporting of recent and local criminal activities. One really had to search for these, however, as usually they did not have a title and they were separated by a mere dash from a gossipy story of someone's marriage just above and a recording of the visit of some dignitary just below. Most papers also carried a "mixed news" or "miscellaneous" section (usually called *Vermischtes*). Here the reports of criminal acts or criminal trials in other parts of Germany or abroad were sandwiched between stories of fires, suicides, diplomatic events, and other brief news items. In addition to all of these regular columns in most papers, one could find an occasional editorial or book review on some matter or another relating to crime and criminal justice. Thus, you may have had to look around a little bit for crime news, but if you did, you were sure to find it. Most papers used a similar format in reporting their crime news, so the well-practiced German reader had little difficulty in finding news of recent trials or crimes.

Crime stories were printed for several reasons. Sometimes, no doubt, it was to arouse the prurient interests of readers, though this was probably less the case in Germany than in many foreign countries, and it applied much more to liberal papers, which seemed to be the only ones to display an increasing interest in covering crime, than to left-wing or right-wing papers. Crime stories may also have acted as a kind of "Dear Abby" column, especially as so many cases of libel were reported in most papers that one begins to think this was the primary means by which Germans got hold of the smutty gossip that seems to entertain people of all countries. Sometimes a crime report could even be printed for its humor value, but this was more often the case with the lusty Bavarians than with the more sober Prussians. All papers were similar in that they reported a large volume of cases involving honor and morality (two of Germany's greatest concerns) and a somewhat excessive number of stories about crime in foreign lands. If they felt themselves constrained in reporting domestic crime cases, they certainly showed very little restraint in their lurid and animated coverage of crime elsewhere.

The most striking feature of crime reporting, however, was its ideological and political bias. If you add up systematically the types of crimes that were reported in different newspapers, and if you pay attention to which details were or were not mentioned in each of the different reported crime cases, you get a very different picture of what kinds of crimes were being committed, who committed them, and what caused them to be committed. If you read a conservative paper, you would get an almost mirror-image opposite picture of criminality than if you read a socialist paper. And if you read a liberal paper you would get still another picture. Unless you read newspapers of all different political leanings, you would get a very unbalanced view of criminality. Arguably, this is what most Germans had.

A COMPARISON OF FOUR BERLIN NEWSPAPERS: *VORWÄRTS, KREUZZEITUNG, BERLINER TAGEBLATT,* AND *VOSSISCHE ZEITUNG*

These four Berlin newspapers, each a major daily, and each read by a different segment of the Berlin population, have been selected to demonstrate the gross differences that existed in the crime reporting of various German newspapers. The four newspapers spanned a wide range of political interests. Farthest to the left was *Vorwärts,* the leading organ of the huge and doctrinaire-Marxist Social Democratic Party. Farthest to the right was the *Kreuzzeitung,* the mouthpiece of the powerful Conservative Party, a party that had strong ties to the Prussian aristocracy and the Lutheran church. Between these were two important liberal dailies, the *Berliner Tageblatt* and the *Königlich Privilegirte Berlinische Zeitung* (more popularly known as the *Vossische Zeitung*). Both of these newspapers were associated with the progressive branch of German liberalism as opposed to the more conservative National Liberal branch. The *Berliner Tageblatt,* however, was probably favored by progressive financial and business interests, whereas the *Vossische Zeitung* catered especially to academic and intellectual interests. By analyzing all reported court cases in each of the four different newspapers in the month of November 1902, a month selected randomly, it is possible to gain an appreciation of how German newspapers used the issue of criminality more for the purpose of promoting their ideological biases than for objectively reporting important news to their readers.

News of criminal activities appeared daily in each paper. With the exception of the conservative *Kreuzzeitung,* most of the crime news was carried in rather lengthy columns devoted to the coverage of important ongoing and recently completed court cases. Both *Vorwärts* and the *Berliner Zeitung* carried these daily columns under the title *Gerichts-Zeitung* (Court News). The *Vossische Zeitung* carried a similar daily column with a slightly different name, *Gerichtliches* (Court Matters). On an average day each of these papers would carry news of from one to four cases. The space devoted to each case would vary in length from a few lines to several paragraphs with the average court case being reported in about one solid paragraph. Each case would have a title in boldface type, and sometimes boldface would also be used to emphasize a key word in the story.

The *Kreuzzeitung* also carried news of court cases on a daily basis, but it avoided using boldface titles and did not carry a separately designated column on court affairs. Rather, it handled crime news somewhat more discreetly by placing its reports of criminal cases and recently committed crimes alongside other recent events in its *Berliner Zuschauer* section ("Berlin Observer," which resembled the *Lokales* section in the other papers) when the crime or trial occurred locally, or in its *Vermischtes* (Miscellaneous) section when the crime or trial took place in other parts of Germany. At this time the *Kreuzzeitung* usually reported its news on criminal trials more briefly than the other papers, but it was more apt than the others to use boldface type in the middle of its crime articles to denote some key aspect of the story. Although the *Kreuzzeitung*'s coverage may have appeared somewhat more discreet, its daily volume of crime news was, if anything, more substantial than that of the other papers.

Whereas the socialist paper *Vorwärts* almost never carried news of reported crimes, and usually the two liberal papers would only print crime reports on days when they carried no interesting court trials, the *Kreuzzeitung* printed articles on reported crimes just as regularly as it carried news on criminal trials, and it did this far more regularly than any of the other papers. In the month of November 1902, the *Kreuzzeitung* had 55 articles on court cases, *Vorwärts* 42, the *Berliner Tageblatt* 61, and the *Vossische Zeitung* 89. But, in the same period, the *Kreuzzeitung* also published 55 separate articles on reported crimes, whereas the two liberal papers carried only two dozen of these articles apiece, and *Vorwärts* carried none.

One can take any day at random and observe how very different the news on crime was. On the very first day of the month, Saturday November 1, *Vorwärts* reported on only one court case, the *Berliner Tageblatt* reported on four court cases, the *Vossische Zeitung* also reported on four cases, and the *Kreuzzeitung* reported on two court cases, but also on two recently committed crimes.

Vorwärts's sole case was entitled "Eine Polizeithat schwerster Art" (A Police Misdeed of the Most Serious Kind). The case involved the acquittal of a Polish bricklayer named Max Musowski for the crime of *Widerstand* (resistance to authorities). Musowski had been falsely arrested and brutally treated by a Berlin policeman. After reporting the case in the same matter-of-fact words that were issued by the court authorities to all of the newspapers, the editors of *Vorwärts* inserted one brief sentence in the form of a rhetorical question asking what would happen to the *schlagfertigen Beamten* policeman (normally translated as the "quick-witted" policeman, but literally meaning the "violence-prone" policeman). Would he be punished or not?

The *Berliner Tageblatt* was the only other paper to cover this story, but it covered three others as well: one a brief report of a murder conviction in Brunswick of a servant for killing his fiancée, another a longer report on a salesman convicted of a robbery, and the last a brief report on two Polish soldiers convicted of highway banditry. Its coverage of the Polish bricklayer's acquittal for resisting arrest was similar to that in *Vorwärts*, except in two subtle respects. The title it used was *Ein polizeilicher Missgriff* ("A Police Blunder") rather than the harsher words used by *Vorwärts*, and its story ended without the rhetorical question. Otherwise the words were exactly the same as in *Vorwärts;* but the impact of the story was obviously quite different. The fact that both papers chose to carry the story shows that they did not hesitate to criticize the authorities if they erred, but only *Vorwärts* would go the extra mile to rub the authorities' faces in their misdeeds.

On this day the *Vossische Zeitung* also chose to cover the murder conviction of the Brunswick servant, but its other three stories dealt with the acquittal of a Berlin businessman for embezzlement, the conviction of a local

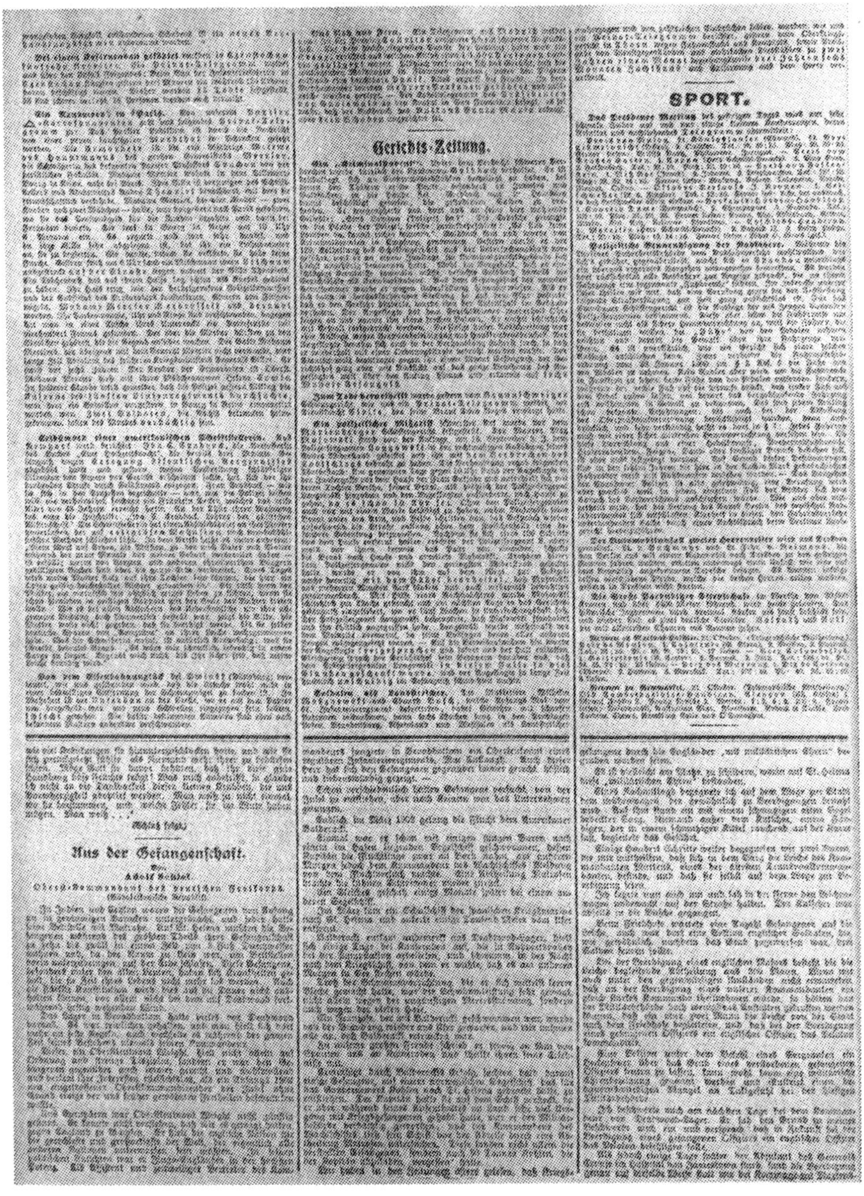

Plate 2.1. "Gerichts-Zeitung," *Berliner Tageblatt*, November 1, 1902.

Table 2.1 *Court Cases Reported in Berlin Newspapers in November 1902 (Acquittals, Convictions, Ethnicity, Social Class)*

Feature of Case	Vorwärts (Socialist)		Berliner Tageblatt (Liberal)		Vossische Zeitung (Liberal)		Kreuzzeitung (Conservative)	
	N	%	N	%	N	%	N	%
Total N of cases	42	100	61	100	89	100	55	100
Decided cases	28	67	42	72	60	67	49	89
Convictions	13	46[a]	31	74[a]	49	82[a]	47	96[a]
Acquittals	15	54[a]	11	26[a]	11	18[a]	2	4[a]
Ethnicity of Defendant								
All non-German ethnics	4	10	8	13	4	5	5	9
Poles	4	10	3	5	4	5	4	7
N and % convicted	0	0	4	50	1	25	5	100
Social Class of Defendant								
Worker	9	27[b]	13	30[b]	14	19[b]	19	49[b]
(N and % convicted)	(1)	(11 %)	(10)	(77 %)	(11)	(79 %)	(19)	(100 %)
Bourgeois	7	21[b]	13	30[b]	31	42[b]	12	31[b]
Peasant/farmer	1	3[b]	3	7[b]	2	3[b]	2	5[b]
Aristocrat	3	9[b]	3	7[b]	6	8[b]	0	0[b]
Academic, gov't. official, journalist, intellectual	13	39[b]	11	26[b]	20	27[b]	6	15[b]

[a] = % of cases decided.
[b] = % of cases when occupation is known.

Junker aristocrat for libel, and the conviction of a few Polish workers for a minor political infraction. The *Kreuzzeitung* also covered the murder case, but its other case dealt with the conviction of a Berlin medical doctor for fraud.

The figures and trends reported in Tables 2.1 and 2.2 and in Figures 2.1 and 2.2 demonstrate that these differences in crime reporting were not fortuitous. Table 2.1 and Figure 2.1 deal with the conviction/acquittal rates of all court cases reported in the four newspapers for the month of November 1902. A quick glance demonstrates that great differences separated the four papers. Whereas only 46 percent of the cases with a known verdict reported in the socialist newspaper ended in the conviction of and 54 percent ended in the acquittal of the defendant, in the conservative *Kreuzzeitung* 96 percent of the cases involved convictions (there were only two acquittals in fifty-five cases). The two liberal papers fell in between the two with conviction rates of 74 percent and 82 percent. One might hypothesize that these trends show that the conservatives wished to demonstrate that nearly all people who were arrested were arrested fairly and were deserving of punishment. In the conservative paper the only two cases in the entire

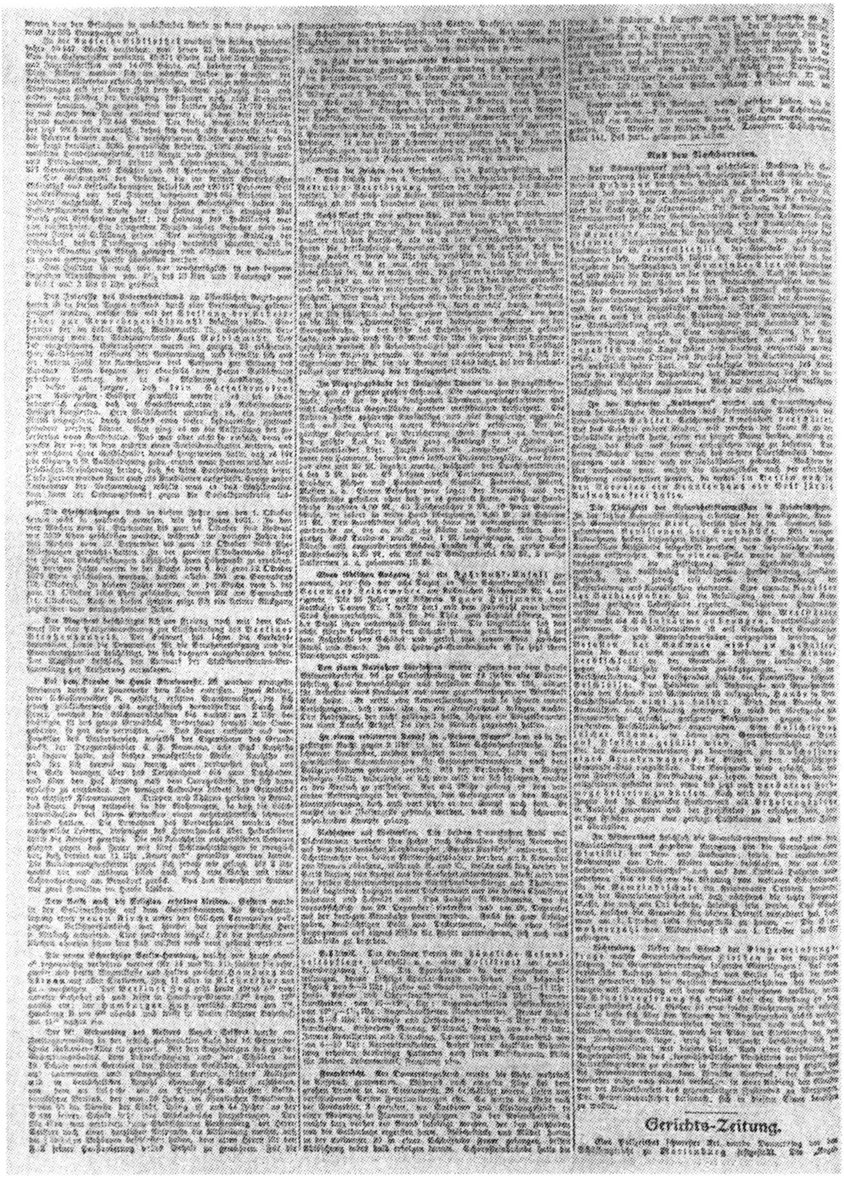

Plate 2.2 (*above and opposite*). *Vorwärts,* November 1, 1902.

Table 2.2 *Court Cases Reported in Berlin Newspapers in November 1902 (Type of Crimes)*

Type of Crime	Vorwärts (Socialist)		Berliner Tageblatt (Liberal)		Vossische Zeitung (Liberal)		Kreuzzeitung (Conservative)	
	N	%	N	%	N	%	N	%
Crimes against Persons								
Insult, libel	10	24	11	18	22	25	6	11
Murder, manslaughter	1	2	4	7	7	8	15	27
Assault and battery	1	2	1	2	5	6	6	11
Rape	0	0	2	3	0	0	0	0
Other moral offenses	0	0	1	2	0	0	1	2
Totals		28		32		39		51
Crimes against Property								
Theft	1	2	9	15	3	3	7	13
Poaching	0	0	0	0	0	0	1	2
Embezzlement	11	26	12	20	15	17	2	4
Fraud, swindling	2	5	2	3	9	10	5	9
Faulty weights and measures	1	2	3	5	8	9	4	7
Totals		35		43		39		35
Crimes against the Gov't.								
Perjury	1	2	1	2	4	5	2	4
Opposition, rebellion	1	2	2	4	1	1	0	0
Treason, spying	1	2	3	5	4	5	3	5
Disobeying police ordinances	2	5	2	3	1	1	2	4
Other political crimes	3	7	3	5	3	3	1	2
Totals		18		18		15		15
Crimes by the Gov't.								
Police brutality and abuses	2	5	1	2	0	0	0	0
Other	3	7	3	5	2	2	0	0
Totals		12		7		2		0
All other crimes	2[a]	5	2[b]	3	3[c]	3	0	0

[a] Both blackmail.
[b] One case of blackmail and one of bearing false witness.
[c] Duelling, copyright violation, breach of trust.

month that involved the acquittal of the defendant were reported on Saturday, November 8. One dealt with the acquittal of a landowner for murdering his wife and her lover, whom he had come across accidentally while they were making love; the landowner was acquitted by the court for the reason of temporary insanity (could it not be that the conservative paper was here advocating its patriarchal views on marriage?). The other dealt with the case of a professor's wife who was acquitted of petty theft (would they have carried the case if it had involved a worker's wife?).

If the conservatives believed that professors' wives and landowners were

Crime as a "Foreign" Concept

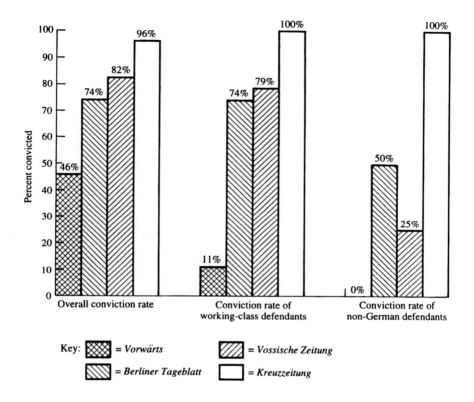

Figure 2.1

unlikely criminals, who then did they believe were deserving of punishment? Clearly not aristocrats. In this whole month not one aristocrat was ever mentioned by the *Kreuzzeitung* as a criminal defendant. *Vorwärts* and the *Berliner Tageblatt,* on the other hand, each carried three different cases dealing with aristocratic misdeeds, and the *Vossische Zeitung* carried six cases (see Table 2.1). In nearly half the cases reported in the conservative paper, the criminals were workers; in about 10 percent of the cases they were of some non-German ethnic group, and otherwise they were middle-class types of some variety.[24] Even more indicative of the conservatives' view on the social class and ethnicity of the criminals were the conviction

---

24 Actually, the percentage of cases involving nonethnic Germans might be considerably higher, because the 10 percent figure only represents those cases when the ethnicity of the defendant was either directly stated in the newspaper or when the defendant's name and the circumstances of the case made it obvious that a nonethnic German was involved.

Urbanization and Crime

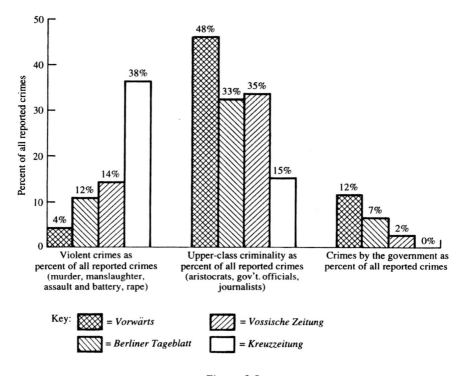

Figure 2.2

rates of these people. Of the nineteen articles dealing with working-class defendants reported by the *Kreuzzeitung* and the five articles dealing with non-German ethnic groups, all resulted in convictions. Thus, in the conservative view of things, the courts were busy with cases involving crimes by workers and "ethnics," and these people were always guilty and deserved punishment.

The socialist newspaper *Vorwärts* had a completely different viewpoint. Although 27 percent of the cases they reported involved working-class defendants, only one out of the total of nine of these was guilty and eight were acquitted. Similarly, of the four cases dealing with the non-German ethnic group, all four ended in acquittal. Thus, in the socialist view, workers and non-German ethnics were often arrested by the German authorities, but they were almost always arrested wrongly. As the socialists saw it, the real criminals were from the more favored classes. *Vorwärts* combed the courtrooms of all of Germany to find cases of crimes committed by the propertied and the powerful. Almost half of all the cases reported by *Vorwärts* in the entire month dealt with aristocrats, government officials, nonsocialist intellectuals, and nonsocialist academics (see Table 2.1), and almost all of these cases involved convictions.

The bourgeois liberal dailies took the middle position once again. Their defendants were spread out among the various social classes and ethnic groups; and although working-class and "ethnic" defendants were usually convicted, the conviction rates of these less fortunate Germans did not differ much from the conviction rates of other types of people. Thus, if one considers the trends in conviction rates presented in the four newspapers, one must conclude that the farther to the right on the political scale one goes, the more likely one is to discover criminal cases that ended in the conviction of the defendant and of guilty defendants that came from lower social and economic positions in German society. Also, one might conclude that no matter what the political slant of the newspaper, a sizable number of its crime cases involved persons of non-ethnic German extraction.

What also should be pointed out, but is hidden in these figures, is that the differing conviction rates of the "ethnic" and lower-class defendants are not the only indications of the selective ways in which the various papers demonstrated their social and ethnic biases. One has to read the entire text of the papers' crime reports to appreciate fully how the conservative *Kreuzzeitung* would nearly always point out directly (often by using boldface type) that a defendant was of Polish, Lithuanian, Russian, or some other non-German extraction or was from the working class with probable socialist leanings,[25] and how this was so very different from the socialist and liberal papers, which seldom made direct mention of the political or ethnic character of the defendants (often the only way of determining that the defendants were Polish or of some other non-German ethnic group is to draw inferences from their names, occupations, and residences, when given).

The data displayed in Table 2.2 and Figure 2.2 point out other notable differences in crime reporting in the four newspapers. Here information relating to the types of offenses the papers reported is displayed. All papers

---

25 Thus, for example, in the afternoon *Berliner Zuschauer* section on Monday, November 24, 1902, the *Kreuzzeitung* reported on a case involving a Russian swindler: "The swindler is by his speech and appearance undoubtedly Russian. He is between twenty-five and twenty-eight years old, pale and thin, with a long face, dark hair and a dark moustache. He wears dark clothes and a black, stiff, round hat. . . . He calls himself Barclay de Tolly and says he is here to study at the agricultural Hochschule. His mode of operation is to say that he needs a few hundred marks to help himself out of an embarrassing situation – then he bolts." In the month of November 1902, the *Kreuzzeitung* directly mentioned the involvement of socialists in four different criminal cases.

reported on a large number of cases dealing with honor, a prime value in German society and one that was frequently linked to criminal activity. Thus, in each paper a large percentage of the crime news dealt with cases of libel, fraud, perjury, faulty weights and measures, and other crimes where honor was at stake. The *Kreuzzeitung* was perhaps the least likely to mention such cases, especially libel, which were either the most numerous or second most numerous cases in the other papers. One might conclude that conservative newspapers did not carry such cases very often because they might have perceived this as acting dishonorably themselves by exposing such affronts to the honor of upper-class Germans, who usually were the ones libeled. But here the similarity ends. Again, the political and ideological leanings of the different papers are highly apparent and, with the exception of cases involving honor, the papers reported on remarkably different kinds of criminal cases.

If you read a socialist paper like *Vorwärts* you might come away with the view that criminal violence almost did not exist in Germany; if you read a conservative paper like the *Kreuzzeitung* you might think that criminal violence was threatening you at every moment. In the entire month of November 1902, the socialist paper only reported on one murder or manslaughter and, in fact, this was only a case of attempted murder that resulted in the acquittal of the defendant.[26] The case involved the divorced wife of a wealthy Berlin merchant who had not been given custody of her nine-year-old son and twelve-year-old daughter even though both she and her husband had been ruled as guilty parties in their divorce settlement in 1901. Soon afterward she was denied visitation rights as well, and this led her, presumably out of desperation, to the attempted murder of her son. But at her trial she was able to convince the jury that she had not wished to kill her son and had only shot past his ear, as all she had wanted to do was draw attention to her misery and find some way of seeing her children again. Obviously this case was selected because it helped to expose the unfair and patriarchal legal system that led even wealthy people to serious criminal acts.

Besides this case, the only other violent crime reported by *Vorwärts* was a simple case of assault and battery, and this too ended in acquittal.[27] The

---

26 This case was reported in both *Vorwärts* and in the *Berliner Tageblatt* on November 22, 1902.
27 On November 11, 1902, *Vorwärts* carried a long article about the case of a Polish master carpenter named Stanislaus Stelmaszyk, who was acquitted of the crime of assault and battery. *Vorwärts* explained that Stelmaszyk was an upstanding family man with a wife and three children and that he also owned a successful carpentry shop. One evening while in a Berlin bar he was accosted by two Germans, who tried to involve him in a fight by calling him all sorts of names. He left the bar and immediately asked a policeman for help. The policeman should have offered him protection but did

Kreuzzeitung, on the other hand, devoted nearly 40 percent of its coverage of criminal trials to cases of violent criminality (fifteen murders or manslaughter, six cases of assault and battery). To make it further appear that violence was omnipresent, the *Kreuzzeitung* also carried articles on twelve reported murders or manslaughters and five cases of assault and battery during the same month, whereas the socialist paper carried no articles on reported crimes at all. As Figure 2.2 shows, the liberal papers again occupied the middle position between these two widely divergent poles. Clearly, these figures on violent criminality show that, at this time at least, the more conservative the newspaper, the more likely it was to be concerned with violence and to give the impression to its readers that violence was a very present danger in German society.

The ideological differences among the papers are also evident in regard to other types of criminal offenses. The socialist paper suggested that almost all property offenses were cases of embezzlement, fraud, or swindling (together accounting for nearly a third of all cases of any type reported). Obviously, these were usually middle- and upper-class crimes. Cases of lower-class economic crimes were, conversely, unfit to print in socialist papers.[28] The conservative paper, on the other hand, reported a large number of lower-class economic crimes but few cases of upper-class economic crimes. In addition to the eight court cases of theft or poaching reported in the *Kreuzzeitung,* the paper also carried reports of eighteen theft and three poaching offenses that were reported by the police but had not yet gone to trial. The liberal papers once again stood the middle ground by reporting even-handedly on both lower- and upper-class economic crimes, but they perhaps demonstrated their bourgeois concerns for property and money by devoting a larger percentage of their crime news to cases of property crime (43 percent for the *Berliner Tageblatt* and 39 percent for the *Vossische Zeitung* compared to 35 percent for both the *Kreuzzeitung* and *Vorwärts*).

A final important difference among the types of cases reported on by these papers involves crimes committed against or by the government. All papers

---

not, and left. Soon afterward the two men who had accosted him forced him into a cab, where a fight followed, resulting in the death of one of the men. Because he acted in self-defense, Stelmaszyk was acquitted. But he had been forced to spend some days in jail while awaiting his trial, and, as a result, he could no longer maintain ownership of his carpentry shop. The obvious reason why *Vorwärts* carried the case was that it afforded the opportunity of casting shame on the policeman, who presumably did not help Stelmaszyk because he was biased against Poles. Also, it gave the newspaper another chance to cite a case involving the wrongful arrest of an upstanding Pole and worker.

28 The only case of theft carried in the entire month of November 1902 involved the conviction of an ex-convict named Ernst Bast. The case was reported on November 14, 1902.

carried several cases in which the government had been offended. Interestingly, the socialists tied with the liberal *Berliner Tageblatt* for reporting the highest percentage of cases of this sort (18 percent). As will be discussed shortly, one of the prime concerns of the socialists was to demonstrate that they were loyal, patriotic Germans and that they, too, hated criminality and thus were upstanding citizens. By not hesitating to point out spies, traitors, and political criminals, the socialists hoped to make their point. On the other hand, the socialists also took the lead in pointing to criminal activities by those in authority. Twelve percent of the crime cases they reported involved police brutality, the misuse of authority by members of the German government and administration, or other illegal activities of the government's officials while acting in their official capacity (it should also be pointed out that a large proportion of the cases presented in Table 2.1 under the heading of crimes of academics, government officials, and so on involved crimes committed by government officials while they were not acting in official capacities). The *Kreuzzeitung* again was the polar opposite of the socialist paper, as it reported not one single case of a crime committed by an employee or official of the German government while acting in an official capacity.

Thus the image of criminality presented by individual Berlin newspapers was sharply differentiated along political and ideological lines. The socialist newspaper *Vorwärts,* from which all other German socialist newspapers took the lead, gave its readers the impression that crime was a kind of upper-class or bourgeois phenomenon; that workers, ethnics, and poor people were not criminals but were often involved unfairly in criminal trials; and that government officials were just as likely to break their own laws as anyone else. Furthermore, random criminal violence was not something that existed in large measure in German society. The conservative newspaper, *Kreuzzeitung,* gave its readers a completely different impression. Violence was rife, in their view of things; crime was mostly a lower-class phenomenon; and the government always acted properly. The liberal papers took the middle position between these two ideological extremes in their crime reporting, just as the liberal political parties stood between these two political and ideological enemies.

To understand more fully why each of these political interests took such different stands in the handling of crime in their newspapers, and how the issue of crime reporting evolved in all newspapers during the years of Imperial Germany, I shall now discuss separately each of the three major political positions, socialist, liberal, and conservative, and the crime reporting in their newspapers.

CRIME IN THE SOCIALIST PRESS

The growth in size and influence of the Social Democratic Party in Imperial Germany was mirrored by and perhaps partially attributable to the growth in size and influence of the socialist press. Soon after the party officially established itself in 1875,[29] it established the newspaper *Vorwärts* in the city of Leipzig to act as its principal organ. At the time of its first issue, on Wednesday, January 3, 1876, the paper, which was published only three times per week, like the party itself, only had a few thousand followers and limited influence. In 1878 both the paper and the party were outlawed by Bismarck's Anti-Socialist Laws. When the laws were allowed to lapse in 1890, the party and the paper quickly made their reappearance, but the paper shifted its lead organ from Leipzig to Berlin. In its new home both the paper and the party thrived. Between 1890 and 1914 the party grew rapidly, and by shortly after the turn of the century had become the largest single party in all of Germany. In this same period the readership of *Vorwärts* grew from 25,000 to nearly 175,000. Although after 1890 *Vorwärts* was published daily (with the exception of Mondays) as the party's mouthpiece and was clearly its largest and most influential newspaper, other socialist newspapers followed its lead and also recorded tremendous increases in their readership. By 1914 the party press in general had in excess of one and a half million readers, and all areas of Germany were covered by a locally published socialist daily, with the notable exceptions of Posen, Hohenzollern, Lippe, and Waldeck.[30]

Although *Vorwärts* and other party papers differed little in form and appearance from other newspapers and reported on the same range of news items, covering the day's news was not the prime purpose of party papers. Rather, the socialist press consciously acted to mold the public opinion of the German working class: it kept the party leadership in contact with the party faithful (many leading party officials acted as editors of the leading party papers); it promulgated the party's ideological and political aims and positions; and it also acted to serve as a recruiting ground for new party members. The party newspaper was so important to its working-class readers that, as Rolf Engelsing puts it, they would read it "three or four times and regard it as a sermon."[31]

Beginning with the very first issues of *Vorwärts*, the party used the news-

---

29 The party was officially established in May 1875, when the Allgemeinen Deutschen Arbeiterverein and the Sozialdemokratische Arbeiterpartei, along with several other minor socialist groups, decided to merge into one party.
30 Hall, *Scandal, Sensation and Social Democracy*, pp. 31–7.
31 Cited in ibid., p. 26.

paper to expose the evils of Imperial German society, not least of which was its practice of *Klassenjustiz,* which the party claimed discriminated against and oppressed the working classes and made a mockery out of the *Rechtsstaat* principles. Karl Liebknecht, one of the party's most important leaders, explained the four major features of *Klassenjustiz* at a party meeting in Stuttgart in 1907: "the way physical appearance influenced character assessment, always to the detriment of the working class; the one-sided evaluation of legal material and evidence; the application and use of specific laws; and the severity of sentencing policy against known political dissidents."[32]

The party press's attack on *Klassenjustiz* began with the very first issue of *Vorwärts* in 1876, when a lead article entitled "Wie Recht ist Unrecht, und wie Unrecht ist Recht" (How Justice is Injustice and How Injustice is Justice) cited a case of a Berlin mechanic who went to court against his master and, despite the overwhelming evidence in his favor, lost.[33] From then on, the party press used the issues of crime and criminal justice as the basis for an attack on the German authorities that, despite the turn toward revisionism and away from the orthodox Marxism of many of the party's leaders, never decreased in virulence and intensity in all the years of the Reich. Many would argue that the attack, if anything, increased. Thus, a Bremen police report in 1909 stated: "There has been a noticeably coarser tone in the SPD press than in recent years . . . every government measure is an outrage and a slap in the face of the proletariat, every policeman is a pig, and Prussia itself is a state of barbarism, inferior to all other civilized lands."[34]

The figures cited earlier for the reporting of crime in November 1902 show that the party made its attack in two major ways. The first was to demonstrate that socialists were not criminals, but that workers and non-German ethnics, people who often became socialists, were often unfairly accused of criminal activities. As early as May 1878, the party newspapers began the practice of carrying crime cases in which the workers and socialists were unfairly linked to criminal activity. Reporting on a case of theft that was committed in February 1878, the Leipzig-based *Vorwärts* took issue with the common charge that socialists were criminals. Citing a police warrant entitled "Soll Sozialdemokrat sein" (probably a Social Democrat), the paper

32 Ibid., p. 73. Many cases of the unfair and unequal application of laws can be found in the socialist daily the *Hamburger Echo,* on August 19, 1909. One of the cases involved a woman who stole a bundle of firewood from a neighbor's cellar in order to heat some milk for her newborn child and was given a year's imprisonment. This case was contrasted with that of a building manager who received a fine of only 300 marks for breaking his walking stick over a woman's head.
33 *Vorwärts,* January 3, 1876.
34 Hall, *Scandal, Sensation and Social Democracy,* pp. 26–7.

went on to editorialize that socialists resented being made the scapegoats for all evils (*Sündenböcke für alle Schlechtigkeiten*). Whereas in the Middle Ages the Jews had played such a role, now, in the last quarter of the nineteenth century, the finger of blame was constantly and unfairly placed on the socialists. Socialists, the paper argued, were simply not criminals: "The regular readers of this paper do not need to be assured that the thief is no Social Democrat. The readers of *Vorwärts* know, that whoever has understood the high and pure teachings of socialism is incapable of being not only a thief but of committing any kind of immoral act."[35]

In almost every issue of *Vorwärts* and other Social Democratic Party newspapers that followed it was possible to read cases of workers who went to court but were acquitted. Despite the fact that a large number of German criminals were of the working classes and many of them no doubt considered themselves socialists, one never discovers a case of a socialist who was justly convicted of a crime and seldom any type of worker at all, in any socialist paper.[36]

The second way in which the party made its attack was by pointing out the crimes of upper- and middle-class Germans and cases of police brutality and unfair application of the laws. Seldom did the paper ever print a case in which an upper-class German was not convicted. The only exceptions to this rule were when they had the chance of calling attention to an unfair application of the law.[37]

With the passage of time very little changed in the image of crime and criminal justice that socialist newspapers conveyed to their readers. The form of their coverage may have changed somewhat over the years (in the first issues of *Vorwärts* in the 1870s there were no formal *Gerichts-Zeitung* columns; like most other German papers this regular column only began to appear in the 1890s), but the contents and message remained remarkably consistent. In general, the socialist papers always dealt with crime in a sober fashion. But though they avoided lurid reporting, they made no attempt whatsoever to report all crimes, or even a representative sample of all crimes.

35 *Vorwärts*, May 29, 1878.
36 Whenever *Vorwärts* reported on a case involving the conviction of a working-class person, poverty was almost always the motive. Thus, two examples: On May 8, 1878, *Vorwärts* reported on a case involving the conviction of several unemployed workers for the crimes of begging and vagrancy. "It is a very sad symbol of our times, that for many people who would love to find work, but cannot, an arrest is frequently a blessing." On June 1, 1904, *Vorwärts* reported on a murder and attempted suicide case under the heading "Eine Tragödie der Armut" (A Tragedy of Poverty). In this case a poor Berlin shopgirl, Margaret Mittelstadt, was shot and killed by her fiancé, a hard-up barman's helper named Karl Markgraf, who then attempted unsuccessfully to kill himself. Both Markgraf and Mittelstadt had decided to end their lives because they did not see any way they would ever be able to make enough money to support a family.
37 See note 21.

Certain types of crime, such as violent crimes, were almost never mentioned. Thus, in November 1902, the paper only cited one case of attempted murder and one of assault and battery, and this was the rule, not the exception. In June 1904, the paper again only presented one case of murder and overlooked numerous other cases reported in other papers. It even failed to mention the murder case of a nine-year-old Berlin girl named Lucie Berlin that earned lurid and bold-type headlines almost daily in most Berlin papers (the *Berliner Tageblatt* frequently reported on the case under the huge boldface heading *Entdeckung eines Lustmordes,* "Discovery of a Lust Murder")[38] and was covered in great detail in papers as far away as Munich.[39]

Socialist papers wanted to report criminal activity only when it served their own political and ideological purposes. Reporting on irrational acts like murder was avoided because it might help justify the already overbearing presence of German policemen and arouse the public to call for even more stringent enforcement of the criminal justice system. On the other hand, by carrying a constant stream of cases which demonstrated that the authorities overstepped their bounds and that the fortunate classes of Germany themselves might find reason to lament the long arm of the German law, the socialist press made the issues of crime and criminal justice a primary basis for conveying its political and ideological viewpoints. The socialists were on the offensive in the crime battle and their attack never called for retreat. During the First World War all nonsocialist papers completely stopped reporting crime, but the socialist press continued with business as usual. Even on Christmas Day, 1914, *Vorwärts* published its normal *Gerichts-Zeitung.*

CRIME IN THE CONSERVATIVE PRESS

The reporting of crime in the conservative press bore some similarities to that in the socialist press. Both attempted to show that they did not stoop to such a low practice as devoting great attention to news of criminality; both, however, were intensely concerned with using the crime issue for their own distinct political and ideological interests, and both remained very consistent in their reporting of criminal stories and trends. But there end the similarities. Just as the German socialist and conservative parties had completely

---

38   The case was first reported in the *Berliner Tageblatt* on June 3, 1904. This was truly a lurid murder case reported in uncharacteristic length and gruesome detail. Lucie Berlin was the nine-year-old daughter of a Berlin cigar manufacturer. She had been sexually molested and dismembered, her corpse "lacked a head, arms and legs."

39   The Munich liberal paper *Allgemeine Zeitung* reported on the case several times in June 1904. The first day it was reported was June 13, 1904, under the bold-print heading LUSTMORD.

different views of the world, so their two presses painted completely different portraits of criminality. The socialists depicted the rich as corrupt and exploitative and the poor as victims or honest citizens; the conservatives portrayed the well-to-do – unless they were Jewish – as intellectually, morally, and spiritually elevated and the lower-class workers, Poles, and socialists as debased and dangerous. The socialists thought crime resulted from the greed and poverty engendered by capitalism and the authoritarian German class structure and government; the conservatives viewed crime as resulting from irrationality, inferior moral and spiritual development, big-city life, political hooliganism, and race.

Using the conservative main organ *Kreuzzeitung* as a guide, it appears that the types of crimes reported in the conservative press, who committed them, and why they committed them did not change very much over the years in Imperial Germany, but there were some changes in the style in which crimes were reported. As time progressed, the number of crime stories may have escalated, the length of the crime stories started to grow, and, toward the end of the period, there was a greater tendency to use larger and bolder type to alert the reader's eye. Eventually the *Kreuzzeitung* even established a regular column strictly devoted to crime news called *Aus den Gerichtsfällen* (From the Court Cases) similar to the *Gerichts-Zeitung* columns in other papers.[40]

But the process of devoting more attention to crime news was a gradual one. It reflected the gradual broadening in length and scope of the paper itself (in the 1870s and 1880s it only came out once a day and six times a week; by the 1900s it came out twice daily), and it jibed with the practice, adopted by all other newspapers, which gradually introduced the use of bolder print and more regularly carried columns on a wide variety of topics as time wore on. Still, it should be stressed that the conservative *Kreuzzeitung* seemed extremely concerned to make it appear that it was so high-minded that it would not involve itself in the cheap trade of using crime stories to sell newspapers. It kept crime off the front page, except in some rare instances when it was soberly discussing criminal justice as opposed to reporting on some lurid crime case; it gave less space to the coverage of reported crimes and criminal trials than other newspapers; and throughout the period it reported most crime news in seemingly inconspicuous places.

The conservatives were of two minds about crime reporting. They could not completely resist reporting it, as it offered such fertile ground for scoring

---

[40] This column appeared occasionally as early as 1902, but it was not until just before the war that the column appeared regularly.

political and ideological points against their enemies. But all the while they seemed to be conscious that crime was somehow not a proper topic for god-fearing, aristocratic, and patriotic Germans such as themselves. What crime they did report was selected solely to serve their own self-interests, never to inform their readers objectively. On July 29, 1914, all news of crime ceased abruptly in the *Kreuzzeitung,* and presumably in other conservative papers as well. Although, as the socialist papers proved, crime did not end with the war. It merely ceased to be newsworthy for the conservatives.[41]

The conservative papers may have concealed their interest in reporting crime, but they certainly did not conceal the types of crime they were interested in. Similar to the figures presented for the month of November 1902, one can pick almost any month at random over the entire Imperial German period and discover that violent crime was perhaps the principal criminal activity of concern to conservatives. Whereas the socialists in November 1902 only reported on one case of murder or manslaughter and one case of assault and battery (together making up less than 4 percent of their crime stories), and the two liberal papers only mentioned eleven cases between them (an average of 7.5 percent of all of their cases), the *Kreuzzeitung* reported on fifteen criminal trials for murder or manslaughter (27 percent of their criminal trial cases in general) and also carried articles on twelve other reported murders (22 percent of all reported crimes) and a raft of cases of violent assaults and other violent crimes.

Using two other months, April 1879 and July 1914, for the purpose of comparison, it appears that the conservatives' interest in violent crime remained relatively constant. In April 1879, the *Kreuzzeitung* reported on a total of thirty-four court cases, nine of which, or 26 percent, were of murder or manslaughter. The paper also reported on forty-six other crimes that had not yet gone to court, of which fourteen, or 30 percent, were murders or manslaughters. Although it might appear that there was slightly less attention devoted to crime in general in 1879 as opposed to 1902 (a total of 80 crime stories of any type versus 144), much of this may have been because the paper was published twice as often in 1902 as in 1879. Certainly there

---

41 The *Kreuzzeitung* reported regularly on crime in its "Court News," "Berlin Observer," and "Mixed News" columns until July 29. After that date all mention of criminal activities ended abruptly and the paper no longer printed a "Court News" column. Crime news was not the only news to be curtailed. Up to July 29, the paper had carried daily reports of violent accidents, suicides, burnings, and bombings alongside its crime news in the "Berlin Observer" and "Mixed News" columns. After July 29, however, this kind of tragic news also disappeared. In its place was substituted good news like the August 4, 1914, "Mixed News" article on the prevention of a severe train accident (*Ein grosses Eisenbahnunglück verhütet*). Thus it appears that the *Kreuzzeitung* no longer found bad news to be politically expedient. Like its reporting on Germany's battles throughout the war, only good news was now fit to print.

was no great increase in the attention devoted to murder and manslaughter. Even if there were a few more cases mentioned in 1902 than in 1879 (a total of twenty-seven versus twenty-three), the percentage of all crime stories represented by murder and manslaughter was slightly less in the later period. But it must be remembered, that in both periods murder and manslaughter represented a far greater proportion of all crimes reported in the *Kreuzzeitung* than in other newspapers.[42]

Moving ahead to the very last month in which crimes of any type were reported in the *Kreuzzeitung*, July 1914, it turns out that the paper continued its torrid pace of reporting on violent crimes such as murder and manslaughter until the eve of the war. In this month there was a total of thirty-three stories on murder and manslaughter,[43] fifteen of which were court cases and eighteen reported crimes. If, in any of these periods, one were to add the number of other types of violent crimes the paper mentioned to the number of murders and manslaughters, one would find that nearly half of all the crime stories ever mentioned in this conservative newspaper were of extreme forms of violent crime. To the large volume of violent crime reported in the newspaper might be added a daily flood of articles on bombings, burnings, suicides, and accidents, most of which resulted in death. Clearly there was a reason why the paper chose to deal so often with such morbid subjects.

The *Kreuzzeitung* and other conservative newspapers wished to convince their readers that Germany was under attack from within. Violence threatened the good Germans on almost every streetcorner. And who committed these violent acts and most other types of crime? Of course, the enemies of the Reich, or at least the enemies of the conservatives – workers, socialists, Jews, foreigners, and non-ethnic Germans such as Poles or Lithuanians. In at least two-thirds of all the articles on murder or manslaughter in the three months mentioned above, the paper pointed out directly that workers were the perpetrators. In nearly one-third of the cases the violent criminals were Poles or other non-ethnic Germans. The paper had a harder time finding

---

42   As the comparative figures for November 1902 show, the *Kreuzzeitung* devoted a large percentage of its crime-news reporting to homicide cases. Whereas less than 10 percent of all court cases carried in the other papers involved homicide, homicide represented over 25 percent of the court cases reported in the *Kreuzzeitung*. In April 1879, nine of the thirty-four court cases (26%) reported in the *Kreuzzeitung* involved homicide. But in the *Vossische Zeitung* in this same month there were no court cases involving homicide reported at all, even though the paper reported on fifty-two other types of court cases. When one considers that in an average year homicide cases represented less than one out of one thousand court cases in Berlin and in the rest of the country, it is clear that the *Kreuzzeitung* was inordinately interested in this type of criminality and that the overall picture of criminality rendered by the newspaper to its readers was greatly distorted.

43   The last case of a murder reported was in the morning edition on July 27, 1914.

violent crimes on which to report that involved socialists or Jews, but it certainly did not hesitate to implicate these hated enemies even if it required making some large inferential leaps.

On November 14, 1902, an article appeared in the "Miscellaneous" column of the evening edition under the boldface heading "Sozialistische Einflüsse" (socialist influence). Two men had been sentenced to death for killing a woman in Jena, but it was not at all certain that they were socialists. The only proof the paper could give came in the form of an excerpt from their testimony at the trial, where one of them was quoted as saying: "The world is terrible and the rich won't allow it to be otherwise. That's why we kill and steal." When the paper lacked even such flimsy evidence upon which to make their case against socialists and Jews involved in violent crimes, it would devote more attention than was normal to other types of criminal activity such as swindling or embezzlement, so long as Jews or socialists were involved.[44] Thus, for example, on November 4, 1902, the paper reported on a case of a Berlin SPD trade-union leader arrested for embezzling union funds: ". . . for the third time in recent memory one of their number has been found to have embezzled funds from the SPD trade unions in Berlin. All of this despite the SPD claim that they are 'unparalleled models of honesty and probity.'"[45]

Crime, the conservatives argued, was a constant feature of German society, especially in the big cities. Those who committed crimes were primarily urban types who either were not really Germans, like Jews, Poles, and foreigners, or who were political malcontents, like socialists and most workers. They committed crimes not because of poverty or hardships of any type, but because they were unruly, irrational, and morally and spiritually inferior. The way to reduce crime was by increasing police surveillance of these people, enforcing the laws more stringently, and bringing God into

---

[44] The *Kreuzzeitung* relished reporting on crimes involving Jews. Although Jews were involved in very few crimes compared with other types of Germans, the paper made it seem that Jews were often criminals. In particular, the paper conveyed the impression that Jews were either capitalistic swindlers (as in the case of a Jewish swindler reported on November 11, 1902) or dangerous radicals (see the case of the Jewish nihilist reported on November 13, 1902). In a truly offensive front-page article in the morning edition on November 29, 1902, entitled "Das Judenthum in Amerika," the paper lays out in great and disturbing detail its position on Jews in general. Stating that Americans were finally waking up to the realization that the great racial mix poses grave dangers and that Americans were finally coming to the realization that Jews in particular were an evil influence, the paper warned that Germans should recognize the evil influence of Jews in their own country. Sometimes the article even sounded as if it might have been written in 1933 instead of 1902: "The truth about the Jews is that they can only live as either oppressed or oppressors [*Unterdrückter oder als Unterdrückten*], for the Jew it is not possible to respect the rights of another person equal to his own rights."

[45] Evening edition in the "Berliner Zuschauer" column.

their lives. In a front-page article on November 4, 1902, entitled "The Value of Prison Pastoral Care," the paper explained at length the virtues that would be derived were a greater number of pastors assigned to German prisons. It would "soften hard attitudes . . . [and] restore self respect," and, as a result, "the number of repeat offenders will decline, there will be fewer court cases, less need to hire prison officials and build prisons."[46] It was certainly no accident that the arch-patriotic and chauvinistic Lutheran and aristocratic-backed organ *Kreuzzeitung* found criminality to be a feature of the godless, the foreign, and the urban – the Jews, the Poles, the workers, and the socialists.[47]

CRIME IN THE LIBERAL PRESS

The reporting of crime in the *Vossische Zeitung*, the *Berliner Tageblatt*, and Germany's other liberal newspapers was less ideological but more plentiful and dynamic than in the conservative and socialist press. Crime was reported when it was considered interesting and newsworthy; it did not have to fit a predetermined ideological mold. Liberal newspapers felt freer than socialist ones to report on crimes by the lower classes, and they had no qualms about reporting both acquittals and convictions. If there was a rash of murders in a particular city, the liberal papers of that city would probably mention them. If there were no murders, as was the case in many cities for periods of as long as a year, the liberal papers would not look over hill and dale to find some to report. Free of the ideological imperatives that restricted the crime coverage of the conservative and socialist press, the liberal press may have reported on crime more objectively.

Over the years of Imperial Germany there were some distinct changes in the way in which crime was reported in the liberal papers. In the 1870s and 1880s most liberal papers did not carry a separate column devoted to court cases, police reports, or criminal matters of any type. The only crime news one could find in these years was contained in short, untitled notices placed in inconspicuous places in the newspapers.[48] There were a few notable exceptions, as in the *Vossische Zeitung*, which did feature a regular column

---

46 Evening edition.
47 The *Kreuzzeitung*'s view that urban life was crime inducing comes through graphically in a large review article printed in the morning edition on November 22, 1902, on a book by Arthur Dix concerning juvenile delinquency and social conditions, *Die Jugendlichen in der Sozial und Kriminalpolitik*. In this review the paper argues that it is a sad development that so many young people have moved into the big cities to take up work in factories. The big cities and the factories stunt the moral and religious development of these youths and lead many of them into lives of crime.
48 See, for example, the *Allgemeine Zeitung*, which was based until 1882 in Augsburg before moving to Munich.

Table 2.3 *Court Cases Reported in the* Vossische Zeitung *in April 1879, November 1902, and June 1908*

	April 1879		November 1902		June 1908	
	N	%	N	%	N	%
Total cases	52		89		104	
Decided cases	47	90	60	67	46	44
Acquittals[a]	4	9	11	18	7	15
Convictions	43	91	49	82	39	85
<u>Major Types of Crime</u>						
Libel, insult (*Beleidigung*)	12	23	22	25	14	13
Homicide	0	0	7	8	15	14
Assault and battery	6	12	5	6	4	4
Theft	11	21	3	3	11	11
Embezzlement, fraud, and swindling	6	12	24	27	15	14

[a] Acquittal and conviction rates are the percentage of decided cases.

(called *Gerichtsverhandlungen*) reporting important court cases in the 1870s and 1880s, but this column did not appear in every edition of the paper or even every day, as it did by the turn of the century, and its cases were brief, dispassionate, and rather inconspicuous. At this time, the paper used only a mere dash to separate a report on one court case from another. By the turn of the century, however, great changes had come about. By 1900 almost all liberal papers carried regular and separate "court news" columns.[49] These columns frequently used liberal measures of bold print and stirring captions to alert the reader's eye and to arouse curiosity; the articles were longer in length; and occasionally they even seemed almost lurid. It was not uncommon, for example, to come across an article with the caption LUSTMORD (Lust Murder) in half-inch-high bold letters.

By the turn of the century, crime was simply bigger news. It grew bigger and bigger with each passing year until the outbreak of the war. In terms of the volume and types of crime reported, the changes were dramatic also. Some evidence for this is found in Table 2.3, which summarizes the reporting of court cases in a single month in each of three different years – April 1879, November 1902, and June 1908 – in the *Vossische Zeitung*. A definite progression in the number of court cases is immediately evident. In April

---

49 Such columns were found in all the major liberal papers that the author researched. In addition to the *Vossische Zeitung* and the *Berliner Tageblatt*, they include the *Frankfurter Zeitung*, the *Kölnische Zeitung*, and the *Allgemeine Zeitung*.

1879, the paper carried articles on only 52 cases; in November 1902, it carried 89; and in June 1908, it carried 104. If this were at all representative of the *Vossische Zeitung*'s and other liberal newspapers' reporting in different months and years (some quick spot checks through other periods in this and other liberal papers like the *Berliner Tageblatt*, the *Frankfurter Zeitung*, and the *Allgemeine Zeitung* seems to indicate that it was), then there was roughly twice as much crime reported in the last years of the Reich as there was in the early years of Imperial Germany. Actually, the volume of reported crime may have been as much as four or five times higher, because these figures do not reveal the fact that the articles on crime were much longer in the later years, and that in later years there were many more lengthy articles on crime not contained in the "Court News" section.[50]

The most striking change of all, however, was in the reporting of homicide. In the early years of the Reich, one could read a liberal paper for weeks and not find one article on a court case of homicide. But in the years just before the war broke out, homicide was reported on an almost daily basis. In April 1879, there was not one single case of homicide in the *Vossische Zeitung*. In November 1902, the "Court News" section carried articles on seven cases, and in June 1908, it carried articles on fifteen ongoing or recently completed court cases of murder or manslaughter. In the early years, there also would seldom be a case of a reported murder in the paper; and if there was one, it would only get a few lines. By 1908 there were numerous police reports of homicide each week, and often these would be given considerable space. Whether this tremendous growth in homicide reporting occurred because of the increase in the actual number of homicides[51] or because the newspaper reflected a growing liberal and perhaps general societal concern for and interest in violent criminality is uncertain. Since there were always more homicide cases actually taking place than were ever reported in the newspaper, the paper's editors must have been making some conscious decisions about which and how many of them they should report to their readers. In April 1879, the *Vossische Zeitung* reported no cases

---

50 In June 1908, for example, the *Vossische Zeitung* carried eleven large articles on homicides and numerous large articles on other criminal activities separate from its "Court News" column.

51 In 1879, in Berlin there were only 2 cases of murder or manslaughter according to coroners' records, and in all of Prussia only 455. In 1902 there were 27 in Berlin and 580 in Prussia. Although no figures are available for 1908, it is certain that the number of homicides had continued to rise. In 1907, in Berlin there were 41 homicides and in Prussia, 788. Thus the number of homicides was increasing rather steadily, but this was mostly because the population of Berlin and the rest of Germany was increasing rapidly as well. Although the absolute number of homicides was rising, the rate of homicides was not rising in most places; in fact, the homicide rate actually decreased in most areas between the 1870s and the early 1900s, and only increased gradually thereafter. See the discussion of these figures in Chapter 3.

of homicide at all, but in the same month the *Kreuzzeitung* reported on nine homicide cases; in November 1902, the *Vossische Zeitung* carried seven cases, and the *Kreuzzeitung* carried fifteen.

Despite the increases in the volume of homicide cases and in the volume of all criminal cases reported in liberal newspapers over the years of Imperial Germany, the general view of criminality rendered by liberal newspapers remained rather constant. Even the increase in reported homicides need not be taken to mean that liberal newspapers after the turn of the century were all that much more concerned with criminal violence than they had been earlier. As the figures in Table 2.3 show, the increase in the reporting of homicides was almost matched by a decrease in the reporting of other kinds of violent crime such as assault and battery. Thus in April 1879, when the *Vossische Zeitung* reported no homicides, it reported six cases of assault and battery, which amounted to 12 percent of all cases of any type reported. In June 1908, when the paper reported fifteen cases of homicide, which constituted 14 percent of all cases, it reported only four cases of assault and battery, which made up only 4 percent of all cases. Hence, it might be argued that liberal papers like the *Vossische Zeitung* may have reserved a certain portion of their crime news for news of violent criminality, and the form of that criminality may have changed but the volume was not all that different. Also the figures in Table 2.3 point out that, despite some fluctuations, the relative reporting rates of most other types of criminal activity remained rather stable over time. And if one compares these rates with the rates in November 1902, of the *Berliner Tageblatt* (see Table 2.2), or with similar analyses for other liberal newspapers such as the *Allgemeine Zeitung* in Munich,[52] then it appears that there was a rather distinct and consistent pattern to the reporting of crime in liberal newspapers.

Germany's liberal press always devoted more space to crime reporting than did the socialist or conservative press. Socialist papers only wanted to report on crimes perpetrated by the upper classes or in which the authorities had acted improperly; conservative papers only wanted to report on crimes committed by the lower classes and would never report official improprieties. The liberal press, on the other hand, would report on crimes committed by anyone, provided the crimes seemed interesting and newsworthy. Nevertheless, certain types of crime were considered more interest-

---

52 The *Allgemeine Zeitung* in Munich in November 1902 reported on 53 court cases. Of these, there were 5 homicides (9%), 5 assault and batteries (9%), 5 thefts (9%), 7 cases of libel (13%), 9 cases of faulty weights and measures (17%), 8 cases of fraud or swindling (15%), 5 cases of embezzlement (9%), 2 violations of police ordinances, 2 drunk and disorderly cases, and one case each of abduction, perjury, disloyalty, violation of religious laws, and misuse of authority.

ing and newsworthy than others. Crimes involving honor, such as libel, swindling, and fraud, regularly received great play in liberal papers (see Tables 2.2 and 2.3). Violent crimes were interesting and newsworthy too. Simpler criminal activities such as petty thefts and mild assaults, although they represented the bulk of the crimes that were actually committed,[53] were not deemed all that interesting and therefore did not get much space in liberal newspapers.

In sum, the liberal papers provided their readers with a more balanced and accurate, though less pointed, portrayal of crime and criminal justice than did the conservative or socialist press. Compared to both the conservative or socialist newspapers, the liberal papers appear relatively unbiased.[54] Compared with the conservatives, they were far more willing to criticize an occasional impropriety of the German officials, but compared with the socialists, they were far more accepting of the criminal justice system and the society in general.[55] They concerned themselves mainly with reporting of cases in which the defendant was convicted, and this reflected the actual performance of German courtrooms; but as in the German courtrooms, occasionally their defendants were acquitted. Their criminals came from all social classes and occupations: workers, businessmen, professionals, and even aristocrats. Most of their criminals were ethnically German, though a considerable percentage had non-German ethnic origins such as Polish. But even when the criminals were of non-German ethnic background, the liberal papers generally refrained from slandering them or their people by printing their ethnic origin in bold print, by making negative comments about their inferior ethnic backgrounds, or by drawing particular attention to them in any way. The liberal press was, therefore, quite unlike the conser-

---

53 Simple theft was the most common crime prosecuted by the German authorities, with assault and battery the second most common. In an average year, these two offenses made up nearly 50% of all crimes that went to court. Libel was the third most frequent crime, making up slightly less than 15% of all criminal cases in an average year.
54 The word "relatively" is important, for certainly the liberal press did have biases. On the ethnic biases of one liberal (more nationalistic than progressive) newspaper, see Johannes Daun, "Die Innenpolitik der Kölnischen Zeitung in der Wilhelminischen Epoche 1890 bis 1914" (diss., University of Cologne, Cologne, 1964). Poles were the biggest ethnic concern. One indication of the liberals' feelings and possible biases toward them was written in an editorial in the Cologne newspaper in 1907: "Our German Reich is a national, unified, federated state. . . . We have to assimilate the Poles to our national characteristics, or, as far as it is possible, we have to drive them out" (cited in Daun, p. 28). For other expressions of views on Poles, see pp. 127–32; for views of other minorities, see pp. 127–71.
55 See, for example, the front-page articles under the heading "Missgriffe der Beamten" (Abuses of the Authorities) in the *Vossische Zeitung* of November 22 and 23, 1902. In these two articles it was argued that German policemen too often acted brutally and too seldom were brought to task for their actions. In England, the paper argued, the police were much more restrained and were much more likely to receive punishment if they got out of line.

88   Urbanization and Crime

vative or socialist press in not making crime an offensive weapon with which to attack their enemies.

The liberal press, like the liberal political parties, did, however, have some serious weaknesses. Part of the reason they did not make crime an offensive weapon may have been because they did not know whom or what to attack.[56] They did a relatively good job of recording criminal activity as it was, but they did a poor job of providing their followers with an understanding of the origins of that activity. Almost never did they make a serious attempt to analyze and explain the social, economic, and political factors that caused crime in the first place. They did little to explain the impact of poverty, class conflict, governmental discrimination toward minorities, or the hardships of urban or rural life. About the only time when they would expand beyond reporting the bare facts of a criminal case was when they were reporting on criminal activity on foreign soil. Whereas German crimes only merited cautious reporting in regular "Court News" sections of liberal papers, foreign crimes often got full front-page treatments. When the liberal papers had the opportunity to report on a *Lustmord* in France or a mass murder aboard a Greek ship, they threw all caution to the winds and explained in great detail how and why crime occurred in these foreign lands.[57] Thus their readers may have been left with the impression that crime in Germany was a kind of aberration, but that crime abroad was a normal state of affairs.

CRIME IN MIDDLE-CLASS MAGAZINES

As most German magazines were read by middle-class audiences, their handling of crime and criminal justice matters bore marked similarities to

---

[56] See Ralf Dahrendorf's discussion of the insipid and weak-kneed nature of German liberalism on the part of the German bourgeoisie, in his *Society and Democracy in Germany* (Garden City, N.Y., 1967).

[57] The *Allgemeine Zeitung* carried several front-page articles in November 1902 dealing with the murder of several officers on board the ship *Loreley* anchored near Athens. On November 3, 1897, the *Frankfurter Zeitung* reported in great detail on a case involving a French *Lustmorder* under the heading "Massenmord und Parlamentsreform" (Mass Murder and Parliamentary Reform). The article involved an insane twenty-eight-year-old French mass murderer by the name of Joseph Bacher. Bacher was the son of a well-to-do farmer but had become a vagabond after being dismissed on grounds of insanity from the French military. Between 1895 and 1897, he killed at least nineteen people, mostly young women whom he had sexually assaulted. The paper went into great detail to deride the French government, police, and general populace for allowing such a madman to roam about and to make it seem that only in France could such atrocities occur. Although the paper made no reference to Germany, preferring instead to compare the French system with what the paper argued was the much more intelligent English system of dealing with the criminally insane, it was rather obviously implied that Germans dealt more intelligently with such criminal matters as well. Also implied in the article was that the French could only deal more intelligently with criminals if they had a more intelligent government. But the German paper did not think the French were capable of that.

that of liberal newspapers. The majority of the magazines, like the popular *Vom Fels zum Meer* and *Die Gartenlaube*, were rather apolitical and unconcerned with crime and matters of criminal justice.[58] In the few instances when they did deal with these issues, they would either print quasi-scientific articles written by scholars, who explained to the lay public that crime was caused by opportunity, passion, or physical instability, or they would print journalistic travelogue-type pieces dealing with crime in sensationalist fashion.[59]

A large share of all the articles, particularly those of the latter type, dealt with crime abroad. For example, in the six-year period between 1880 and 1886, *Vom Felz zum Meer* carried roughly six hundred articles, but only nine dealt with crime or criminal justice, of which over half were about crime in foreign countries like America, Italy, or France. These articles could sometimes be a bit offensive, though probably not to their readers. In an article entitled "New York und seine Polizei" (New York and its Police),[60] the author recounted his travels to New York City in such a way as to give a ridiculously biased and awful impression of crime in New York and America, by implication assuring Germans how much better things were in their own country. The author's main point was that in America there was an incredible discrepancy between unspeakable poverty and unbelievable wealth, which usually existed cheek by jowl. Understanding English poorly, he lands in New York and immediately asks a policeman to escort him to the richest and the poorest sections of the city. Having taken almost an entire day to walk along Fifth Avenue and through the slummy "Five Points" section, he had learned enough to complete his investigation and write his article. His method of operation would find its parallel if an ingenuous American were to report on German vice after spending an evening in Hamburg's red-light district and an afternoon at Neuschwanstein castle.

[58] See note 11 for figures on the readership of *Die Gartenlaube*, one of the most popular German magazines.
[59] See, for example, the article by the criminologist Ludwig Fuld, "Aus der Kriminalpsychologie des weiblichen Geschlechtes" (The Criminal Psychology of the Female Sex) in volume 3, Band 1 of *Vom Fels zum Meer* (October 1885–March 1886), pp. 155–61. Fuld argued that women are moved primarily by passion. He started off with the example of a twenty-six-year-old Frenchman who had shot the husband of his lover, a forty-year-old French woman. She had enticed him unwittingly into his murderous act, argued Fuld, by writing him numerous love letters full of complaints about her husband. Another illuminating article carried in the same volume was an unsigned article entitled "Gelegenheit macht Diebe" (Opportunity Causes Theft). People were warned to guard their wallets, jewelry, and other possessions more carefully. In another unsigned article in the same magazine, but in volume 4, Band 2 (April–September 1886): pp. 581–4, entitled "Wiedererkennung der Verbrecher" (Recognition of the Criminal), one learned how to stave off possible criminal assaults by recognizing the types of eye color most common among already convicted criminals.
[60] F. Kiessling, "New York und seine Polizei," *Vom Fels zum Meer*, volume 1, Band 2 (April–September 1882): 692–7.

There were some magazines, however, that devoted more of their attention to crime and criminal justice and which actually treated these subjects critically and intelligently. To avoid censorhip and imprisonment, most of them, like the Berliner Tageblatt's *Ulk* and the independent but left-liberal *Fliegende Blätter, Kladderadatsch,* and *Simplicissimus,* used humor, satire, and cartoons to make it appear that they were only joking. Such journalistic means made it possible for them to make some trenchant observations and criticisms, but the authorities recognized that they were only "kidding on the square" and the editors of these magazines often faced convictions for lèse-majesté.[61] The editors of these magazines were, nonetheless, not scared off and their exposés of societal conditions conducive to criminality and critical attacks on the faults of the German criminal justice system seemed to grow in frequency and intensity with the passage of time.

The Munich satirical journal *Simplicissimus* (published weekly since 1896) led the charge. As Derek Van Abbe notes, "It must be mentioned as one influence which opened the minds of its many readers (who were, above all, members of the middle classes) to 'subversive' thoughts."[62] Frequently concerning itself with poverty, discrimination, psychopathology, and other factors that caused criminality, the magazine also constantly criticized German policemen for being stupid and brutal, German judges for being capricious, haughty, and politically controlled by aristocratic reactionaries, and the German criminal justice system in general for being overbearing and inhumane. (See the accompanying cartoons of heavily armed policemen patrolling the parks; two judges saying that "now that we have a verdict, all we need is an offense"; a judge who decides on a harsh sentence because he does not like the taste of the wine he's drinking while sitting in his chambers; and a judge who, while hunting with a Junker who has just shot a human being, points out that according to the law he will have to prosecute the Junker, while the Junker boldly replies, "[only] if you let yourself be influenced by the law.")

In nearly every issue between 1896 and 1914, one finds a cartoon or satirical article lampooning the criminal justice authorities or the harsh conditions under which many Germans lived. Although one does not recognize any serious increase or decrease in the frequency with which these cartoons and articles appeared, it seems that over time the magazine focused more and more on grave criminal violence and death. In its first year of

---

61 On their criticisms and on their not infrequent brushes with the law, see Harry Pross, *Literatur und Politik. Geschichte und Programme der politisch literarischen Zeitschriften im deutschen Sprachgebiet seit 1870* (Freiburg, 1963), especially pp. 50–66; Ann Taylor Allen, *Satire and Society in Wilhelmine Germany: "Kladderadatsch" and "Simplicissimus" 1890–1914* (Lexington, Ky., 1984); and Masur, *Imperial Berlin,* pp. 151–203.

62 Van Abbe, *Image of a People,* p. 95.

Plate 2.3. "Spring Flowers."
"The heart in the policeman's breast also beats more happily when the flowers are again in bloom."

Plate 2.4. "Our Judges."
"We have here a major case of lèse-majesté, Herr Colleague. The guilt is proven, now all we have to do is come up with an offense."

Plate 2.5. "The Judges in Their Chambers."
"Damn it, the wine tastes like cork. I say give him ten years in the pen."

Plate 2.6. "From East Elbia."
"You can be assured, Count, that it was embarrassing enough for me. However, because of the injury you inflicted, the man was not able to work for three months. According to the law, I'll have to sentence you."
"Yes, dear judge, if you let yourself be influenced by the law."

publication (April 1896 to April 1897), only one article or illustration was of this type, but in the issues appearing in the last year before the war (April 1913 to April 1914) at least six articles or illustrations were concerned with these themes. This development appeared to mirror the growing preoccupation of the liberal newspapers with homicide and violent criminality.

CRIME IN GERMAN LITERATURE

Few German novelists and playwrights in the second half of the nineteenth and the first decade and a half of the twentieth century gained the international renown of Dickens, Zola, Hugo, Dostoevsky, Tolstoy, and other European writers, and fewer still concerned themselves with crime and justice issues. Nevertheless, there are some – like Karl May, Hermann Sudermann, Wilhelm Raabe, Theodor Fontane, Max Kretzer, and Gerhart Hauptmann – whose works are worth consulting to add to the portrait of crime and justice provided by the analysis of newspapers and popular magazines. Their works, though reflecting different shades of political and ideological opinion, largely reinforce the image of crime and justice that has already been drawn. Crime, to many authors, was a rather foreign phenomenon linked to foreigners and non-German ethnics of weak character and dishonorable behavior; crime was seldom linked to urban settings or the growth of cities, and in fact was depicted as at least as much of a rural as an urban phenomenon; poverty and hardship were seldom considered the causes of illegal behavior save for in the works of a few left-liberal naturalist writers like Hauptmann, whose writings came the closest to resembling the view of crime and justice provided in the social democratic press (there were no socialist writers of note).[63] Homicidal violence was rarely encountered except when it occurred abroad, as in the popular novels of Karl May, which were often set in America, Spain, or other foreign lands, or in the penny dreadfuls of other less esteemed writers,[64] or was perpetrated by Poles, Lithuanians, and other foreigners residing on German land. Women were virtually never seen as violent actors, though they not uncommonly, as in the Lucy Berlin *Lustmord* case, figured prominently as victims. In addition, in serious literature at least, almost no trace of normal, upstanding, ethnic Germans, or even Jews and socialists, could be found among the *violent* criminals (one remembers how even the conservative press had a hard time

---

63 On the uneasy relationship between bourgeois authors and the socialist party, see Vernon Lidtke, "Naturalism and Socialism in Germany," *American Historical Review* 79 (1974): 23ff.
64 See Rudolf Schenda, *Die Lesestoffe der Kleinen Leute: Studien zur populären Literatur im 19. und 20. Jahrhundert* (Munich, 1976); Schenda, *Volk ohne Buch;* Carl Müller Fraureuth, *Die Ritter und Räuberromane. Ein Beitrag zur Bildungsgeschichte des Deutschen Volkes* (Halle, 1884).

finding reports of Jewish violence, though they claimed to be more successful with the socialists). And although several authors, if somewhat less directly than Hauptmann and other left-liberal writers, joined in the socialist's condemnation of *Klassenjustiz* and criticism of Germany's officialdom, most literature of the period was rather uncritical of the society and the leadership and was moderately to extremely xenophobic.[65]

These points can be expanded by considering some of the most prominent authors' work. Although this method of proceeding is similar to that used by Tobias and Chevalier in their studies of England and France, it will admittedly serve to understate the generally conservative and chauvinistic nature of the most widely read pulp literature of the period, which a fuller study of German literature on crime and justice would need to consider in much more detail. Keeping this in mind, however, one can gain an impression of the main lines of German authors' thinking on crime and issues of justice in the period by examining briefly some of the most important novels and plays written on the theme of crime and justice in the Kaiserreich.

CONSERVATIVE AND MODERATE WRITERS: MAY, SUDERMANN, RAABE, AND FONTANE

The most widely read literature of the period was extremely conservative in its political message. Rudolf Schenda, the author of a massive study of popular German literature from the late eighteenth to the early twentieth century, argues strongly that this literature had a very unhealthy effect on the German population. In his words: "The consumers of popular reading material have played a role which is as deplorable as it is indictable. In two world wars, millions of readers – manipulated, thoughtless, blind – trusting in their tradition, supporting authority, and weaned on the 'old values,' believed in the lying fiction of false reports, sought adventure on the field of honor, and dreamed of a greater Fatherland or an idyllic peace."[66]

When violence and lawlessness was the theme, which it frequently was in this *Trivialliteratur*, the setting was often in foreign lands. Tales of rape, robbery, murder, and plunder had no problem getting by eagle-eyed government censors and attracting a large readership so long as the victims and

---

65 Jörg Schönert explains in his "Kriminalgeschichten in der deutschen Literatur," p. 66, that "the criminal literature of the time [drew] . . . a picture of a stable society, where crime was only confronted in the margins of the society, and where the danger of crime could be overcome by the spirited work of the police and the courts." George L. Mosse argues that "Germany, in the second half of the nineteenth century, was barren of a tradition of letters that might have called for liberty and equality against the inherited inequalities of life." *Masses and Man: Nationalist and Fascist Perceptions of Reality* (New York, 1980), p. 22.
66 Schenda, *Volk ohne Buch*, p. 494.

offenders were Italians, Spaniards, Mexicans, Blacks, or Native Americans. As Schenda explains, for example: "The [German] author was free to work out his fantasies when writing about Italy, and in this way he could protect Germany from being considered to be an uncivilized land."[67]

This was also true in the works of the period's most widely read author, Karl May, who wrote many novels about the exploits of a German settler on the American frontier named Old Shatterhand. Old Shatterhand was a paragon of German virtue, manhood, courage, and honor. He fought a one-man war against evil and lawlessness, usually perpetrated by Indians, Blacks, and other non-German American bandits. Law and order always won out in his novels; foreigners were unruly, weak, and immoral. "The confrontation between good and evil is direct and simple. For Karl May, king, fatherland, and law are necessary institutions that give roots to man."[68]

These themes were echoed in higher-class literature as well, as in the works of many German naturalists – for instance, the most popular German naturalist author of the period, Hermann Sudermann. The best known of his works is *Frau Sorge* (1887, translated as *Dame Care* in 1891). Although this is not a crime novel per se, crime and criminal justice figure prominently in the story, and the novel represents an excellent example of the dominant conservative strand of serious German literature on crime or any other social topic. The tone of the novel is extremely gloomy and depressing; the setting is somewhere in a rural part of northeastern Germany in the late 1880s; the major character is a lower-middle-class, peat-farmer youth named Paul Meyerhofer.

As a kind of *Bildungsroman* (a popular genre of the time dealing with the moral growth of, typically, one middle-class character), the novel traces Meyerhofer's physical and psychological development from the neglected third son whose parents and peers thought puerile and incapable, through many harrowing hardships – including public disgrace for failing to safeguard his two younger sisters' virtue, a two-year jail sentence for arson, and the death of his beloved mother – to his eventual blossoming into an upright adult worthy of everyone's respect. Following Meyerhofer's path, the reader is introduced to the various social types existing in rural Germany (aristocrats, peasants, foreign farmhands, and small-townspeople). The only crit-

---

[67] Ibid., p. 398. On literary censorship in the period, see several works by H. H. Houben such as *Verbotene Literatur von der klassischen Zeit bis zur Gegenwart* (Wittemburg, 1923); *Hier Zensur – wer dort? Antworten von Gestern auf Fragen von Heute* (Leipzig, 1918); and *Polizei und Zensur. Längs- und Querschnitt durch die Geschichte der Buch- und Theaterzensur* (Berlin, 1926). See also the special issue in *Central European History* 18 (1985) on "The Censorship of Literary Naturalism."

[68] Mosse, *Masses and Man*, p. 44.

icism of society that one encounters deals with various individuals' lack of honor and moral virtue, with which the author is obsessed. Meyerhofer, on the other hand, always acts morally and honorably, in that many of the difficulties he met arose in his attempt to act honorably and defend virtue.

Crime, law, and justice issues come into view at several points in the tale. Crimes committed by German citizens, in Sudermann's view, stemmed only from cowardice or passion, tied to a lack of honor or to an attempt to preserve it. A different yardstick was applied to foreigners, however, whose criminality seemed only "natural." Crime was never occasioned by poverty or by social or political injustice.

The main character's brush with the law comes when he tries to defend his father's honor and is convicted of arson for burning down his own barn before his father, acting out of passionate but misguided rage, can burn down his neighbor's home. At another point in the novel, Meyerhofer buys a revolver and almost uses it on two local bullies who have taunted and mocked him since childhood and have recently deflowered his two younger sisters. Having bolstered his nerve with drink, he finds his tormenters asleep and takes aim. But upon reflection, he decides to wake them and encourage them to fight like men, as shooting them in their sleep would be cowardly and dishonorable. To describe his bearing at that moment, the author writes that he "trembled and shook like a criminal." It is interesting that this simile "like a criminal" is employed several times in the novel, meant each time to conjure up images of cowardice, weakness, and dishonorable activity. It is never used to convey the image of a violent, wicked, impoverished, or even greedy person that is often associated with the term.

The other person to commit a crime in the novel is a silent and surly Lithuanian farmhand named Michael Raudszus, who "lived in a miserable hovel . . . had a slatternly wife who had already been in prison twice, and who sent her children out to beg." In a drunken rage, and seeking revenge against Meyerhofer's abusive and bullying father, Raudszus also turns to arson and burns down the Meyerhofer barn anew. Although his act is also connected with honor, and although the author takes a neutral stance toward him and his hardships, the primary message conveyed to the reader is that a life of misery and even prison was the "natural" fate of such semiliterate, pathetic, and surly foreigners, who often got into trouble because they could not control their drinking or keep their emotions in check.

The criminal justice authorities in the novel are all portrayed in a favorable light; the wheels of justice turn fairly and efficiently, though Raudszus receives a five-year sentence and Meyerhofer a two-year one. The chief judge at Raudszus's trial is portrayed as kindly and omniscient: he "smiled constantly... was feared by all the world... [and had eyes which] no speck of dust in the court escaped."

Thus, in the works of Sudermann and May, the justice system and justice officials were honorable, efficient, and fair. There was little emphasis placed on social and economic conditions. Crime was associated with a lack of honor and weakness. And crime, dishonor, and weakness were typical of foreigners and not of Germans.

More balanced and critical in their treatment of crime, law, and justice were politically moderate authors like Wilhelm Raabe and Theodor Fontane. Raabe, who has been compared to Dickens, and Fontane, who has been compared to Thackeray and Trollope, were perhaps the most respected standard-bearers of Germany's comparatively weak "realist" literary tradition in the second half of the nineteenth century.[69] Although both writers were most at home and best known for their critical portraits of the German bourgeoisie's social manners and mores, both treated crime and criminal justice as at least a minor theme in several of their works. Fontane, in fact, actually wrote two bona fide crime novels, *Quitt* and *Unterm Birnbaum*, which some consider to be the only two real representatives of this genre in the literature of the Kaiserreich. Neither of Fontane's crime novels was very successful economically, however, and Raabe also met with little encouragement from the reading public to write about crime and criminal justice.[70]

Although Raabe's works have done well with foreign twentieth-century audiences, his contemporaries apparently did not appreciate the Dickensian type of social criticism so prominent in his many works.[71] Like Dickens, Raabe was particularly critical of the hardships imposed on youth and the poor by the industrial age, the harsh life in the reformatories and poverty schools, and the smugness of the bourgeoisie. But Raabe's criticism was less direct than Dickens's, and there was often a fairy-tale quality in his works, as in his urban pastiche of Hänsel and Gretel, *Im Alten Eisen*, where two lost children roam about, lost in the big city of Berlin instead of in the wild forest.

Horacker, published in 1875, is probably Raabe's most significant novel to treat crime as a major theme. This time, his youth, a nineteen-year-old vagabond and former thief named Horacker, really is in the wild forest. At the beginning of the story one learns that Horacker has escaped from a

---

69 On Raabe, see Doernenburg and Fehse, *Raabe und Dickens*; and Barker Fairley, *Wilhelm Raabe: An Introduction to His Novels* (London, 1961). On Fontane, see Wolfgang Eberhardt, *Fontane und Thackeray* (Heidelberg, 1975); and A. R. Robinson, *Theodor Fontane: An Introduction to the Man and His Work* (Cardiff, 1976); and Hans Scholz, *Theodor Fontane* (Munich, 1978).
70 Scholz, ibid., pp. 163, 170–1.
71 Fairley, *Wilhelm Raabe*, pp. 164ff.

reformatory and is hiding out from the authorities in the forest surrounding his native village. The reader is encouraged to feel sympathy for the youth because he had been forced, by poverty and the unfeeling treatment he received from his wealthier neighbors and the authorities, into petty thievery and vagabondage, for which he was sentenced. Also, one is led to feel compassion for him because his former neighbors offer him none. Upon hearing rumors that he has escaped from the reformatory and is now a dangerous vagabond lurking in the woods, his neighbors spread new and more pernicious rumors that he killed two schoolmasters.

Although this as well as his other works were not really crime novels, Raabe's books often made strong comments on crime and criminal justice. By displaying compassion for the criminal, by ridiculing the false propriety and greed of the propertied classes, and by depicting the grim nature of poverty schools and reformatories, Raabe clearly suggests that the real criminals in German society were the state and the unfair class system and the real victims were defenseless lower-class youth and the poor.

Theodor Fontane, the London-based foreign correspondent for the conservative *Kreuzzeitung* in the 1850s and later the chief diplomatic and drama critic for the more academic and liberal *Vossische Zeitung,* though milder and less judgmental than Raabe, also offered important insights into the problem of crime. Today this "gentle critic," as he is sometimes called, holds the reputation of being Imperial Germany's foremost novelist. Like his masterpiece *Effi Briest,* which shares similarities with Tolstoy's *Anna Karenina,* most of his novels are critical yet balanced portraits of the social conventions, mores, and problems of the upper bourgeoisie. As one critic said of him: "If he has any message, it is that all messages are contradictory and that it is false to think that anything or anybody can be wholly right or wholly wrong."[72]

Attempting to present the strengths and weaknesses of all sides of a person, issue, or argument, Fontane made some poignant criticisms of German society, its values, and its leaders. His two crime novels, *Quitt* and *Unterm Birnbaum,* are good examples. Both involve murder and both take place in rural settings (the former in the Silesian Riesengebirge and the latter along the Oder River). Whereas both novels make it clear that murder under any circumstances is morally wrong, they both offer criticisms of lawmen as well as of criminals.

Quitt, first published in serialized form in 1890 in the popular middle-class magazine *Die Gartenlaube,* involves a struggle between a poacher and a

---

[72] Douglas Parmee, in his introduction to his translation of Fontane's *Unwiederbringlich (Beyond Recall)* (London, 1964), p. vii.

gamekeeper. The poacher is a liberal-thinking and basically honorable wheelwright who eventually murders the ultraconservative gameskeeper, who had once been his superior officer in the military and who had previously abused him and denied him well-deserved military honors. Throughout the novel, Fontane suggests that one should have sympathy both for the poacher and for his liberal values; and, usually through the poacher's voice, he frequently criticizes German society for being authoritarian and rigidly class-based: "It is so close and stifling here, [it is] a police state, a country with a few lords and counts . . . otherwise serfs and mere servants."

Fontane has less sympathy for the murderer in Unterm Birnbaum, a somewhat greedy pub owner of Czech background named Abel Hradschek, but through the novel's intricate plot and numerous characters, the author makes many criticisms of police and justice officials, capitalist greed, and ethnic bias. Near the beginning of the story, the gambling and debt-ridden pub owner Hradschek kills a Pole named Szulski, who as a business emissary for a Kraków firm, had come to collect on a loan that Hradschek could not afford to pay. Hradschek cleverly and remorselessly conceals the murder by making it appear that Szulski had drowned in the Oder River on his return home. The balance of the story revolves around the attempt to find Szulski's missing body. Eventually, some of the villagers suspect Hradschek, and the criminal justice authorities are called in to prove his guilt.

The village policeman, named Geelhaar, is depicted as altogether a "good policeman but a better drinker," who is close to the villagers with whom he gambles and drinks. But he is also somewhat stupid and unsympathetic, both to the Polish victim and to the possible murderer, Hradschek. The judge, Vowinckel, although more intelligent and respectable, is equally incapable of solving the crime, despite his overoptimistic view of the power of the law and his high appraisal of himself. Speaking confidently to his brother, a local pastor, about how the criminal will soon be found, the judge boasts, "All guilt paralyzes, guilt and courage make poor company." Despite this apparent conception among middle-class Germans (note the similarity with Sudermann's Dame Care), Hradschek acts cleverly and boldly to the end, showing that Fontane did not share a belief in this bourgeois folk wisdom. Rather, Fontane found more wisdom in a place where few middle-class Germans would look. The only person to figure out the mystery and continue suspecting Hradschek all along is a semiliterate and elderly peasant woman named Jeschke, whom most everyone overlooks save the judge, who threatens her with a libel conviction if she doesn't keep her opinions to herself.

These were the realistic but limited portraits of crime and criminal justice offered by two of Imperial Germany's most critically acclaimed novelists. Both found criminal activity morally reprehensible, but both were capable of finding sympathy for the criminals as well as for the victims, and both had critical things to say about criminal justice officials. Although both were otherwise best known for novels set in urban Germany, they picked rural settings when they wrote about crime.

Considering that May and Sudermann also chose rural locales, it appears that conservative and moderate German novelists seldom singled out urbanization and city life as major causes of criminality. For May and Sudermann, crime was associated with cowardice, ethnicity, honor, and morality; for Raabe and Fontane, honor and morality played a part, but poverty, discrimination, and greed seemed even more important. In the works of these writers there is no mention of criminal mobs, slums, street violence, urban hustlers, fencing operations, pimps, or mobs; yet they were writing during a period of fantastic urban expansion. Their criminals always acted alone, and crime therefore seemed to be an isolated and rare event.

LEFT-LIBERAL WRITERS: KRETZER AND HAUPTMANN

The only group of German authors to give crime in general, and crime and urban conditions in particular, a real airing was the more radical branch of the naturalist literary movement. Although with a few exceptions their works were less well known and less popular than the more conservative and moderate authors, writers like Max Kretzer and Gerhart Hauptmann were intent upon exposing the seamier side of German society and occasionally concerned themselves with the problem of urban criminality.[73] Their works often focused on the lower orders of society, frequently depicting them as poor and pressed by circumstances and discrimination into petty criminal activity. The state was repressive and unjust, police officials were often overbearing and drunken, and judges were biased, egotistical, and concerned more with upholding the political order than with prosecuting real criminals.

Max Kretzer was one of the very few German authors with a claim to working-class roots. The author of several novels and short stories about

---

73 Ernst Rose, *A History of German Literature* (New York, 1960), pp. 275ff.; Ronald Gray, *The German Tradition in Literature* (Cambridge, 1965), pp. 132ff.; and Klaus Hildebrandt, *Gerhart Hauptmann und die Geschichte* (Munich, 1968).

social conditions in Berlin,[74] his novel dealing most directly with justice issues was *Der Irrende Richter*.[75] The story of "an errant judge" in Berlin who falls into heaps of personal difficulties bearing directly on his judicial performance, at the end of the story the judge learns that he too can make mistakes "just like the people," and that judging directly according to the letter and not the spirit of the law can lead to serious injustices.

In the novel, the haughty upper-middle-class judge, Sonter, who fancies that he possesses a *Napoleonblick* and has everyone, including his own mother, address him by the title of Herr Landgerichtsrat, gets drunk and compromises the virtue of his housemaid. Even though he insists on marrying her, as it seems the only honorable thing to do, he cannot admit this to his mother or to society and thus carries on a charade that he is still a bachelor and that the maid is not his wife. The maid plays along with this outwardly, but inwardly shows her displeasure by continuing to address him in private by the formal "Sie" or by his title.

Sonter continues, so he thinks, to perform his professional duties with the utmost objectivity and probity. But he is brought low when he falls in love with a wealthy socialite whose divorce case is pending in his court. Before meeting her, he had planned to rule against her and claimed that she probably deserved the beatings her husband had given her. She, as it turns out, is a reprehensible adulterous and egocentric flirt, who uses her beauty and charm to influence the judge to decide in her favor. After her divorce, he gets a divorce as well, and then proceeds to marry her. But at the end of the story he learns that she continues in her adulterous ways, and he comes to regret having been blinded by arrogance and greed and having lost his first wife, who, though common and uneducated, was always faithful and decent.

Insightful as Kretzer's exposure of the hollowness of the German criminal justice system's pretentions to objectivity, compassion, and fairness was, his criticisms were far milder than those of Gerhart Hauptmann, the most significant left-wing (before his later rightward change of course) naturalist author to deal with crime and justice issues in Imperial Germany. Born the son of a Silesian hotel keeper and the grandson of a Silesian weaver, Hauptmann had ample opportunity to observe the tragic lives of Silesian miners and textile workers suffering under capitalistic exploitation and political repression, which he wrote about in his first important play, *Vor Sonnenaufgang* (Before Sunrise), in 1889 and his masterpiece, *Die Weber* (The Weavers), in 1892. With these plays he gained the reputation of being the

---

74   Günther Keil, *Max Kretzer: A Study in German Naturalism* (New York, 1928).
75   Max Kretzer, *Der Irrende Richter*, 3d printing (Dresden, 1914).

foremost literary critic of German social, economic, and political conditions, which he preserved in later works dealing with crime and justice like *Der Biberpelz: Eine Diebskomödie* (The Beaver Coat: A Comedy of Thieves) and *Die Ratten* (The Rats).

Hauptmann's most acclaimed work, *The Weavers*, treats the historic revolt of the Silesian textile workers in the late 1840s, which came about after a long period of excruciating labor and privation. In one of the more graphic scenes, he depicts the plight of one poor family as they sit down to a dinner of roast dog. Before they sit down, Jaeger, a weaver who has just returned home from military service in Berlin, notes the dreadful poverty in which he finds the weavers: "This can't go on much longer. I'm amazed at how things are with you people around here. Why, dogs in the city live better than you live."

Later on in the play, Hauptmann makes it plain that the weavers often resorted to petty criminal acts like stealing wood or poaching game and fish because they had no other recourse, given their poverty and impending unemployment. Later he demonstrates that the manufacturers and the authorities were no less culpable than the poor weavers. In one scene, a forestry official, carrying an axe that he has just taken from some poor people attempting to steal wood, comes into a tavern full of weavers. One of the elderly weavers retorts that it is unfair to punish poor people for such petty acts when the really big criminals, often the manufacturers themselves, never seemed to be punished: "Beggin' your pardon, it's the same here as everywhere else with the big and the little thieves; there are those that carry on a wholesale lumber business and get rich from stolen wood, but if a poor weaver so much as. . . ." In several other scenes, common policemen slander the poor weavers before their superiors and abuse their police authority by punishing the poor weavers far out of proportion to their petty offenses. An example of this is when Old Wittig, a blacksmith friendly with the weavers, talks about the actions of a local policeman named Kutsche, who was sitting at a bar with Old Wittig and some weavers: "Who has blabbed to the manufacturers and to the nobles, and reviled and slandered me so I don't get a lick of work no more? Who set the farmers and millers against me so that, for a whole week, I haven't had a single horse to shoe or a wheel to put a rim on? I know who that is. I once yanked the damned scoundrel off his horse because he was thrashing a poor little nitwit boy with a horsewhip for stealin' a few green peas."

Hauptmann's strongest condemnation of the repressive German authorities who blindly meted out class justice and of the class-based authoritarian society that made crime the only avenue of escape for many poor people is found in *The Beaver Coat* and *The Rats*. The hero of *The Beaver Coat* is a hard-working Berlin washerwoman named Frau Wolff. No one, least of all the local judge, suspects her of being a criminal, even though she is the clever leader of a small band of local thieves. Hauptmann neither condones nor condemns her activities. He implies that her motivation is to provide better opportunities for her teenage daughters.

Frau Wolff eventually steals some firewood and an expensive beaver coat from a local landlord named Krüger. She is not caught or even suspected because of the incompetence of the reactionary, biased, and arrogant local judge, von Wehrhahn. "He gives the impression of being a Junker . . . he speaks in an almost falsetto voice and has cultivated a military abruptness of expression." Von Wehrhahn proves to be concerned solely with keeping the lid on any liberal or radical ideas, no matter how mild and unthreatening they may be. Displaying no concern at all for administering justice, he presides over a host of informants, who constantly snoop around and tattle on common citizens if they display the least liberal leanings.

When Krüger reports to the judge that his firewood has been stolen, the judge immediately suspects Krüger's lodger, a modest, liberal-thinking, and fully honest person named Dr. Fleischer. When Krüger returns with his more serious complaint about the stolen beaver coat, the judge shows no interest. Rather, he devotes his full attention to trying to get informants to squeal on Dr. Fleischer, who may have made some derogatory remarks about a high official. In the final words in the play, the judge tells Frau Wolff: "You look at all men from the outside. People like myself look somewhat deeper. And it is as true when I say here that Mrs. Wolff is an honest soul as it is when I tell you with the same certainty that your Dr. Fleischer is an extremely dangerous fellow."

In *The Rats*, a grim naturalist tragedy first performed in 1911, Hauptmann depicts the miserable lives of some poor Berlin workers juxtaposed to the more fortunate existence of some wealthy theatrical people. One misfortune after another is piled upon the lives of a childless working-class couple named John and a poor Polish servant girl named Pauline Pipercarcka. Mrs. John is desperate to have a child and arranges secretly to buy Pauline's illegitimate baby and to pretend that she bore it naturally while her husband – a decent, decorated-in-battle, hard-working mason of socialist sentiments – was away for several months on a job. Mr. John, too, is ecstatic to hear the news when he returns, but problems arise when Pauline decides she wants the baby back.

Mrs. John lies to the authorities in protesting that the child is her own, and the authorities refuse to listen to the real mother, presumably because she is Polish and of an even lower class. Things only get worse for Pauline and the John family, as Mrs. John's brother, a bad apple since childhood and constantly on the run from the police, ends up raping and murdering Pauline. The upstanding Mr. John finds out the truth and says that they must turn both the child and Bruno over to the authorities. Mrs. John then kills herself, leaving Mr. John without a wife or a child.

Whereas the obvious moral of the story is that poor people live like rats and tragedy is their fate, it also is important to point out that Hauptmann did not blame urban conditions for this, though he notes that a bias against the city existed among the propertied classes. In a subplot dealing with a wealthy theatrical family led by an aging adulterer named Hassenreuter, he begs his audience to ask themselves if the miserable lower-class "rats" were really the most morally reprehensible. Hassenreuter's daughter falls in love with a young actor named Spitta who had recently come to Berlin from the countryside to pursue his career. His sanctimonious father, a conservative small-town pastor, had forced his move, driving him from the family home for seeking a theatrical instead of a theological career. Pastor Spitta had previously expelled his daughter as well when she became pregnant out of wedlock, an act that led to her suicide shortly after she moved to Berlin. Completely unconscious of his own moral irresponsibility, he casts all blame upon the wickedness of the modern metropolis and continues to do this when he comes to Berlin to rescue his son from a similar fate. Using the voice of the play's most respectable character, Mr. John, the author asserts that the city is not at fault, when John scolds his wife for taking their child off to the countryside when it fell ill: "Why did you have to go an' take the child on the train an' outa town? The city is healthier. That's my notion."

CONCLUSION

Ending the discussion of popular opinion with Hauptmann's observation about the falsely placed bias against the city is especially appropriate because it reinforces the argument to be demonstrated statistically in the following chapters. His observations and those which can be gained from other authors and from newspaper and magazine articles confirm that the conservative ruling elite's association of crime with urban conditions and urban populations was not supported by most novelists and playwrights, including the most respected conservative ones, or by moderate, liberal, and left-wing opinion makers. Hence, if the criminal statistics support the views of those who wrote about crime for a popular audience, then rural crime should emerge as prominently as urban crime. Were it to be otherwise, one would have to suspect the serious biases of the conservative authorities as the real culprit, not the city.

From the popular discussion of crime, law, and justice issues, one would also expect to find an overrepresentation of foreigners, a predominance of offenses dealing with honor, morality, and politically motivated activity, and a large contingent of youth in the criminal statistics. On the other hand, women, as they were so infrequently mentioned, would be expected to figure less prominently in crime totals, except perhaps as victims. Whereas the population's gender, class, age, and ethnic background were frequently cited in the popular arena as determinants of criminal activity, religious denomination was less so, except in arch-conservative circles that had clear biases against Catholics and Jews.

On the whole, the portrait drawn by the leaders of popular opinion was one of an orderly society with its populace kept in check by a rigid class structure and repressive authorities. Curiously, perhaps this view of crime in Germany during its most rapid period of industrial and urban expansion does not fit the picture of surging urban crime and violence in France and England during their industrial revolutions as presented by Louis Chevalier and J. J. Tobias in their respected works.[76] Were the German popular observers wrong? The statistics will show that largely they were not. To be sure, crime existed in late nineteenth- and early twentieth-century Germany. A concern about violence may have increased over time, as attested particularly in the liberal media. But as the discourse surrounding the problems of crime and violence was so often tucked away in the backs of newspapers, confined to the *Stammtisch,* or hidden as a subplot in a few successful authors' novels and plays, dealing openly with the issue of crime seemed somewhat out of the ordinary to many Germans. Even crime itself was made to appear rather foreign to German audiences.

---

76 Chevalier, *Laboring and Dangerous Classes;* J. J. Tobias, *Urban Crime in Victorian England.*

3

Long-term Trends: The Modernization of Crime and the Modernization of German Society?

The qualitative treatment of crime and justice in the last two chapters, though important in itself, provides a necessary contextual foundation for the largely quantitative examination of these issues that begins with this chapter. With an understanding of how crime was defined, how it was prosecuted, and how contemporaries thought about it, one can more effectively evaluate the immense body of criminal and social statistics that the often-biased German legal system generated and state administrators recorded in their conscientious attempt to keep tabs on their society and its lawbreakers.

The following examination of the statistical evidence relating to criminal activity during nearly fifty years of rapid industrial and urban expansion between the foundation of the Reich and the onset of the First World War overlaps in many ways with the picture of crime and justice drawn in the previous chapters by using qualitative evidence. Furthermore, it adds considerably to a growing body of empirical evidence demonstrating that many long-maintained assumptions about the causes of crime, based on the supposed dislocations engendered by urban and industrial growth, "modernization," and urban living have very little explanatory power.[1] It shows, rather,

---

1   Much of the most significant work on this subject in a long-term sense has been done on the history of English crime. For reviews of the English evidence, see Lawrence Stone's chapter on "Homicide and Violence" in his *The Past and the Present Revisited* (London, 1987), pp. 295–310; J. A. Sharpe, "The History of Violence in England: Some Observations," *Past and Present* 108 (1985): 206–15; and Sharpe, "Quantification and the History of Crime in Early Modern England: Problems and Results," in Eric A. Johnson, ed., *Quantification and Criminal Justice History in International Perspective*, special issue of *Historical Social Research/Historische Sozialforschung* 15 (1990), 17–32. For other recent reviews considering the evidence from other societies, see Jean-Claude Chesnais, "The History of Violence: Homicide and Suicide through the Ages," *International Social Science Journal* 132 (1992): 217–34; and Helmut Thome, "Gesellschaftliche Modernisierung und Kriminalität. Zum Stand der sozialhistorischen Kriminalitätsforschung," *Zeitschrift für Soziologie* 21 (1992): 212–28. For earlier but still useful reviews of the evidence, see Ted Robert Gurr, "On the History of Crime in Europe and America," in Hugh Davis Graham and Ted Robert Gurr, eds., *Violence in America: Historical and Comparative Perspectives* (Beverly Hills, Calif., 1979), pp. 353–74; and several of the articles in James

that the genesis of criminal activity during, and likely before and after, the industrial revolution was far more directly related to economic hardship, repression of ethnic and political "undesirables," and changing legal definitions and enforcement patterns, all of which applied both to the countryside and to the metropolis. Finally, it demonstrates that although Germany had a deserved reputation for upholding order and maintaining safety, German society was becoming increasingly intolerant of and repressive toward stigmatized foreigners such as Poles and Lithuanians and urban dwellers like socialists and other workers, more threatening to women seeking independence and employment outside the home, and more violent in general.

To demonstrate these facts requires some effort and elaboration. This chapter begins to do so by examining long- and short-term crime trends from the early decades of the nineteenth century to the third decade of the twentieth, hence from a time when the first signs of the industrial revolution were beginning to be noticed in the 1830s to well after it had run its course in the 1920s. Once the longitudinal patterns in criminal and justice activity are established here, the following chapters go on to investigate the demographic characteristics of the criminals and the victims and the socioeconomic and ethnic makeup of the communities and regions in which they lived.

MODERNIZATION AND CRIME?

A careful examination of Germany's voluminous criminal statistics in the nineteenth and early twentieth centuries not only promises to demonstrate how crime-ridden or crime-free German society and individual German regions and communities were and which types of German people were most prone to crime or most repressed by the German government and criminal justice system, it also affords an excellent opportunity to help clarify several historical and theoretical issues related to the important debate over the "modernization" of crime and the "modernization of German society."

Few would dispute that German society modernized economically in the nineteenth century. An industrial revolution took place bringing in its wake a decline in the agricultural population and a huge rise of cities and an urban work force. But did social and political modernization follow in the industrial revolution's wake? Did power relations change significantly? Did people's attitudes change? Did Germany follow the same developmental path as other European and North American societies like France, Britain, and the

A. Inciardi and Charles E. Faupel, eds., *History and Crime: Implications for Criminal Justice Policy* (Beverly Hills, Calif., 1980).

United States, or did it embark on its own special path (*Sonderweg*), which ultimately resulted in the horrors of Hitler's Germany in the twentieth century? These questions are at the center of one of the most important debates in modern German history.[2]

Clearly there were some manifestations of political and social modernization in Germany similar to that of other countries in roughly the same period: constitutions were granted; education became universal; national sentiment started to replace local and regional allegiances; liberal and socialist ideas, institutions, and political parties developed. But in other important ways Germany's modernization seemed incomplete, half-hearted, and, many think, dangerous. Perhaps most importantly, many liberal scholars have argued that the German bourgeoisie failed to become a strong force in moving the society toward democratic values; important sections of it slavishly acquiesced to the political and ideological dominance of the powerful aristocracy, cared more for titles and honor than for freedom and liberalism, and in a sense became "feudalized." This "feudalized bourgeoisie" then conspired with the entrenched aristocracy to ensure that Germany, at least until the end of the First World War and possibly until the end of the Second, would, at its core, uphold conservative and antimodern principles beneath a thin and ultimately doomed veneer of democratic trappings.

This view of German history, so popular among liberal historians and sociologists since it was first elaborated by Dahrendorf, Moore, Wehler, Kocka, and others in the 1960s and early 1970s, though obviously one that is anathema to conservative scholars, has also been challenged in the last decade by the British scholars David Blackbourn and Geoff Eley.[3] They argue, among other things, that this "social-liberal" view of German history overestimates the liberal and democratic sentiments of the bourgeoisie in other lands; exaggerates the holdover of supposed feudalistic tendencies in Germany, such as the concern for honors and titles, which motivated middle-class people in other lands, too; assumes falsely that the apparent

---

2 For an excellent evaluation of the most important arguments and scholarly literature involved in this debate, see Richard J. Evans, *Rethinking German History: Nineteenth-Century Germany and the Origins of the Third Reich* (London, 1987), esp. chap. 3 on "The Myth of Germany's Missing Revolution." For defenses of the *Sonderweg* thesis, see especially Hans-Ulrich Wehler, "'Deutscher Sonderweg' oder allgemeine Probleme des westlichen Kapitalismus?", *Merkur* 35 (1981): 477–87; and Jürgen Kocka, "Der 'deutsche Sonderweg' in der Diskussion," *German Studies Review* 5 (1982): 365–79.

3 Ralph Dahrendorf, *Society and Democracy in Germany* (London, 1968); Barrington Moore, Jr., *Social Origins of Dictatorship and Democracy* (London, 1967); Hans-Ulrich Wehler, *Das deutsche Kaiserreich 1871–1918* (Göttingen, 1973); Jürgen Kocka, "Vorindustrielle Faktoren in der deutschen Industrialisierung," in M. Stürmer, ed., *Das Kaiserliche Deutschland* (Düsseldorf, 1970), pp. 265ff.; David Blackburn and Geoff Eley, *The Peculiarities of German History* (Oxford, 1984); and Blackburn and Eley, *Mythen deutscher Geschichtsschreibung. Die gescheiterte bürgerliche Revolution von 1848* (Frankfurt, 1980).

failure of Germany's 1848 revolution meant that Germany had no "bourgeois revolution"; and in general tends to whitewash the role that moribund capitalism and bourgeois elites played in the rise of fascism. In sum, they, like Germany's traditional and conservative historians, but for different reasons, reject the notion of a German *Sonderweg* and prefer to see the nineteenth-century development of German society as simply another variant of the modernization process, that, according to Marxist scholars, takes place in all societies.

Crime rates and trends seldom figure prominently in these debates about Germany's modernization or lack of it, but perhaps they should. As law is developed to codify and represent a society's values, an investigation of criminal activity and its repression can help to shed light on what those values were. If the progression of criminal activity "modernized" in Germany as it did in other countries in the nineteenth and early twentieth centuries, then the argument that Germany followed a special developmental path would be seriously weakened.

Like the debate in German history over Germany's political and social modernization, there is an important debate brewing in criminal justice history over the issue of "modernization and crime." Although less directly ideological, and perhaps closer to resolution than the German history question, this debate also has important ideological implications. But standing in the way of resolution are conceptual and methodological problems, as the German sociologist Helmut Thome pointed out recently in a lengthy and insightful article addressing the current state of the sociological and historical literature on the problem.[4] What does modernization in crime trends mean, how should it be measured, on which time periods should one concentrate?

Until very recently there was no consensus on what "modernization" in relationship to criminal trends and patterns meant, though the term itself, or what the term implied – development or change or urbanization – was often used to explain why crime rates rose or fell. Going back at least to the nineteenth century and continuing until today in many countries, conservatives have assumed that the modernization of society – most associated with the growth of cities, which in their view are in themselves detrimental to orderly behavior – necessarily brings about crime, violence, disorder, and other unruly forces in conflict with the status quo. Thus, they argue, there is little society can do to combat modernization's evil influences except to

---

4 Thome, "Gesellschaftliche Modernisierung und Kriminalität."

develop more powerful and efficient means of repression, such as police forces and prisons.

Although they would likely dispute what the remedies should be, the conservatives' views on the crime-inducing nature of modernization were supported by classical sociological thinkers like Durkheim and Tönnies in the late nineteenth century, who also saw the change from "community to society" as deeply unsettling and the growth of the modern metropolis as injurious to mental health and social order. In several societies, the conviction that modernization and, above all, urban growth led to crime and disorder was echoed in the twentieth century by urban-bashing fascists whose antimodern ideas and movements joined with those of traditional conservatives in extolling the virtues of the countryside. Finally, it became almost an article of faith among the general populace in America and in some other democratic societies, when American sociologists started in the 1920s to "prove" statistically that crime was a necessary correlate of urban growth and urban life, which were thought to be conducive to gang behavior, organized crime, and anxious, anomic city residents who turn to crime out of desperation or social pressure.

In the 1970s, a new wave of scholars studying Europe and America started to employ refined quantitative methods and began to argue for more precise terminology and conceptualization. American sociologists and historians like Charles Tilly, Howard Zehr, Roger Lane, and Ted Robert Gurr used powerful statistical techniques and modern computers to examine crime trends in several nineteenth-century societies and found that "crime" as a general term was too unmeasurable and too varied in definition from one society to another to have any meaningful theoretical utility.[5] Furthermore, they found that trends in different types of crime, especially property and interpersonal crime, often diverged and seemed to be explained by different types of phenomena. Although some thought their works added up neatly to a new theory of modernization and crime, most of them realized that their

---

[5] Abdul Quaiyum Lodhi and Charles Tilly, "Urbanization, Crime and Collective Violence in Nineteenth-Century France," *American Journal of Sociology* 79 (1973): 196–218; Howard Zehr, *Crime and the Development of Modern Society: Patterns of Criminality in Nineteenth Century Germany and France* (London, 1976); Roger Lane, *Violent Death in the City: Suicide, Accident and Murder in Nineteenth Century Philadelphia* (Cambridge, Mass., 1979); Ted Robert Gurr, Peter N. Grobasky, and Richard C. Hula, *The Politics of Crime and Conflict: A Comparative History of Four Cities* (Beverly Hills, Calif., 1977). See also David Cohen and Eric A. Johnson, "French Criminality: Urban-Rural Differences in the Nineteenth Century," *Journal of Interdisciplinary History* 12 (1982): 477–501; Vincent E. McHale and Eric A. Johnson, "Urbanization, Industrialization and Crime in Imperial Germany," *Social Science History* 1 (1976–77): 45–78 and 210–47; and Eric A. Johnson, "The Roots of Crime in Imperial Germany," *Central European History* 15 (1982): 351–76.

studies were too tentative and extended over too brief a period of time to do more than help resolve some mid-range theoretical issues and to point in the directions that other scholars might want to pursue.[6]

Quietly in the last decade, and especially in the last couple of years, several European criminal justice historians began to meet formally and informally, in an association called The International Association for the History of Crime and Criminal Justice, and started to address the issue of modernization in a more theoretically and conceptually unified manner. Most typically early modernists of liberal sentiment, hailing from countries with perhaps a stronger sense of tradition than America and living or having lived in cities like Stockholm, Amsterdam, London, and Paris, which have not witnessed the urban decay and staggering levels of crime and violence of such American cities as Detroit, Washington, and Los Angeles, these scholars are not pessimistic about the impact of modernization over the long haul of European history.[7]

The fruits of their research have recently come or are just now coming into print.[8] Already the efforts of these criminal justice historians have started to stir up the scholarly community in Europe and America, as evidenced especially by the new attention they have brought to a long-unnoticed German emigré scholar named Norbert Elias, whose ideas are central to many of their publications.[9] Similarly to Foucault and other French scholars who espoused the "de la violence au vol" argument about the change over time in crime patterns from a predominance of violence and personal crime in premodern society to a predominance of theft and other

[6] For one attempt at integrating the empirical studies into a general theory, see Louise I. Shelley, *Crime and Modernization: The Impact of Urbanization and Industrialization on Crime* (Carbondale, Ill., 1981).

[7] See, for example, Pieter Spierenburg, "Justice and the Mental World. Twelve Years of Research and Interpretation of Criminal Justice Data, from the Perspective of the History of Mentalities," *IAHCCJ-Newsletter* 14 (1991): 38–79; Spierenburg, *The Spectacle of Suffering. Executions and the Evolution of Repression: From a Preindustrial Metropolis to the European Experience* (Cambridge, 1984); Eva Österberg and Dag Lindstöm, *Crime and Social Control in Medieval and Early Modern Swedish Towns* (Lund, 1988); Jan Sundin, *För Gud, Staten och Folket. Brott och rättskipning i Sverige 1600–1840* (Lund, 1992); and James A. Sharpe, *Crime in Early Modern England 1550–1750* (London, 1984).

[8] See, for example, the essays by Eva Österberg, Pieter Spierenburg, J. A. Sharpe, Herman Diederiks, Jan Sundin, Eric A. Johnson, and Eric H. Monkkonen on long-term trends in violent crime from the Middle Ages to the present in Sweden, England, the Netherlands, and other societies, in Johnson and Monkkonen, eds., *Violent Crime in Town and Country since the Middle Ages* (Urbana: University of Illinois Press, forthcoming). See also the essays by Österberg, Sundin, and Johnson in a special issue on "The History of Urban and Rural Crime," in *Social Science History* 16 (1992).

[9] Norbert Elias, *The Civilizing Process* (Oxford, 1982, first published as *Über den Prozess der Zivilization*, 1939). Elias's work was discussed in two panel sessions at the 1993 Social Science History Association Convention in Baltimore, Maryland (November 4–6, 1993) and was at the center of a lively discussion on "Modernization and Crime over the Long Haul of European History," at the 1991 SSHA Convention in New Orleans, Louisiana (November 2, 1991).

property crimes in modern bourgeois society,[10] Elias and his new adherents argue that over the long term a "civilizing" tendency takes place in modernizing societies. Feudalistic fetishes of protecting one's honor and resorting to violence to resolve disputes become less prevalent over time, they argue, and murder, assault, and other crimes of violence decrease with the rise of the state's power in increasingly bourgeois society. Whereas their findings show an unmistakable and significant decline in personal violence from the late Middle Ages to the nineteenth century, their evidence is less supportive of Foucault's and others' contention that property crimes rise in step with modernization to take the place of crimes of violence in the modern criminal courtroom.[11]

Although these studies have done much to refine and clarify the debate on modernization and crime, and even if a civilizing process probably did take place in many countries, resulting in lower levels of interpersonal violence in the last two centuries as compared with the more distant past, none of their authors believes these findings add up to an acceptable general theory, and many of them in fact remain skeptical about the notion that crime modernizes at all.[12] Having to work with fragmentary data, as their focus is more on the data-poor distant past than on the last two centuries, their findings beg for analogous treatments of the modernization problem that are supported by more plentiful data and cover more localities (they usually focus on one city, like Amsterdam or Stockholm, or one county, like Essex) and that tackle the problem during the time of the most rapid economic and social change, usually coinciding with the industrial revolution of the nineteenth century, when one would expect the shift in crime patterns from violence to theft to have been the most powerful.[13] All this means that an in-depth

10 Michel Foucault argues that "a general movement shifted criminality from the attack of bodies to the more or less direct seizure of goods," and that "the shift from a criminality of blood to a criminality of fraud forms part of a whole complex mechanism, embracing the development of production, the increase of wealth, a higher juridical and moral value placed on property relations, stricter methods of surveillance, a tighter partitioning of the population, more efficient techniques of locating and obtaining information: the shift in illegal practices is correlative with an extension and a refinement of punitive practices," in his *Discipline and Punish: The Birth of the Prison* (New York, 1979: first published as *Surveiller et punir: Naissance de la prison*, 1975), pp. 76–7.
11 See the introductory essay by Johnson and Monkkonen in their *Violent Crime in Town and Country since the Middle Ages*.
12 See J. A. Sharpe, "Crime in England: Long-Term Trends and the Problem of Modernization," and Pieter Spierenburg, "Long-Term Trends in Homicide: Theoretical Reflections and Dutch Evidence, 15–20th Centuries," in ibid.
13 Modernization theory, as Helmut Thome recently has suggested, also needs to take into consideration the upsurge in post–World War II crime rates and the torture practices and violent excesses in state-sanctioned violence in many countries in the twentieth century. Thome, "Gesellschaftliche Modernisierung und Kriminalität," p. 226.

investigation of crime patterns in nineteenth- and early twentieth-century societies like Germany should have much to offer in adding to the understanding of the impact of modernization on crime.

To this point, although several scholars have written on nineteenth-century crime patterns in European and American society, most have either paid little direct attention to the statistical evidence[14] or have studied only relatively brief time periods.[15] For Germany, at least, the only scholar to use the abundant available statistical evidence for the balance of the nineeenth century with an eye to sorting out the relationship between modernization and crime has been Howard Zehr, who published a seminal work on the topic in the mid-1970s, which also compared French trends with German trends.[16] His argument that crime modernized in line with the "from violence to theft" thesis will be shown to rest on tenuous empirical foundations. The following discussion will demonstrate that nineteenth-century German crime patterns did not demonstrate a shift from violence to theft, as he argues. It will cast some doubts on the utility of the "civilizing process" concept in explaining developments in societies like nineteenth- and twentieth-century Germany. And it will make one question if Germany itself modernized in step with other industrializing societies, if it followed a special developmental path, or if all societies follow any clearly definable developmental paths. Finally, it will show that urbanization and industrialization did not generally lead to crime and violence even though urban workers and other urban residents were often unfairly stigmatized and persecuted by the society's leaders and the justice system.

YEARLY CRIME TRENDS PRIOR TO UNIFICATION

It is a difficult task to reconstruct German criminal trends prior to 1882, when the Reich first offered a complete set of criminal statistics based upon a uniform criminal code, criminal procedure, and method of collecting and publishing criminal statistics. Before this time, different German states used different criminal codes and somewhat different criminal procedures, and they published much less voluminous criminal statistics. Furthermore, the official criminal statistics for the various regions of Germany often lumped crimes into such diverse categories that comparisons are extremely difficult

---

14 Perhaps the most notorious example is J. J. Tobias, *Urban Crime in Victorian England* (London, 1972).
15 See note 5 above for citations. See also Dirk Blasius, *Kriminalität und Alltag. Zur Konfliktgeschichte des Alltagslebens im 19. Jahrhundert* (Göttingen, 1978).
16 Zehr, *Crime and the Development of Modern Society*.

to make.[17] Part of the problem with Zehr's work is that he often compared apples and oranges. But in that one cannot reconstruct German crime patterns without using many of the same statistical sources Zehr used, any interpretation of the available evidence is open to question. A new interpretation of the evidence benefits, however, from the opportunity to use the important work of Dirk Blasius, whose two important studies of preunification criminal trends were published after Zehr's.[18]

It is best to start with a reexamination of the two most important nineteenth-century contemporary works on criminal trends in the first three quarters of the nineteenth century. One is a major study of criminal trends in Bavaria written by one of Germany's first and foremost criminologists and statisticians, Georg von Mayr. The other is a famous study of Prussian criminal trends in mid-century written by a leading German government official and criminologist, Wilhelm Starke.[19] Table 3.1 presents the very same figures Zehr used to draw the conclusion that both theft and assault and battery were increasing rather steadily in nineteenth-century Germany prior to the time when the Reich offered a set of uniform criminal statistics in 1882.

Zehr's conclusion that assault and battery was on the rise finds support in these figures. Both Mayr's and Starke's evidence points to a continual rise in this type of offense, but it should be noted that the measure of assault and battery they use is "simple assault and battery" (*leichte Körperverletzung*), a far less common offense and perhaps a far less useful indicator of the level of assault and battery than "aggravated assault and battery" (*gefährliche Körper-*

---

17 Police statistics are available for only very few areas of Germany in the nineteenth century and were not published on a national basis at any time. The states with the most voluminous crime statistics of any sort prior to unification are Baden, Bavaria, and Prussia. See the discussion of the availability and the differences in nineteenth-century German criminal statistics in Graff, *Die deutsche Kriminalstatistik*. Graff explains that Bavaria published the first criminal statistics in Germany in 1803, but they were fragmentary and irregularly reported. Not until the 1840s did the Bavarian statistics become very well developed; and only after 1867 were they truly voluminous. Bavaria first started to publish police statistics in 1833, but these were even more irregular and fragmentary than the court statistics. Nevertheless, Bavaria had the most highly developed crime statistics of any German state prior to 1882. The only other states ever to publish police statistics prior to World War II (Graff, p. 225) were Baden, Württemberg, and some Prussian cities like Berlin, which published police statistics after 1885 in its annual statistical yearbook, *Statistisches Jahrbuch der Stadt Berlin*. For a fuller discussion of the availability of German police statistics, see Friedrich Zahn, "Aufgaben und Leistungen der Polizeistatistik," *Allgemeines Statistisches Archiv* 9 (1915): 364–96.
18 Blasius, *Bürgerliche Gesellschaft und Kriminalität* (Göttingen, 1976); and *Kriminalität und Alltag*.
19 Georg von Mayr, *Statistik der Gerichtlichen Polizei im Königreiche Bayern* (Munich, 1867). Mayr's work is the first major empirical treatment of crime and socioeconomic conditions in German society. This was but the first work in a long career lasting more than fifty years. Mayr continued publishing even after the First World War and at the same time held the editorship of one of Germany's most important sociological magazines, the *Allgemeines Statistisches Archiv*. W. Starke, *Verbrechen und Verbrecher in Preussen 1854–1878. Eine Kulturgeschichtliche Studie* (Berlin, 1884). Starke was a leading official in the Prussian justice ministry, and his book remains a classic in German criminology.

Table 3.1 *Criminal Trends in Bavaria and Prussia, 1835–1878*

Period	Mayr's Bavarian Statistics[a]	
	Theft	Assault
1835–39	269	46
1840–49	290	49
1850–59	322	62

Period	Starke's Prussian Statistics[b]	
	Theft	Assault
1854–59	293	40
1860–69	236	51
1870–78	215	63

Period	Blasius's Prussian Statistics[c]		
	Theft	Assault	Wood Theft
1835–39	245	25	1,269
1840–44	259	27	1,620
1845–49	282	26	1,750
1850–54	286	33	1,908
1855–59	302	34	2,299
1860–65	239	44	2,102

Note: All crime rates are yearly averages per 100,000 population.

[a] The source for Mayr's theft figures is Zehr, p. 36; for assault and battery, Zehr, p. 88.
[b] The source for Starke's theft figures is Zehr, p. 36; for assault and battery, Zehr, p. 88. These figures are based on new judicial investigations.
[c] Blasius's figures have been adapted from his tables in *Kriminaltät und Alltag*, pp. 81–82. They do not include Rhineland Province, and the figures themselves are based on court convictions.

verletzung). Zehr's argument that theft was clearly increasing is more problematic. It is true that Mayr's figures point to a rise in theft offenses between 1835 and 1859; but Starke's figures demonstrate a declining trend in theft offenses from the mid-1850s to the late 1870s.

Why Zehr accepted the Bavarian trends reported by Mayr and not the Prussian trends reported by Starke is unclear. Perhaps he had more faith in Mayr's figures, as they are based upon "crimes known to the police," as opposed to Starke's, which are based on "new judicial investigations." Perhaps he considered Mayr's figures to be measures of criminal activity that most closely represent the actual amount of wrongdoing that occurred and thus that they are less hampered by the notorious "dark figure" than Starke's. But even if one were to accept this as a reason to place more trust in Mayr's figures, there are other reasons to believe that Starke's evidence is better than Mayr's. The best weighing of the evidence, however, might be to accept both sets of figures. In all eventualities, the available evidence shows that theft was certainly not increasing consistently throughout Germany after the middle of the nineteenth century even though there might have been some increases in the first half of the century.

Starke's figures might be considered more reliable than Mayr's for two reasons: one is that they come from Prussia, which was a much larger state than Bavaria, hence Starke's Prussian figures may have been more representative of Germany as a whole; the other is that Mayr's figures are not purely for theft alone, as they are actually a kind of grab-bag of economic offenses, including embezzlement, poaching, and assorted other crimes, whereas Starke's figures are only for simple and serious theft, and theft when repeated.[20] But in that the Bavarian figures and the Prussian figures provided by these two criminological experts come from different periods, overlapping only in the late 1850s, is it not possible to conclude that both were basically correct? Had Starke provided earlier figures overlapping with Mayr's, might it not turn out that theft was in fact rising in both Bavaria and Prussia, and probably in the rest of the German lands, until slightly after mid-century, but declining thereafter?[21]

This is precisely what the Prussian figures provided by Dirk Blasius show (see Table 3.1). Although Blasius's figures are somewhat different from Starke's in that they do not include the Prussian Rhineland Province and are based on court convictions instead of judicial investigations, and they are obviously different from Mayr's because they come from Prussia instead of Bavaria, they coincide quite neatly with both Mayr's and Starke's statistics. Thus, theft offenses were rising both in Prussia and in Bavaria at least from the mid-1830s to the mid-1850s;[22] but after this time they declined quite steadily. This trend was also evident in the yearly and periodic progression of wood-theft offenses according to Blasius's figures; convictions for wood

---

20 Starke, *Verbrechen und Verbrecher in Pruessen*, pp. 100–15.
21 Zehr reports that rates of persons tried for theft offenses rose rapidly from the 1830s to the 1880s. Zehr, *Crime and Development*, p. 38.
22 Blasius's figures show that the rate for simple theft reached a peak in 1856, when it stood at 416 convictions per 100,000 population; in 1857, however, the rate declined precipitously to 257. According to his figures, the theft rates corresponded closely with the price of rye, which was at a premium between 1854 and 1856, but dropped by nearly 40% in 1857 (Blasius, *Kriminalität und Alltag*, p. 82). In his earlier work, Blasius presented other measures of the theft rate, such as the rate of new judicial investigations for the period 1835–50; these figures also confirm the conclusion that theft rates were rising in Prussia in this period. Blasius, *Bürgerliche Gesellschaft und Kriminalität*, p. 141.

theft increased quite steadily in Prussia up to 1859, after which time they declined just as steadily as they had increased earlier.

In that Blasius's figures support Mayr's, Starke's, and Zehr's observations concerning assault and battery, there is no reason to dispute Zehr's argument that violence was on the increase in nineteenth-century Germany. Blasius did not employ any measures of homicide offenses in either of his two studies of crime in pre-Bismarckian Germany, but both Mayr and Starke did. In both cases, it appears that homicide followed a pattern not unlike that of assault and battery.[23] Prior to mid-century there was little increase in homicide, and there were even some periods of decline after mid-century; but beginning with the period of Bismarck's wars with Austria and France, and particularly after the financial crash of 1873, there was a precipitous rise in homicide offenses.[24] Hence both common and severe forms of criminal violence were increasing in Germany from about mid-century on. It will soon be argued that these trends basically continued, with some minor exceptions, during the period of Imperial Germany.

From the evidence brought forward so far, it appears that violent crime was increasing in the first three-quarters of the nineteenth century and that property crime increased some in the two decades preceding the 1848 revolution but declined rapidly shortly thereafter. During the hard economic times of the 1840s and the period of rising food prices in the mid-1850s, theft, wood theft, and other forms of property crime did rise; but thereafter, most property offenses were on a distinctly downward course. Hence, nineteenth-century German crime trends prior to unification display no evidence of a shift from "violence to theft," as Zehr and other modernization theorists have posited. Rather, the opposite was more the case.

YEARLY CRIME TRENDS IN IMPERIAL GERMANY

Beginning with the year 1882 it becomes possible to trace the progression of crime trends for the whole of Germany. Every year the government published a huge volume of criminal statistics filled with statistical tables, maps, charts, graphs, and commentary by the government officials working in the

---

23 Mayr's figures are perhaps somewhat less reliable than Starke's, as his homicide indexes combine all kinds of offenses against life; Starke sorts them out into different major categories. Starke, *Verbrechen und Verbrecher in Preussen*, pp. 133–45.

24 Starke's figures show that the yearly total of new homicide investigations rose in Prussia from 640 in 1873 to 836 in 1874 and continued increasing up to 1877, when they hit their peak of 909. In 1878 they finally took a huge drop to 808. Starke, *Verbrechen und Verbrecher in Preussen*, p. 133.

Reichjustizamt (Reich Bureau of Justice).[25] There is a true wealth of useful information in these volumes: the statistical information is often broken down in such a way that one can determine what the crime rates were for each year in numerous different regions, cities, and districts; one can determine how many of the crimes were committed by women or juveniles; one can be sure that the statistics themselves were uniformly applicable to each of the cities, regions, and districts, and that they were compiled in exactly the same way for each year.

Despite the many good features of the government's crime statistics, they all suffer from one major flaw: They are all based on court records.[26] As all students of criminal justice realize, it is impossible to know exactly how many crimes ever occurred in any society at any time, as all crime records record a mere fraction of the actual amount of criminal wrongdoing; they represent only those crimes that come to the attention of the authorities and those crimes that the authorities choose to place in their records. Court records are often considered to be some of the worst kind of statistical material for measuring the actual state of criminal activity, for they represent only a fraction of the crimes reported to the police, and crimes reported to the police represent only a fraction of the actual amount of criminality. Thus, although there is some reason to believe that the German court records were particularly good, and although contemporary German crimi-

---

25 On December 15, 1881, the German government decided to produce yearly volumes of criminal statistics, beginning with the very next year. The statistics were compiled in the same fashion from 1881 up to the Second World War. As Graff explains: "Despite various developments – world war, dictatorship, Kaiserreich, democracy, inflation – the continuity of the gathering and representation of the criminal-statistical data from 1881 up to the Second World War was preserved" (Graff, *Die deutsche Kriminalstatistik*, p. 55). The statistics, however, were presented in much fuller detail during the Reich than during Weimar; as, for example, in the Weimar period they were no longer published by the "Place of the Criminal Offense" (*Ort der Tat*) so it becomes very difficult for the scholar to use them for cross-sectional studies in Weimar. The yearly criminal statistics volumes were entitled *Kriminalstatistik für das Jahr* and were a part of the massive Reich governmental series of official statistics, *Statistik des Deutschen Reichs*. The latter series contains all major population, business, and industrial consensus. Also, it reported yearly on a host of other pertinent goings-on of the Reich, including trade, schooling, finance, military matters, and so on. There is, unfortunately, no overall index accompanying these volumes. The appropriate volumes one needs can be found, however, by using the *Quellenverzeichnis* (Source Index) contained in the Reich's statistical abstracts, *Statistisches Jahrbuch für das Deutsche Reich*. Criminal statistics can also be found in many state statistical abstracts such as the Prussian *Jahrbuch für den Preussischen Staat*, and for several cities such as Berlin, which published their own statistical abstracts.
26 The government's decree to start publishing these figures stated that they were to be a "representation of statistics of legally settled cases [*rechtskräftig erledigten*] of felonies and misdemeanors against Reich laws." This statement was printed in each of the *Kriminalstatistik* volumes. All of the figures are based on information obtained from lengthy forms known as a *Zählkarte*, which the defendants filled out. These cards provide information on the defendant's religion, age, occupation, sex, and previous criminal record. At the end of each year, each locality forwarded these *Zählkarte* to Berlin, where they were compiled, then published about a year or two later in summary form. For a discussion of these *Zählkarte*, see Graff, *Die deutsche Kriminalstatistik*, pp. 53–8 and 72–83.

nal justice scholars trusted them implicitly and used them so successfully that many of their works were regarded throughout the world as classic models of criminal justice scholarship,[27] they must be used cautiously and skeptically. But, even if they are far from perfect indicators of actual criminality, they are accurate measures of the criminal justice activities of the German authorities.

From the figures presented in Table 3.2, it is apparent that the government's official figures did not record any tremendous increase in crime during Imperial Germany. In this table, the total number of trials, convictions, and acquittals transacted by German courts for all felonies and misdemeanors are broken down into average yearly totals for five-year periods, beginning with the first year that such figures became available on a national basis, 1882, and continuing on into the middle of the Weimar period. This table also lists, in five-year periods, yearly conviction rates per 100,000 people of criminally liable age (twelve or older) for all crimes in general, and for the three major categories into which the government divided the "total crime rate": crimes against state and religious laws, crimes against the person, and crimes against property. Although these figures, if taken at face value, do not point to any staggering increases in crime or criminal justice activity, they do reveal that German courts were becoming increasingly active from the 1880s until just after the turn of the century (the highest yearly crime total came in 1902, when the rate reached 1,246). In these two decades the total crime rate grew in each five-year period, and almost in each year itself. After 1902, however, the total crime rate was on a steady decline until it grew rapidly in the early 1920s before declining again in the later Weimar years.

If one considers the years of Imperial Germany in sum, and if one admits these court figures to be at all indicative of the actual incidence of criminal activity, one might conclude that crime in general had increased from the early years of the Reich until the outbreak of the First World War. Between the periods of 1882–5 and 1911–13 (see Table 3.2), the total crime rate grew from 1,003 to 1,191, an increase of 17.2 percent. The conviction and acquittal figures presented in this table make it clear that the increase did not come from a tendency to convict ever larger numbers of persons on trial, as the overall acquittal rate actually grew slightly over the period, roughly in

---

27   Many German criminologists of this period gained a worldwide reputation writing books and articles based on these figures, and criminologists from other lands used them liberally as well. See, for example, the classic studies of Gustav Aschaffenburg, *Crime and Its Repression*, trans. Adalbert Albrecht (Boston, 1913, originally published 1906); William Adrian Bonger, *Criminality and Economic Conditions*, trans. Henry Horton (New York, 1967, originally published 1905).

Table 3.2 *Time Series Trends in Conviction and Acquittals, 1882–1927 (All Offenses and Major Types of Offenses*

Period/Year	Convictions and Acquittals for All Felonies and Misdemeanors[a]			
	Total Tried	Total Convicted	Total Acquitted	Acquittal Rate[b]
1882–5	396,722	320,890	70,338	17.7%
1886–90	425,152	342,195	76,214	17.9%
1891–5	519,485	410,565	100,496	19.3%
1896–1900	578,640	453,730	115,652	20.0%
1901–5	635,840	497,798	127,884	20.1%
1906–10	678,226	535,962	135,785	20.0%
1911–13	702,165	558,121	131,780	18.8%
1914	560,024	454,054	97,047	17.3%
1915–18	366,250	302,786	58,814	16.1%
1919	418,064	348,247	61,643	14.7%
1920–4	805,021	683,416	123,330	15.3%
1925–7	703,250	591,237	98,778	14.0%

Period/Year	Crime Rates for Major Types of Offenses (convictions per 100,000)			
	All Offenses	Against State and Religion	Against Persons	Against Property
1882–5	1,003	118	369	511
1886–90	1,020	126	414	476
1891–5	1,155	150	478	523
1896–1900	1,197	173	530	491
1901–5	1,220	186	530	501
1906–10	1,210	196	494	518
1911–13	1,191	201	461	528
1914	940	157	346	435
1915–18	—	—	—	—
1919	736	81	135	517
1920–4	1,430	221	243	959
1925–7	1,232	407	274	545

Note: These figures were compiled by adapting the tabular information found in *Kriminalstatistik für das Jahr 1928*, vol. 370 of the series *Statistik des Deutschen Reichs* (Berlin, 1930).

[a] All figures are average yearly totals.
[b] The acquittal rate was computed by dividing the total number acquitted by the total number tried.

step with the progression of the total crime rate.[28] Also, the increase in the total crime rate did not stem from an increase in prosecutions for property offenses, which held very stable over the entire period. Most of the rise,

---

28 Acquittal rates grew in manslaughter and assault and battery cases, but declined in rape cases and stayed relatively stable in premeditated murder cases. Of these personal crime offenses, the acquittal

then, had to come from increases in the categories of crimes committed against state and religious laws and crimes committed against the person.

The rate of crime against state and religious laws was the major area of growth in German criminality. Between the periods of 1882–5 and 1911–13, it grew from 118 to 201, a staggering increase of more than 70 percent. Most of this growth, however, was in a sense "manufactured" by the German government.

This was done in several ways and mainly at the expense of the working class. Not only were existing laws often enforced more rigidly, but with increasing intensity after 1890, when Bismarck left office and the antisocialist laws were allowed to lapse, most local governments enacted a host of local police ordinances and the national government itself passed several additional new laws to slow the socialists' advance.

As Klaus Saul explains in his important study of the workers' movement, "after the fall of the [anti-] socialist laws, the justice and administrative authorities, in close cooperation, strove to use all of the possibilities of the criminal law, the association and press laws, and the ordinances regulating industrial practices to fight against the socialist workers' movement and to stem their advance [especially] through a highly discriminatory usage of police and administrative ordinances."[29] Richard Evans provides several examples of the new police ordinances that were passed in the 1890s in his study of the Hamburg political police's reports on the working class and explains that these were often "criticized by many people in Hamburg as further proof of the advance of Prussiandom."[30] Punished as *Übertretungen*, these police ordinances did not affect the national crime rate directly (as it was limited to *Verbrechen* and *Vergehen*). But their indirect effect was signifi-

---

rate was highest in premeditated murder and lowest in manslaughter (the former averaged about 22% yearly and the latter about 12%). Acquittals resulted in about 18 percent of rape cases and about 20 percent of assault and battery cases. In crimes against property, acquittals were more common in embezzlement and fraud (white-collar crimes) and less common in simple theft and serious theft cases (blue-collar crimes). The acquittal rate in fraud cases was rising quickly, whereas the acquittal rate in serious theft cases was declining. Acquittal rates grew slowly in both simple theft and embezzlement cases. One striking fact about the acquittal rates for property offenses is that acquittals in fraud offenses were about twice as high as they were in serious theft offenses in the early 1880s (22.4% to 10.7% between 1882 and 1885), but were over three times more common after the turn of the century (31.4% to 9.4% in 1906–10). We might note that though there is some evidence that acquittals were more common for upper-class than for lower-class people, they were obviously not extremely common for anyone. This overall average of about 20 percent, however, is a figure very similar to the percent of acquittal cases reported by the liberal newspapers and very different from that of either the socialist or conservative papers. See the discussion in Chapter 2 on the acquittal rates of the reported cases in the various newspapers.

29 Klaus Saul, *Staat, Industrie, Arbeiter-bewegung im Kaiserreich: Zur Innen – und Sozialpolitik des Wilhelminischen Deutschland 1903–1914* (Hamburg, 1974), p. 189.
30 Richard J. Evans, *Kneipengespräche im Kaiserreich: Stimmungsberichte der Hamburger Politischen Polizei 1892–1914* (Hamburg, 1989), p. 205.

cant. Many workers, feeling themselves unfairly harassed by the police – who could pass and enforce these ordinances on the local level basically by fiat and thus without having to get them through legislative bodies – reacted in a hostile fashion to their arrest and were subsequently charged with offenses that did indeed figure in the national crime totals.

New national laws pushed the crime totals still farther. In the commentary accompanying a special volume on the national trends in crime from the 1880s to the late 1920s, the Weimar ministry of justice reported that many new laws, "especially regarding workers' protection and workers' insurance legislation as well as other laws of a social-political character," were enacted after 1883, and especially after 1890, making "numerous cases punishable" that previously were not.[31] A table in that volume, comparing the registered, national crime rate over time with the national crime rate that would have resulted had these new laws not been passed, showed that the effect of the new laws alone accounted for an increase of nearly 80 points in the overall crime rate between 1890 and 1912. Although the largest percentage upsurge occurred between 1890 and 1895, the effect of these new laws on the national crime rate continued to be of importance up until the First World War.

The final way in which the government "manufactured" the apparent growth in the crime rate is explained by Dirk Blasius in his study of the history of political criminality in Germany from 1800 to 1980. "Especially through the use of paragraph 130 of the criminal code (incitement to violence), the justice authorities" employed harsher enforcement of previously existing laws to crack down "against the 'leftists' criticism and agitation." He cites several cases as examples. One occurred in July 1893 in which a tailor was tried for incitement to violence merely because, in the course of a strike meeting, he publicly said that he was "absolutely for the strike, because every strike weakens the bourgeoisie, and that capital must in every case be pushed out of the way either by legal or illegal means."[32]

In sum, had the ordinances, laws, policing, and prosecution practices in effect in 1882 been held constant throughout the period of the Kaiserreich, there would hardly have been any increase in the rate of crimes against the state and religious laws. Furthermore, when one takes into account the rise in the overall crime rate that was attributable to these "manufactured" crimes of a "social-political character," one finds that the overall rise in the "total crime rate" between 1882 and 1913 was measurably smaller. If one

---

31 *Kriminalstatistik für das Jahr 1927, Statistik des Deutschen Reichs*, 370: 32. Hereafter cited as *STDR*.
32 Dirk Blasius, *Geschichte der politischen Kriminalität in Deutschland 1800–1980: Eine Studie zu Justiz und Staatsverbrechen* (Frankfurt am Main, 1983), pp. 60–6.

subtracts these manufactured crimes from the increase in the total crime rate, one finds that the increase in the total crime rate was less than 11 percent over the years of Imperial Germany rather than over 17 percent, as approximately 42.5 percent of the apparent increase in the total crime rate was attributable to the rise of politically manufactured criminal offenses.

TRENDS IN VIOLENT CRIME

The addition of new laws and ordinances was not a major factor in the trends in crime against the person or crime against property, and since the rate of crime against property did not show much of an increase, much of the increase in the "total crime rate" of Imperial Germany had to be attributable to an increase in prosecution for violent criminal activity. As will be demonstrated shortly, there are strong reasons to think that Imperial Germany experienced a real rise in violent crime and not just an increase in governmental efforts to curb such behavior. But, if one starts with the court records, one finds that, between 1882 and 1913, the crime rate for personal crime grew rapidly until the turn of the century, reaching a peak of 539 in 1901 and 1902. Thereafter, the rate declined mildly but remained at a higher level than it had been at the beginning of the period.

Howard Zehr employed many of these same figures and also argued that violent crime was increasing. However, he sensibly distrusted using such "total crime indexes" and based his comments mostly on separate offenses such as homicide and assault and battery. In his view, most of the increase in violence was attributable solely to increases in assault and battery, as he believed that the homicide rate was actually declining steadily throughout Imperial Germany. If one uses only the court records, it appears that Zehr is correct, with some qualifications. Table 3.3 lists official figures for six major types of personal crimes beginning with the period of 1882–5 and continuing until the middle of the Weimar years. Although there were no serious increases in libel or in simple assault and battery, there was a significant increase in the most frequent offense in this category, serious assault and battery. Reaching a peak shortly after the turn of the century, this offense grew steadily from 1882 until just after the turn of the century. Between 1882 and 1901, the peak year, the rate jumped from 121 to 248, more than a 100 percent increase. After the turn of the century, however, the rate declined steadily up to the war, and in Weimar it dropped precipitously.[33]

33 Considering that Weimar had high murder and manslaughter rates, even according to the court

Table 3.3 *Time Series Trends in Personal Crime, 1882-1927*

Period/Year	All Crimes against Persons	Premeditated Murder	Unpremeditated Murder	Rape[a]	Serious Assault and Battery	Simple Assault and Battery	Libel
1882-5	369	.45	.49	8.7	140	56	127
1886-90	414	.36	.41	9.3	169	58	130
1891-5	478	.32	.47	10.0	201	68	139
1896-1900	530	.25	.44	11.7	237	70	144
1901-5	530	.23	.43	12.7	240	66	143
1906-10	494	.20	.44	11.8	217	61	137
1911-13	461	.21	.51	11.9	199	50	134
1914	346	.17	.48	10.5	146	34	98
1915-18	—	—	—	—	—	—	—
1919	135	.35	.56	3.0	49	16	43
1920-4	243	.41	.76	7.2	61	23	99
1925-7	274	.33	.81	12.0	65	27	99

Note: All figures are annual conviction rates per 100,000 legally liable population. For source see Table 3.2.

[a] Includes all major types of rape.

Nonetheless, as the rate of this most frequently committed and prosecuted type of personal crime was far higher in the beginning of the twentieth century than in the early years of the Reich, one must concur with Zehr's observation that common forms of violent crime increased in Imperial Germany.[34]

Zehr believes that homicide, on the other hand, displayed a completely different trend. As he put it: "Homicide rates . . . dropped steadily in Germany after 1882 . . . they bottomed during the first years of the twentieth century, then moved upward slightly in what may have been the beginning of a new trend . . . the incidence of homicides was almost the inverse of that in assaults."[35] Indeed, were one simply to accept the court records, which Zehr does in this case, as he believes that homicide offenses are particularly "hard measures" of criminality, then there would be few reasons to disagree with him. Although the apparent trend in homicide offenses went counter

records, one wonders if the reduction in Weimar of assault and battery offenses might have been due to the overburdened court loads caused by the huge increases in theft offenses and in crimes against the state.

34 Many other forms of personal crime offenses not mentioned in the text were rising as well. For example, convictions for immoral provocations and for coercion and threats rose quickly throughout the period until they peaked in 1908 and leveled off thereafter. The latter offense actually tripled in intensity. *STDR*, 370: 57–58.

35 Zehr, *Crime and Development*, p. 115.

to that of some other extreme forms of violent crime such as rape (see Table 3.3), which showed an upsurge, most of these crimes were types of moral offenses which may have simply been prosecuted more vigorously during this period.[36] As the rates displayed in Table 3.3 show, the rate of premeditated homicide (*Mord*) declined steadily throughout Imperial Germany, and the rate of unpremeditated homicide (*Totschlag*) declined from 1882 until just after the turn of the century, after which time it increased somewhat, but only enough to reach its original level of 1882 just before the war. One might add, however, that even the court records demonstrate that homicide was apparently not on the verge of going out of existence, because in the immediate postwar period convictions for both types of homicide offenses registered huge gains.

There are several reasons, however, to distrust the trends in homicide offenses that the court records display. To begin with, several studies of the sentencing practices of German courts have shown that there was an increasing trend toward handing out ever more lenient punishments and for trying people for ever milder offenses.[37] This was especially true in homicide offenses. In the last three columns of Table 3.4 there is some evidence for this. These figures show that between 1882 and 1914 there was almost no difference from one year to the next in the number of people convicted of a homicide offense, despite the fact that the population had grown upward of 50 percent.[38] This in itself should make one wonder about the "hardness" of the courts' homicide figures. But more direct evidence to support the argument that the courts were trying people for ever less serious offenses comes from a comparison of the trends in premeditated versus unpremeditated homicide. When court statistics were first published in 1882, there was an almost equal frequency of these two offenses (for example, in the period of the early 1880s there were 142 convictions for premeditated homicide in an average year and 157 for unpremeditated homicide). But as the years wore on, more and more people were tried for the offense of unpremeditated

36 The acquittal rate for rape offenses remained relatively constant from 1882 to about 1905: in the period between 1882 and 1885 it was 19.3 percent; and in 1900–1905 it dropped slightly to 18.6 percent. After 1905, it dropped rather quickly to 15.0% in 1911–13, and reached a low of 13.7 percent in 1914. In Weimar the acquittal rate grew once again and even surpassed 20 percent in the late 1920s.
37 Franz Exner, *Studien über die Strafzumessungspraxis der deutschen Gerichte* (Leipzig, 1931). Rupert Rabl, *Strafzumessungspraxis und Kriminalitätsbewegung* (Leipzig, 1936). See also George Rusche and Otto Kirchheimer, *Punishment and Social Structure* (New York, 1939), pp. 193–205. The most complete statistical information on the punishments handed down by German judges is contained in "Die Entwicklung der Strafen im Deutschen Reich seit 1882," in *Kriminalstatistik für das Jahr 1928*, STDR, 384: 64–106.
38 The legally liable population (those over twelve years old) rose from 31,720,049 on December 1, 1881, to 48,311,000 on January 1, 1914. STDR, 370: 61.

Table 3.4 *Average Yearly Trends in Reported Homicide Deaths and Homicide Convictions*

Period/Year	Reported Deaths Due to Homicide in Prussia and Berlin			
	Prussia Total	Berlin Total	Prussia Rate[a]	Berlin Rate[a]
1873–5	540	12	21.0	12.4
1876–80	482	10	17.8	8.8
1881–5	430	13	15.2	9.9
1886–90	356	17	11.8	11.4
1891–5	486	18	15.3	10.7
1896–1900	580	26	16.8	13.8
1900–5	668	38	17.9	18.6
1906–1910	761	37	18.9	17.7
1911–13	847	—	20.2	—
1914	1,459	—	34.3	—
	Convictions for Homicide in Prussia and Berlin			
1873–5	—	—	—	—
1876–80	—	—	—	—
1881–5	180	5	6.4	3.8
1886–90	138	4	4.6	2.7
1891–5	158	5	5.0	3.0
1896–1900	136	5	3.9	2.6
1900–5	141	4	3.8	2.0
1906–1910	160	8	4.0	3.9
1911–13	195	10	4.7	4.8
1914	179	3	4.2	1.4
	Convictions for Homicide in Entire Reich			
	Total Homicides	Premed. Murder	Unpremed. Murder	Total Homicide Rate[a]
1873–5	—	—	—	—
1876–80	—	—	—	—
1881–5	299	142	157	6.4
1886–90	259	122	137	5.2
1891–5	281	114	167	5.4
1896–1900	263	97	166	4.7
1900–5	269	92	177	4.4
1906–1910	283	89	194	4.4
1911–13	337	99	238	5.0
1914	312	82	230	4.6

Note: Homicide figures include premeditated murder *(Mord)* and unpremeditated murder *(Totschlag)*.

[a] Homicide rates are per million total population. They differ from the homicide figures in Table 3.3 in that they are not computed by dividing the homicide total by the criminally liable population (twelve and older) and they are per million instead of per hundred thousand.

homicide and fewer and fewer for premeditated homicide. Might not these figures suggest that the German authorities were becoming more reluctant to prosecute and convict people for homicide offenses, especially as large sections of the German populace, including most of the upper bourgeois classes from which the judges usually came, were so opposed to the death sentence that was mandated by murder in the first degree?[39]

Another reason to distrust the trends in homicide suggested by the court records is that they run counter to coroners' records for homicide deaths (see Tables 3.4 and 3.5). Although the coroners' records themselves may be doubted because they apply only to the state of Prussia, because they include many cases of infanticide, which the courts handled differently from premeditated and unpremeditated murder, and because it is impossible to know how many of the homicide deaths registered by the coroners were really accident or suicide deaths, there are several reasons to consider them equally good or even better measures of the actual rate of homicide than the court records.[40] In the first place, they are far closer in time to the actual homicidal act than the court records, and since most dead bodies eventually show up, they represent a much larger percentage of the actual number of homicides that took place. Beyond this, the coroners' records were recorded in such a fashion that it is possible to control for the deaths that might have been subsequently prosecuted under the offense of infanticide rather than premeditated or unpremeditated homicide. This can be done by subtracting all registered homicide deaths of children less than one year old. When this was done in a previous study, it turned out that it did not change the overall picture of the trends in homicide other than to suggest that the rate of homicide offenses (excluding infanticide) was growing even faster in Imperial Germany if possible infanticide deaths were subtracted from the calculus than if they were left in; over time, the number of homicide deaths listed by the coroners was made up of an ever-increasing number of people over one

---

39 Acquittals in premeditated homicide cases (*Mord*) were twice as common as they were in unpremeditated homicide cases (*Totschlag*). Between 1882 and 1914, approximately 22.4 percent of premeditated homicide cases resulted in acquittals, but only about 11.7 percent of the unpremeditated homicide cases ended with the acquittal of the defendant. See the discussion in Chapter 1 about the great debate over the abolition of capital punishment. Although the proponents of abolition lost in the legislature, perhaps they won in the judiciary.

40 The Prussian coroners' statistics are available from 1873 to 1914 in yearly volumes entitled *Die Sterblichkeit nach Todesursachen und Altersklassen der Gestorbenen*. These volumes were part of the major Prussian statistical series, *Preussische Statistik*. The homicide deaths are listed under the category *Mord und Totschlag*, which was but one of the thirty major causes of death (including separate categories for suicide and accidental deaths) for which these volumes provide statistical information.

year old.⁴¹ Finally, the fact that only Prussian figures are available does not pose a problem, as Prussia was a large and representative part of Germany as a whole. It made up roughly 60 percent of the population and land area; it had roughly the same mix of demographic, social, and economic characteristics as the rest of Germany; and the court records demonstrate that its crime trends mirrored the crime trends for the entire Reich.⁴²

In Tables 3.4 and 3.5, the trends revealed by the coroners' homicide figures are juxtaposed with those revealed by the court records. With the coroners' reports one is able to go back a decade further than with the court records. When one does this, one finds that the rate of homicide offenses declined throughout the two decades of Bismarck's rule, and that it started from a level in the early 1870s that was as high as it ever would be again in all the years of Imperial Germany, except for 1914 when the First World War began.⁴³ In the 1870s and 1880s, parallel to what the court records suggest,

---

41   Randolph E. Bergstrom and Eric A. Johnson, "The Female Victim: Homicide and Women in Imperial Germany," in John C. Fout, ed., *German Women in the Nineteenth Century* (New York, 1984), pp. 345–67. Between the periods 1887–91 and 1902–7, the percentage of female homicide deaths composed of infants less than one year old shrank in Prussia from 42.2 percent to 34.8 percent; for male infants the percentage shrank from 22.6 percent to 15.7 percent. In the city of Berlin, the decline was even more dramatic: from 56.1 percent to 40.0 percent for female infants and from 51.8 percent to 34.8 percent for male infants. In a recent criticism of coroners' data for measuring homicide rates, Margaret A. Zahn explains that coroners' figures probably underestimate, not overestimate, the amount of homicide deaths. She argues that, in the United States at least, if "it was likely that the offender could not be found, as when a victim was found with a slit throat on the highway, or if the victim was of low social value, for example, an infant, then deaths were not likely to be reported as homicides but rather as a ruptured aorta in the case of the slit throat and suffocation for the infant" (Zahn, "Homicide in the Twentieth-Century United States," p. 114). Without detailed microstudies of the practices of German coroners, it is impossible to know if these practices applied in Imperial Germany as well. But the court records do show that the rate of infanticide convictions was declining rather steadily throughout Imperial Germany, just as the coroners' data show that the percentage of infant homicide deaths was declining as well. For the yearly court statistics on convictions for infanticide, see *STDR*, 384: 77–8.
42   The "total crime rate" based on court records in the period 1883–87 was 1,018 for Prussia and 996 for the entire Reich. For assault and battery offenses, Prussia's rate was 145 and the Reich's 153. For theft offenses, Prussia's rate was 296 as compared to 282 for the Reich. In the period 1908–12, Prussia's total crime rate was 1,214 and the Reich's was 1,184. In assault and battery offenses, Prussia's rate was 199 and the Reich's rate was 204. In theft offenses, Prussia's rate was 265 and the Reich's 249. Thus, Prussia had almost the same crime rates as did the entire Reich, though theft offenses were slightly more frequent and assault and battery offenses slightly less frequent in Prussia than elsewhere. These figures come from *Kriminalstatistik für das Jahr 1887, STDR*, Neue Folge, 37 and from *Kriminalstatistik für das Jahr 1887, STDR*, 267.
43   Although Starke's figures apply only to Prussia, they support these observations, as he found that the homicide rate in Prussia was highest just after the war with France but was beginning to decline in the late 1870s. His figures show that in 1878 Prussian courts sentenced 73 people to death for murder, but by 1881 only 42 people were sentenced to death. They also show that the rate of homicide, as measured by the number of new judicial investigations for either precipitated or unprecipitated homicide, was at an exceptionally high level in the 1870s. Starke, *Verbrechen und Verbrecher in Preussen*, pp. 135, 145.

Table 3.5 Yearly Figures for Homicide

	Reported Homicide Deaths[a]		Convictions for Homicide[b]		
	Prussia	Berlin	Entire Reich	Prussia	Berlin
1873	516	9			
1874	556	2			
1875	547	24			
1876	471	10			
1877	543	22			
1878	471	9			
1879	455	2			
1880	470	7			
1881	432	8			
1882	444	21	320	199	3
1883	406	12	317	185	6
1884	419	13	269	162	2
1885	446	10	290	173	8
1886	432	12	298	166	2
1887	374	17	273	153	7
1888	377	23	212	112	4
1889	320	11	255	130	5
1890	275	20	258	130	5
1891	442	24	248	121	1
1892	486	17	316	174	10
1893	516	12	281	180	7
1894	517	18	275	156	3
1895	471	17	283	?	?
1896	587	27	270	?	?
1897	524	28	275	150	5
1898	534	17	269	126	7
1899	569	29	250	128	4
1900	684	27	251	139	2
1901	664	46	242	122	5
1902	580	27	282	154	0
1903	691	39	275	152	5
1904	709	38	273	140	3
1905	697	41	271	135	4
1906	696	33	261	150	1
1907	788	41	272	159	7
1908	?	?	290	155	6
1909	?	?	289	160	11
1910	800	?	303	174	13
1911	?	?	322	185	11
1912	804	?	323	182	6
1913	889	?	367	217	12
1914	1,459	?	312	179	3

Note: Homicide includes both premeditated murder and unpremeditated murder.

[a] These figures are all based on coroners' reports. The data were gleaned from a variety of sources, including yearly volumes of the series Preußische Statistik, Statistik des Deutschen Reichs and Berlin statistical yearbooks.
[b] These figures for Prussia come from annual volumes of criminal statistics (Kriminalstatistik), which are part of the series Statistik des Deutschen Reichs. The figures for the entire Reich come from Kriminalstatistik für das Jahr, 1927, STDR, 370, pp. 45–46.

the coroners' figures show that not only the rate of homicide but also the actual number of homicides declined steadily throughout the first two decades of Imperial Germany. In Table 3.5, for example, one observes that in Prussia in the early 1870s there were over 500 homicide deaths yearly, but by 1890, even though the population had grown considerably, only 275 Prussian homicide deaths were recorded by the coroners. But after the 1890s, the coroners' records and the court records start to diverge. In Table 3.4 the court records point to a slight upsurge in the homicide rate in the early 1890s, but that was followed by a sharp decline lasting almost up to 1910. The coroners' records, on the other hand, point to a very sharp upsurge in homicides in the early 1890s followed by a steady increase all the way up until the war. Considering that in the few years preceding the war the homicide rate, calculated from the coroners' figures, was at about the same high level that it had been in the early 1870s, that it had nearly doubled from the low point in the late 1880s, and that it was made up of a larger percentage of noninfanticide deaths than it had been earlier, the conclusion follows that homicidal violence was steadily becoming a more regular feature of German society in the post-Bismarck period. Furthermore, since the rates for other forms of criminal violence such as serious assault and battery and rape were growing as well, but convictions for criminal libel stayed rather constant (albeit at such a high level that they counted for between one-quarter and one-third of all convictions in personal crime offenses, perhaps demonstrating the Germans' mania for preserving their personal honor, but also the government's continuing need to use libel laws to punish their socialist enemies), it cannot be said that crime in Imperial Germany was "modernizing," with people relinquishing atavistic physical acts of violence and turning ever more to the state to resolve disputes and vent their anger.

One can conclude the discussion of violent crime in Imperial Germany by stating that even though violent criminality was increasing after 1890 according to both the statistical evidence and to our analysis of German public opinion, the increases were far from dramatic, and Imperial Germany was certainly not overrun by interpersonal violence, at least in comparison with other countries. Quite the contrary, for scholars as far back as Emile Durkheim cited Germany as having some of the lowest homicide rates in all of Europe. According to Durkheim, only Holland had a lower rate of homicide, and some societies, like Italy and Spain, had homicide rates that were more than twenty times higher.[44] Of course, comparing homicide statistics between one country and another is an especially dubious exercise,

---

44 Emile Durkheim, *Suicide: A Study in Sociology*, trans. John A. Spaulding and George Simpson (New

but there are other indications supporting the view that Germany was not a violent society.

We might well recall the observation of the American traveler who was cited as saying that, at the turn of the century, German cities had the reputation of being "safer for strangers, perhaps, than any other[s] in the world."[45] Both the figures for reported homicide deaths and for homicide convictions provided in Table 3.5 for the capital city of Berlin support this judgment. Although Berlin had an average population of greater than one million people throughout this period, in an average year it had only about twenty reported homicide deaths and only a handful of people convicted of a homicide offense. In some years, Berlin had no convictions for homicide and almost no homicide deaths; and it is important to bear in mind that nearly 50 percent of all reported homicides in most years in Berlin were of infants.[46] Berlin is the only major city cited here, but the same low levels of homicide were characteristic of most German cities.[47]

TRENDS IN PROPERTY CRIMES

Even though German homicide rates compare favorably with those of many other societies, the apparent upsurge in severe forms of interpersonal violence in Imperial Germany does not support the modernization argument; nor do the trends in property offenses. In 1930, the German criminal justice authorities themselves remarked that the trends in property crimes from 1882 until the time they were writing "displayed a very different development than did felonies and misdemeanors against the person."[48] Indeed, even Zehr argued throughout his book that the procession of property and personal crimes marched to different drummers. He, however, thought that the beat was faster in property crimes. To make his case, Zehr had to dismiss completely the trends displayed by the court records, which is somewhat strange in that he trusted them implicitly for homicide and other violent offenses and that even some of his own charts and evidence point to a decrease in theft, arson, and other property crimes in Imperial Germany.[49]

York, 1951), p. 353. Howard Zehr's figures show that the conviction rate for homicide was four times higher in France than it was in Germany in the period 1900–9. Zehr, *Crime and Development*, p. 114.
45 Ray Stannard Baker, *Seen in Germany* (New York, 1901), p. 8.
46 See note 39.
47 For just a couple of examples: In 1905, the city of Düsseldorf had only nine reported homicide deaths and the city of Cologne had only ten. In 1886, Düsseldorf had six and Cologne had none at all. In 1906, Düsseldorf had nine and Cologne had eight.
48 *STDR*, 370: 35.
49 Zehr, *Crime and Development*, pp. 41–2.

Zehr does, however, employ some evidence to support his assertions that theft and property crimes were increasing. Mainly this is in the form of some case studies of reported theft and property crime trends in various German cities and regions.[50] Although his archival efforts are creditable, they do not prove his case. Whereas most of the cities he chose did display a rise in reported theft offenses, this rise almost invariably came only after the mid-1890s. According to his own figures, the Ruhr cities of Oberhausen, Düsseldorf, Bochum, Duisburg, and Mülheim-am-Rhein in fact all displayed a marked downward trend in reported theft offenses from the beginning of Imperial Germany until the end of the long depression in the mid-1890s. Just because there was a rise after this period in these places hardly means that there was a rise in theft offenses in general. The official statistics show a rise in theft offenses after the 1890s in these Ruhr cities as well. But, as will be explained in the next chapter, this rise was primarily accountable to a huge in-migration of poor easterners, who were often of Polish ethnic background and who, as the analysis of popular opinion demonstrated and the statistics will further show, were often heavily discriminated against and, at least partially as a consequence, often figured heavily in the criminal statistics. In addition, much of the rest of the rise in theft offenses in these heavily working-class areas may also have reflected the government's increasing attempts to punish their socialist and potentially socialist enemies by whatever means they could. Given that theft in other less working-class and foreign-settled areas declined markedly in these same years and that the overall rate of theft declined for the entire country, certainly this information cannot support Zehr's conclusion that theft and property crimes were becoming more frequent because of the modernization of German society. Furthermore, as his own figures show that theft and other property offenses actually fell for as many decades as they rose, even though modernization in his view was progressing steadily throughout Germany, the trends in property crimes also do not fit the model prescribed by Zehr, Foucault, and others who argue for a rise in property offenses with the modernization of society.

Had Zehr consulted the German court records alone, he would have found basically the same trends he found in his archival evidence, as the rates were indeed increasing after the mid-1890s in many German cities.[51] But,

---

50 Ibid., pp. 71–7.
51 If we take, for example, four of the same cities used by Zehr (Berlin, Bonn, Bochum, and Düsseldorf) and compare their theft rates in the period 1883–7 with their theft rates in the period 1903–7, we find that in each case even the court records pointed to a rise in the rate of theft. The rates for these cities in these two periods were, in respective order: Berlin, 298,335; Bonn, 172,288;

Table 3.6 *Time Series Trends in Property Crime, 1882–1927*

Period/Year	All Crimes against Property	Simple Theft	Serious Theft	Robbery	Fraud and Embezzlement	Swindling
1882–5	511	234	25	1.3	46	36
1886–90	476	203	22	1.2	45	42
1891–95	523	209	27	1.2	51	52
1896–1900	491	185	24	1.2	51	54
1901–5	501	183	26	1.4	54	54
1906–10	518	181	31	1.5	62	52
1911–13	528	171	32	1.5	65	53
1914	435	139	29	1.4	54	45
1915–18	—	—	—	—	—	—
1919	517	222	81	2.1	35	24
1920–24	959	423	94	2.9	67	62
1925–7	545	147	29	1.7	69	96

Note: All figures represent annual conviction rates per 100,000 legally liable population. For source see Table 3.2.

even if they were increasing in some cities, they were declining in Germany as a whole. As the figures in Table 3.6 show, the national rate for simple theft, the most common of all property offenses, actually declined steadily throughout the years of Imperial Germany. Thus, if theft offenses increased in many urban areas in the last two decades before the war, they must have declined markedly in many other areas at this same time. This in fact was the case, as many predominantly rural areas of Germany, which in the first few decades of Imperial Germany had very high rates of theft, had great declines in convictions for theft later on. Examples of this are found in many of the northeastern Prussian provinces such as East and West Prussia and Posen, which in the 1800s had theft rates that were more than twice as high as the comparatively urbanized and industrialized province of Westphalia but in the years before the war had nearly a 50 percent reduction in their theft rates. Other less extreme examples can be found in German states outside of Prussia.[52]

Table 3.6 shows, however, that many other types of property offenses were actually increasing in Imperial Germany. This was true both for lower-class types of property offenses like serious theft and robbery and for prop-

Bochum, 333,383; Düsseldorf, 291,462. These trends compare very neatly with those provided by Zehr, *Crime and Development*, pp. 74–5. The court records show that the rise was small in Berlin and steeper in the other cities; and Zehr's figures show the same trends.

52 Between the periods of 1883–7 and 1908–12, the rates for theft decreased in East Prussia from 565 to 286, in West Prussia from 557 to 316, and in Posen from 624 to 308.

erty offenses of an often white-collar nature like embezzlement, fraud, and swindling. These less frequent property offenses acted to balance off the decrease in convictions for simple theft, and therefore the "total property crime rate" remained relatively stable throughout the entire period. During the first five years after the war, a period of political turbulence and economic uncertainty, most property crime rates increased markedly. But with the easing of political and economic chaos that followed in the mid-Weimar years, most property offenses declined in frequency. Simple theft declined so drastically that by 1927 its rate was lower than it had been in any of the years of Imperial Germany.

EXPLANATIONS OF YEARLY CRIME TRENDS AND CONCLUSIONS

An attempt has been made in this chapter to track the path of criminal activity in Imperial Germany and in the years preceding and following it. Most of the evidence has come from official sources, but much has been borrowed from the works of several scholars who have either traveled some of the same ground or have uncovered and analyzed some less accessible records.

To this point the effort has been mainly to describe the course of criminal activity in German society. Whereas this has been a difficult and treacherous task in itself, it is easier than explaining why these trends occurred. So far the only explanatory argument introduced has been modernization theory, which, as will be elaborated on shortly, does not appear to explain long-term German criminal trends. Although no comprehensive theory is intended here as an alternative, there are some broad economic and political considerations that offer at least a partial explanation for the rise and fall of crime rates thus far observed. One is that, although all crime rates are influenced to some degree by economic and political factors, economic factors help to explain long-term trends in economic crime rates (for instance, property offenses) better than they do long-term trends in violent crimes, which are perhaps more closely related to attitudinal and political than economic factors.

By economic factors I simply mean material want and economic hardship rather than the more sophisticated relative-deprivation arguments that many modern theorists have found so attractive.[53] Although the relative-

---

[53] One of the most widely acclaimed examples of the use of relative deprivation theory as an explanation for social action is Ted Robert Gurr's *Why Men Rebel* (Princeton, N.J., 1971).

deprivation arguments are of possible importance, raw economic hardship alone explains a large amount of the ups and downs of economic crimes throughout the nineteenth and twentieth centuries. This can be demonstrated at the simplest level by observing that during the greatest periods of economic hardship the rates of personal crime took their greatest leaps forward, and that during more prosperous times they receded. During the 1840s and early 1850s and the first few years of Weimar, food prices were rising quickly, jobs were scarce – and property offenses were rife.[54] But from the mid-1850s on, the general trend in the economy was toward lower prices and an improved economic outlook for the majority of Germans, and over most of these years there was a decrease in simple theft offenses, which were far and away the most common types of economic crimes and the ones most affected by raw economic hardship. There is less evidence, even at this simple level, to support the argument that other forms of property offenses were as neatly related to major changes in economic conditions; in fact, here the evidence is mixed. Although all forms of property offenses for which there are available data increased rapidly during the extremely tough times of the early Weimar period, no evidence has been presented for most of them prior to the 1880s,[55] and during the period from 1882 to 1914 many of these less common types of property crime even registered some increases despite the general improvements in the economy. Nonetheless, a large number of property offenses, particularly those like simple theft offenses that were most often committed by poor and lower-class people, were clearly affected by periods of economic hardship or improvement.

Periodic and long-term economic trends do not, on the other hand, help much to explain national yearly trends in personal and political crime rates; for if they were closely related to one another, then one would have to believe that good economic times encouraged violence and antigovernmental behavior. During the hard years of the early Weimar Republic and during the 1840s in Prussia and Bavaria, violent crime offenses like assault and battery and most other personal crimes were either remaining stable or decreasing, but during the rest of the years between the 1840s and the Weimar period most forms of violent crime and some forms of political

54 For a literary portrait of the economic hardships of the 1840s, see Gerhart Hauptmann's *The Weavers;* for the years just after World War I, see Erich Maria Remarque's *The Road Back.* For statistics on food prices, see Blasius, *Kriminalität und Alltag,* pp. 81–2; Ashok V. Desai, *Real Wages in Germany* (Oxford, 1968); Ludwig Fuld, *Der Einfluss der Lebensmittelpreise auf die Bewegung der Sozialethik* (Mainz, 1881); and Edward Renger, *Kriminalität, Preis und Lohn. Eine kriminalstatistische Untersuchung für Sachsen von 1882 zu 1929* (Leipzig, 1933).
55 Blasius provides some statistics on the rise of various types of property offenses in the years between 1836 and 1850 in his *Bürgerliche Gesellschaft und Kriminalität,* pp. 141ff. See also Starke, *Verbrechen und Vergehen in Preussen,* pp. 95ff.

crimes were on the rise. The reason these offenses were rising during some of the periods characterized by relatively positive economic conditions might simply be that the courts and police were so devoid of property offenses to occupy themselves with that they concentrated much harder than normal on personal and governmental offenses. And, by the same token, during periods when the criminal justice authorities were swamped by property offenses, they may have relaxed their efforts in dealing with other types of criminal offenses. This is a particularly compelling argument for the early Weimar years, as it is hard to believe that in this period of great hardship and bitter political struggle there were only one-third as many rapes and one-fourth as many cases of serious assault and battery as there had been before the war broke out. Nonetheless, this line of argumentation is really more of a political explanation than an economic one, as it suggests that the increases observed in the crime rates were really because of a rise in criminal justice activity rather than in the real level of violent criminality.

The argument that economic factors are particularly important in explaining property offenses can be supported by technically derived evidence as well. Since the nineteenth century, many criminal justice experts in Germany and elsewhere have used a variety of mathematical means to demonstrate a close relationship between economic conditions and long- and short-term trends in crime rates.[56] Whereas, prior to the development of modern statistical techniques and the advent of the computer, most of these efforts were in the form of graphs juxtaposing cost-of-living indexes like food prices or wage rates with crime trends, scholars today use the more powerful statistical tools at their disposal to lend more mathematical exactness to these relationships. But the enterprise is basically the same, and many scholars choose to support their arguments using both the old and the new methods.

Several studies using both mathematical and graphic means of analysis have shown that a strong relationship indeed existed in nineteenth- and early-twentieth-century Germany between economic conditions and certain types of crime. Disagreement remains as to which types of economic indexes are most indicative of economic hardship or prosperity and as to whether the relationship between economic conditions and crime continued as strongly or, rather, weakened in these years. But all agree that the relationships between economic conditions and property offenses are far

---

56 Time-series graphical treatments linking economic conditions to crime trends in nineteenth-century Germany can be found in Aschaffenburg, *Crime and Its Repression;* Rusche and Kirchheimer, *Punishment and Social Structure;* Fuld, *Der Einfluss der Lebensmittelpreise;* Renger, *Kriminalität;* Starke, *Verbrechen und Verbrecher in Preussen;* Blasius, *Kriminalität und Alltag;* and in so many other places that there is no need to provide more graphs here.

stronger than those between economic conditions and other types of offenses.[57] Certainly it is the case that a strong relationship between food prices and theft offenses existed in the first three-quarters of the nineteenth century. Dirk Blasius found, for example, that between 1836 and 1850 there was a correlation of $r = .94$ between rye bread prices and theft rates in Prussia and between 1852 and 1865 the correlation was $r = .90$.[58] Howard Zehr applied correlational techniques to Mayr's data for Bavaria and Starke's data for Prussia and found correlations similar to those of Blasius.[59]

But, when Zehr applied the same techniques to time-series crime trends in Imperial Germany, he found somewhat lower relationships. Using Starke's figures for Prussia between 1854 and 1878, Zehr found a correlation of $r = .77$ for rye prices and theft and a correlation of $r = .67$ for potato prices and theft, but between 1882 and 1912 he found that the correlation between theft and rye prices in all of Germany was down to $r = .61$. Although he found high correlations between theft and other measures of economic conditions in this same period (for example, $r = .75$ between real food prices and theft; $r = .70$ for real wages and theft; and $r = .60$ for employment and theft) he concluded that the relationship between crime and economic conditions became weaker and less important by the end of the nineteenth century.[60]

It was necessary for Zehr to draw this conclusion, as otherwise his modernization theory, which argued that as society modernized a new kind of opportunity motivation for theft replaced the old raw hardship motivation, would have been disproven by his own facts. But his own figures could indeed serve more to disprove than to support his modernization theory. Clearly, a strong relationship between economic conditions and simple property offenses continued throughout the nineteenth century and into the twentieth century, as Zehr's and other scholars' figures have shown. If the mathematical relationship weakened at all, which it hardly did, it is likely that the mathematical measures themselves became less reliable indicators of economic hardship and that the relationship between hardship and theft

---

57 Blasius, *Kriminalität und Alltag*, pp. 48–60 and 81–2. McHale and Johnson, "Urbanization, Industrialization and Crime," 218. Zehr, *Crime and Development*, pp. 98ff.
58 Blasius, *Kriminalität und Alltag*, pp. 48–9.
59 Zehr also cites the work of W. Woytinsky, who was the first to use correlational techniques on this kind of data in Germany and who also found similarly high correlations. Woytinsky, "Lebensmittelpreise. Beschäftigungsgrad und Kriminalität," *Archiv für Sozialwissenschaft und Sozialpolitik* 61 (1929): 21–62.
60 Zehr also tested a number of business-cycle indicators and found that they were not strongly related to crime trends; but he argues sensibly that they were not particularly relevant measures, as they did not really measure the real situation of the individual offenders. Zehr, *Crime and Development*, pp. 44–8.

offenses continued. The logic is that individual measures of economic hardship are less valid by the end of the century, because the personal economy and diet of most Germans had become more varied by this time. Nonetheless, even if the relationship did weaken somewhat, it weakened only slightly, and economic conditions continued to explain a large amount of the variance in national yearly trends in simple property offenses throughout the nineteenth century and into the twentieth. It is hard to accept that a new opportunity motive explained the patterns of property crime in Imperial Germany. Surely there were more goods to steal because Germany as a whole and individual Germans themselves had grown wealthier, but it is not so sure that property offenses were increasing relative to the growth in population and the population's possessions.

Few would dispute that crime in itself is a political artifact, as political decisions determine what crime is, how it is defined, and how it is to be defended against and punished. But it is not easy to demonstrate the importance of political factors in explaining crime trends mathematically.[61] It has already been pointed out, however, that the development of new laws and ordinances and the more vigorous prosecution of old ones, political acts in themselves, accounted for most of the perceived growth in the rate of crime committed against the state. We have also discussed the likelihood that the criminal justice system concerned itself more or less with violent offenses depending on how heavily burdened it was with property offenses. Beyond this, we have indicated that the decline in conviction rates for homicide offenses came from a relative decline in German society's desire to punish offenders for this offense, as the coroners' figures pointed to a marked increase in homicidal deaths.

The most important way in which political factors played a role in determining the amount of criminal activity in German society, however, may be related to the relative amount of political discord, class conflict, ethnic strife, and militarism that the society generated at different times. Increases in these phenomena probably created parallel increases in interpersonal violence at all levels, but this is especially hard to demonstrate quantitatively. Nonetheless, both our analysis of German public opinion and most accounts of these problems show that all of these were on the rise, especially in the post-Bismarck years. Marked increases in "total crimes against the person," in serious and simple assault, in libel offenses (see Table 3.3), and in reported homicide deaths (see Table 3.4) all came immediately after Bismarck left

---

61 See, for example, Charles Tilly, Louise Tilly, and Richard Tilly, *The Rebellious Century: 1830–1910* (Cambridge, Mass., 1975).

office. Despite all of Bismarck's failings, he was a stabilizing force in German society. When he left office, Germany turned toward a more violent foreign policy, which also reflected a more disorderly, discordant, and violent internal culture. The socialist movement made rapid gains, even though some socialists began to follow Bernstein's revisionist ideas. The strike movement increased in frequency and intensity. The government used libel and other laws more and more frequently to contain the socialist threat. Poles and other ethnic minorities were enraged by Wilhelm's "Germanization" policies, and violent crime rates grew apace.[62] And, since the rates for homicide offenses took major leaps forward, as measured both by court and coroners' records, in the years surrounding the Franco-Prussian war and World War I, one of the major explanations for homicide trends is found in the presence or absence of militarism at particular points in time. Emile Durkheim argued this point nearly one hundred years ago, and some modern sociological research has demonstrated its importance for several societies in the twentieth century.[63]

These few economic and political factors only begin to explain the patterns of criminal behavior in Imperial Germany, especially as national yearly crime trends mask great regional, ethnic, and demographic differences in criminal behavior. In the following chapters the discussion will focus on who the criminals and victims were, on where crime rates were highest and lowest, on the impact of urbanization and industrialization on crime in different types of German communities, on the changing status of women, and on the increasing repression of hard-pressed ethnic minorities.

But, before turning to these issues, a few concluding comments about the question of modernization and crime need to be made. In the conclusion to his book on German and French crime trends in the nineteenth century, Howard Zehr stated that "what we have found, in other words, is a modern-

---

62 Eduard Bernstein, *Evolutionary Socialism*, trans. Etich C. Harvey (New York, 1961). On the German socialist movement, see Saul, *Staat, Industrie, Arbeiterbewegung im Kaiserreich* (Düsseldorf, 1974); Hans-Ulrich Wehler, *Sozialdemokratie und Nationalstaat* (Göttingen, 1972); Carl W. Schorske, *German Social Democracy, 1905–1917: The Development of the Great Schism* (New York, 1955); Gunther Roth, *The Social Democrats in Imperial Germany: A Study in Working Class Isolation and National Integration* (Totowa, N.J., 1963). On the situation of the Poles, see Christoph Klessmann, *Polnische Bergarbeiter im Ruhrgebiet. Soziale Integration und nationale Subkultur einer Minderheit in der deutschen Industriegesellschaft* (Göttingen, 1978); and Charles Murphy, *Guestworkers in the German Reich: A Polish Community in Wilhelmian Germany* (Boulder, Colo., 1983). On the rise of collective violence, see Tilly, Tilly, and Tilly, *The Rebellious Century*. And, on the growing educational illiberalism of Imperial Germany and anti-Polish academic restrictions, see Konrad H. Jarausch, *Students, Society, and Politics in Imperial Germany: The Rise of Academic Illiberalism* (Princeton, N.J., 1982).
63 Durkheim, *Suicide*, pp. 352–3. Dane Archer and Rosemary Gartner, "Violent Acts and Violent Times: A Comparative Approach to Postwar Homicide Rates," *American Sociological Review* 41 (1976): 937–63.

ization of criminal behavior paralleling and accompanying the modernization of society in general."[64] We have not found this to be true. Neither did modernization, as characterized by the rapid and continuous urbanization and industrialization process in nineteenth- and early-twentieth-century Germany, lead to a consistent upsurge in crime in general (as conservative and classical thinkers have warned), nor did the modernization of the economy, the body politic, or the mental universe of German citizens cause crime patterns to shift "from violence to theft" (as contemporary modernization theorists suggest). The only consistent change in criminal offenses was an increase in the prosecution of political offenses. This reflected, above all, the entrenched conservative elite's increasing determination to preserve their power status and to keep their socialist, ethnic, and religious opponents in line by enacting new laws and more vigorously enforcing old ones. Violent offenses, instead of decreasing over time, quite clearly increased from the 1830s to the 1870s, according to Mayr's, Starke's, and Blasius's figures; and, after a downturn during the Bismarck years, increased again during Wilhelm II's reign in the 1890s and 1900s, according to the government's combined criminal and medical statistics. The dominant trend in the most relevant property offenses, like simple theft, rather than showing an increase as modernization theory warrants, actually went in the other direction, declining rather steadily from the middle of the century onward.

So, if crime did not "modernize" during Germany's industrial revolution, other explanatory factors for the trends in its crime patterns need to be considered in more detail in the following chapters. But one reason why crime did not "modernize" is because the society itself did not modernize, or only "partially modernized," as scholars such as Dahrendorf, Wehler, Kocka, and others have argued. In addition to pointing to the continuing dominance of conservative elites in the government, military, and administration, one can find evidence of the persistence of premodern values and practices in the society's perhaps overdetermined concern for honor. This was manifest in the continued resort to dueling and interpersonal violence to resolve disputes,[65] by the frequent criminal prosecution of libel, which continued to fascinate newspaper readers, and by the works of novelists and playwrights who continued to explain criminal acts in terms of weak and dishonorable character.

64 Zehr, *Crime and the Development of Modern Society*, p. 139.
65 Ute Frevert, *Ehrenmänner. Das Duell in der bürgerlichen Gesellschaft* (Munich, 1991), esp. pp. 233–40.

4

Urban–Rural Differences, Ethnicity, and Hardship: Cities Are Not to Blame

Watson: "Good heavens!" I cried. "Who would associate crime with these dear old homesteads?"

Holmes: "They always fill me with a certain horror. It is my belief, Watson, founded upon my experience, that the lowest and vilest alleys in London do not present a more dreadful record of sin than does the smiling and beautiful countryside.... But the reason is very obvious. The pressure of public opinion can do in the town what the law cannot accomplish. There is no lane so vile that the scream of a tortured child, or the thud of a drunkard's blow, does not beget sympathy and indignation among the neighbours, and then the whole machinery of justice is ever so close that a word of complaint can set it going, and there is but a step between the crime and the dock. But look at these lonely houses, each in its own fields, filled for the most part with poor ignorant folk who know little of the law. Think of the deeds of hellish cruelty, the hidden wickedness which may go on, year in, year out, in such places, and none the wiser."

Arthur Conan Doyle, "The Adventure of the Copper Beeches"

The task of demonstrating that Holmes's reply to Watson applies to more places than England is of primary concern in this chapter on regional and urban–rural differences and the often decisive factors of ethnicity and poverty in criminal activity in the Kaiserreich. That rising national-level crime rates do not always follow in the wake of urbanization and industrialization has already been shown by the longitudinal data presented in the last chapter. This longitudinal evidence, though it goes against much sociological argumentation and popular folk wisdom, does not, however, prove directly that the process of urbanization and the urban setting itself are not crime-inducing. It is possible that rather stable national-level crime rates might conceal exceptionally high and possibly increasing urban rates balanced by exceptionally low and decreasing rural rates. This chapter will show that this was not the case. The urban explosion that took place during Germany's industrial revolution in the second half of the nineteenth century and the beginning of the twentieth did not cause crime. Ethnic and political discrimination and repression, often associated with human hardship, did.

Criminologists, clergymen, popular writers, social philosophers, historians, social scientists, and politicians in virtually every country have long debated the influence of environmental factors such as cities and urban growth, ethnicity, and poverty on criminal activity. Their arguments have been and remain of considerable import for structuring policy, as politicians and citizens alike generally view criminality as an evil that society can well do without and for which political measures should be taken to make the social and economic environment less crime-inducing. Unfortunately, for far too long and in too many societies, the basically conservative view has prevailed that crime is not caused by economic hardship or discrimination, which society could do something about, but rather is a product of irrational impulses and moral weaknesses engendered by certain ethnic and religious groups and by big-city living, which no amount of social engineering can hope to influence.

Worse yet, the conservatives' arguments have often been supported by scholarly studies and putative theories that seem to lend credence to their anti-urban, anti-ethnic, and moralistic political policies. This has worked to the detriment not only of certain groups but of whole societies; witness the sorry urban wastelands and soaring crime rates in much of contemporary Britain and America, to name only two glaring examples. Scholars are usually not to be faulted for consciously doing the conservatives' bidding. The problem with their work has generally been that they have often developed their theories on the basis of inadequate and insufficient data having no real historical or cross-cultural validity. Hence a sociologist in the postwar United States might easily find that large cities and black communities have higher crime rates than rural and white communities; but this does not mean that cities and blacks or "ethnics" are necessarily prone to crime in the United States, or anywhere else. And it does not mean that citizens and politicians are making a wise choice when they simply throw up their hands in dismay and disgust and vote for policies that ensure the further degeneration of cities into lunar landscapes and the further demoralization and stigmatization of certain ethnic groups. Indeed, by looking at America's past and that of other western societies in both a historical and a sociological light, a number of scholars have recently begun to build an impressive body of evidence that challenges those assumptions of conservative policymakers and present-minded sociologists that have created self-fulfilling prophecies.[1]

---

1 There is a growing body of evidence, for example, that the most reliable measure of criminality,

The evidence in this chapter, largely generated by employing modern quantitative techniques and a mass of census and justice data to test an array of sociological theories about the impact of urbanization, population growth, human hardship, and ethnicity on the incidence of criminal behavior in Imperial Germany will strengthen the emerging sociohistorical argument that cities are not necessarily dangerous or highly crime-prone environments, and that crime is neither primarily irrational nor the preserve of incorrigible ethnic groups who turn to it, not because of bad social and economic conditions and discrimination, but because they are somehow biologically determined to do so. Furthermore, the evidence has a purely historical function as well. It will reveal how criminal behavior varied among different regions, ethnic groups, large cities, towns, and rural communities in Imperial Germany.

REGIONS

One of the arguments often advanced to explain crime is that it is a kind of culturally determined and learned behavior passed on from one generation to the next, and that it is often rooted in certain definable geographic regions, such as the American south, where a culture of violence and lawlessness is supposed to reside.[2] The criminal justice authorities of the Bismarckian and Wilhelmian Reich were surely influenced by this viewpoint, as is evident from the way in which they presented their statistics on

homicide, was far more prevalent (perhaps as much as ten times) in premodern and preindustrial society than it is today. Until very recently, most of the long-term empirical evidence came from British studies. For important summaries of this evidence, see Ted Robert Gurr, "Historical Trends in Violent Crime: A Critical Review of the Evidence," *Criminal Justice History* 3(1981): 295–343; and Lawrence Stone, "Homicide and Violence," in his *The Past and the Present Revisited* (London, 1987), pp. 295–310, 426–32. For more recent studies tracing homicide trends from the late middle ages to the present in several societies in addition to England, see, among others, the essays by Eva Österberg and Jan Sundin (both Sweden), Pieter Spierenburg and Herman Diederiks (both the Netherlands), and J. A. Sharpe (England), in Eric A. Johnson and Eric H. Monkkonen, *Violent Crime in Town and Country since the Middle Ages* (forthcoming). Other useful discussions of the quantitative evidence on a variety of different types of criminal activities and for several other countries are found in Eric Monkkonen, "The Quantitative Historical Study of Crime and Criminal Justice," in James A. Inciardi and Charles E. Faupel, eds., *History and Crime: Implications for Criminal Justice Police* (London, 1980), pp. 53–73; Dirk Blasius, "Kriminologie und Geschichtswissenschaft: Bilanz und Perspektiven interdisziplinärer Forschung," *Geschichte und Gesellschaft* 14 (1988): 136–49; and Eric A. Johnson, ed., *Quantification and Criminal Justice History in International Perspective*, special issue of *Historical Social Research/Historische Sozialforschung* 15 (1990). For the history of crime in Germany alone, see Richard J. Evans, "In Pursuit of the *Untertanengeist*: Crime, Law and Social Order in German History," in his *Rethinking German History: Nineteenth-Century Germany and the Origins of the Third Reich* (London, 1987), pp. 156–87; and Evans, ed., *The German Underworld: Deviants and Outcasts in German History* (London, 1988).

2 An excellent discussion and large, though now dated, bibliography is found in Hermann Mannheim, *Comparative Criminology* (Boston, 1965), esp. pp. 499–605.

criminal behavior. Each year from 1882 until World War I the Royal Statistical Bureau published huge volumes of criminal statistics that used the location of the crime (*Ort der Tat*) as the central organizing principle. In most of the tables in these volumes, however, the location that was listed and used for the purpose of presenting other information about the criminal acts and offenders was usually not the individual town, village, or small district (*Kreis*) where the deed occurred but the province or large administrative region (in Prussia and Bavaria, the *Regierungsbezirk*,) composed of many of these smaller communities. Nor did the authorities generally use categories such as the age, sex, occupational status, or ethnic origin of the criminals themselves for presenting their data (though they sometimes did). Instead, they chose to focus on the characteristics of the large regions in which the crimes were committed. Operating in this way, if only partly consciously, the authorities laid stress on the geographic and cultural environments in which criminal acts occurred.

Geographic and regional bases of criminal activity were stressed all the more by the use of maps that graphically contrasted the supposed lawless and law-abiding regions of the country. Two examples of these maps are presented here, which chart the regional spread of crime in the late 1880s and in the first decade of the twentieth century. Of course, the broad brushstrokes used to darken the high-crime areas in these maps gloss over the great differences that often existed between individual communities, even in the same general region. For example, in the administrative district of Gumbinnen, in the far northeast, which is darkly shaded on both maps, some communities had less than one-third the "overall crime rate" of others. In the five-year period between 1883 and 1887, the small rural community of Heydekrug had an annual rate of 2,579 convictions per 100,000 legally liable population, whereas the equally small rural community of Darkehmen had a rate of only 801; between 1903 and 1907 Heydekrug's rate was 2,647 and Darkehmen's only 887.

But rough as these maps are, they are useful in helping one to see where, very broadly speaking, there was a relatively large or small amount of criminal activity in Germany (or at least where there were many or few criminal arrests and prosecutions). Furthermore, they help one to see that, despite considerable continuity, a good amount of change took place between the early and later decades of the Reich. The information presented in Table 4.1 brings these regional patterns into less graphic but more precise relief. The shadings in the first map show that in the 1880s there was a threefold geographical division of criminal patterns in Germany. The highest crime rates were to be found along the northeastern border regions of Prussia

Urban–Rural Differences, Ethnicity, and Hardship 149

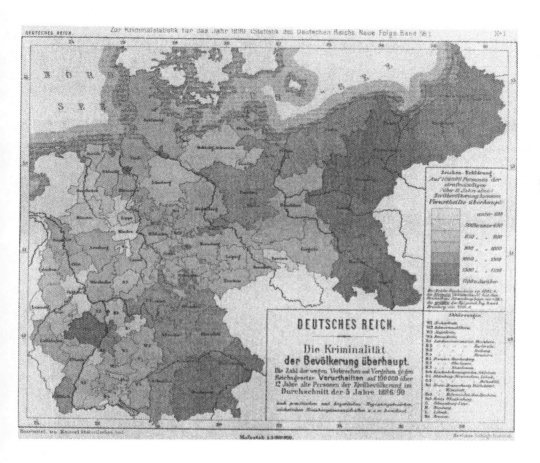

Map 4.1. Regional per-capita crime rates, 1886–90.

(which today all lie in either Poland, Lithuania, or Russia), specifically in the districts of Gumbinnen, Königsberg, Danzig, Marienwerder, Bromberg, Posen, Breslau, and Oppeln. Otherwise, only parts of Bavaria, such as Oberbayern, Niederbayern, and Pfalz, and the city-state of Bremen had exceedingly high crime rates. The lowest crime rates were to be found along Germany's western border with Denmark, Holland, Luxembourg, France, and Switzerland from Schleswig in the north all the way to Konstanz in the south, with only a few exceptions, mostly in central Germany. Moderate levels of criminality prevailed everywhere else, mostly in the German hinterland.

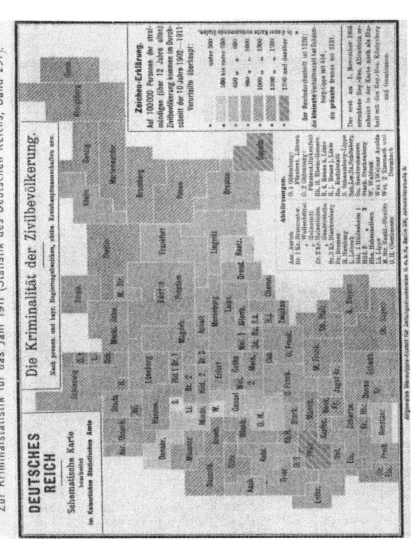

Map 4.2. Regional per-capita crime rates, 1902–1911.

Although these observations are based on the rather dubious classification of convictions per 100,000 legally liable population for all serious crimes and misdemeanors (*Verbrechen und Vergehen*), and adult male criminality accounted for the bulk of the figures (as the adult male rate was roughly five times the adult female rate and three times the juvenile rate), this same tripartite geographic division would seem to apply for women and juveniles and for less suspect individual offenses, such as assault and battery, and especially common theft.[3] Thus, the districts with extremely high or extremely low rates of adult male criminality also had extremely high or extemely low rates of adult female and juvenile criminality (notice in Table 4.1, for example, the extremely high rates for all three groups in the northeastern border districts of Gumbinnen, Bromberg, and Oppeln and the extremely low rates in the western districts of Münster and Minden). Furthermore, if a graph of individual offenses such as theft were presented here, the same kinds of geographic patterns would appear in even bolder relief. During the 1880s some individual *Kreise* in the Prussian northeast, like Labiau in Königsberg, Heydekrug in Gumbinnen, and Obornik in Posen, had theft rates that exceeded 900, and in many more neighboring districts they exceeded 800, ten to fifteen times the theft rates of many individual *Kreise* in western districts in Schleswig, Osnabrück, Minden, Münster, Düsseldorf, Cologne, Koblenz, Aachen, and Trier.[4]

These general patterns of criminality did not hold throughout the years of Imperial Germany, however, as one notices from Map 4.2 and from the figures in Table 4.1. Twenty years later, after the turn of the century, the Prussian northeast and much of Bavaria still had high crime rates, but several formerly low-crime areas along the western frontier, such as the *Regierungsbezirke* of Düsseldorf, Cologne, and Arnsberg, now registered very high rates of crime as well. Some scholars have pointed out that the western frontier was becoming something akin to the American "Wild West," as other western districts, such as Schleswig, Oldenburg, Hannover, Münster, and Trier, also recorded huge increases in their crime rates between the 1880s and the early 1900s.[5] True, the recorded crime rate for Germany as a

---

3   Eric A. Johnson and Vincent E. McHale, "Socioeconomic Aspects of the Delinquency Rate in Imperial Germany, 1882–1914," *Journal of Social History*, 13 (1980): 384–402. Kelley Reed, "Female Criminality in Imperial Germany," unpublished MS, Central Michigan University Senior Seminar Series, Mount Pleasant, Michigan, 1981.
4   In the five-year period between 1883 and 1887, Labiau's theft rate (based on convictions per year per 100,000 population of legally liable age) was 994, Heydekrug's was 922, and Obornik's was 941. In the same period, the Schleswig districts of Hufum and Tondern, for example, registered rates of 54 and 68.
5   See, for example, Evans, *Rethinking German History*, p. 176.

Urbanization and Crime

Table 4.1 A Comparison of Crime Rates in Two Periods, 1882–1891 and 1902–1911 (By Gender, in Large Administrative Districts)

District	1882–91			1902–11			% Change		
	T	M	W	T	M	W	T	M	W
Königsberg	1,538	2,616	618	1,466	2,662	485	-4.7	+0.2	-21.5
Gumbinnen	1,806	3,074	695	1,604	2,801	551	-11.2	-8.9	-20.7
Danzig	1,531	2,584	607	1,510	2,640	516	-1.4	+2.2	-15.0
Marienwerder	1,504	2,466	624	1,407	2,372	533	-6.4	-3.8	-14.6
Berlin	1,316	2,194	554	1,592	2,672	630	+21.0	+21.8	+13.7
Potsdam	1,011	1,695	362	1,235	2,163	393	+22.2	+27.6	+8.6
Frankfurt	922	1,570	345	986	1,767	282	+6.9	+12.5	-18.3
Stettin	1,061	1,798	384	1,352	2,340	448	+27.4	+30.1	+16.7
Köslin	944	1,615	338	889	1,583	251	-5.8	2.0	-25.7
Stralsund	666	1,171	222	1,015	1,808	307	+52.4	+54.4	+38.3
Posen	1,500	2,462	688	1,334	2,345	509	-11.1	-4.8	-26.0
Bromberg	1,886	3,016	872	1,607	2,665	657	-14.8	-11.6	-24.7
Breslau	1,264	2,174	500	1,295	2,342	419	+2.5	+7.7	-16.2
Liegnitz	804	1,395	303	904	1,640	269	+12.4	+17.6	-11.2
Oppeln	1,724	2,925	692	1,969	3,441	665	+14.2	+17.6	-3.9
Magdeburg	950	1,549	371	1,053	1,788	372	+10.8	+15.4	+0.3
Merseburg	934	1,494	401	962	1,608	362	+3.0	+7.6	-9.7
Erfurt	887	1,526	330	891	1,600	285	+0.5	+4.8	-13.6
Schleswig	680	1,164	215	1,002	1,672	343	+47.4	+43.6	+59.5
Hannover	958	1,662	302	1,289	2,199	433	+34.6	+32.3	+43.4
Hildesheim	857	1,445	291	845	1,476	251	-1.4	+1.4	-13.7
Lüneburg	732	1,251	218	1,029	1,757	286	+40.6	+40.4	+31.2
Stade	780	1,356	209	994	1,738	227	+27.4	+28.2	+8.6
Osnabrück	533	957	118	595	1,084	115	+11.6	+13.3	-2.5
Aurich	693	1,140	287	864	1,536	251	+24.7	+34.7	-12.5
Münster	497	897	98	1,111	1,917	262	+123.5	+113.7	+167.3
Minden	449	811	110	659	1,207	141	+46.8	+48.8	+27.3
Arnsberg	854	1,437	223	1,324	2,214	338	+55.0	+54.1	+51.6
Kassel	853	1,517	273	780	1,448	178	-8.6	-4.5	-34.8
Wiesbaden	874	1,523	280	1,097	1,972	290	+25.5	+29.5	+3.6
Koblenz	624	1,095	176	851	1,554	182	+36.4	+41.9	+3.4
Düsseldorf	793	1,374	219	1,413	2,399	399	+78.2	+74.6	+82.2
Köln	778	1,351	235	1,613	2,703	572	+107.3	+100.1	+143.4
Trier	606	1,018	205	1,286	2,132	424	+112.2	+109.4	+106.8
Aachen	628	1,076	192	856	1,503	237	+36.3	+39.7	+23.4
Sigmaringen	562	1,027	151	537	1,020	107	-4.4	-0.7	-29.1
Prussia	1,052	1,769	395	1,248	2,157	403	+18.6	+21.9	+2.0
Oberbayern	1,429	2,369	525	1,430	2,446	507	+0.1	+3.3	-3.4
Niederbayern	1,324	2,324	442	1,588	2,820	432	+19.2	+21.3	-2.3
Pfalz	1,526	2,713	440	1,787	3,233	431	+17.1	+19.2	-2.0
Oberpfalz	1,141	1,923	437	1,399	2,508	389	+22.6	+30.4	-11.0

Table 4.1 *(cont.)*

District	1882-91			1902-11			% Change		
	T	M	W	T	M	W	T	M	W
Oberfranken	1,054	1,823	355	1,219	2,184	335	+15.7	+19.8	-5.6
Mittelfranken	1,213	2,028	471	1,381	2,420	428	+13.8	+19.3	-9.1
Unterfranken	1,058	1,906	299	1,114	2,058	253	+5.3	+8.0	-15.4
Schwaben	1,038	1,797	356	1,240	2,210	335	+19.5	+23.0	-5.9
Bavaria	1,243	2,141	424	1,409	2,498	405	+13.4	+16.7	-4.5
Dresden	941	1,543	420	1,020	1,772	375	+8.4	+14.8	-10.7
Leipzig	1,015	1,634	438	1,084	1,837	387	+6.8	+12.4	-11.6
Chemnitz	—	—	—	838	1,462	272	—	—	—
Zwickau	988	1,676	353	1,029	1,810	342	-5.5	-2.4	-13.0
Bautzen	696	1,202	258	656	1,171	197	-5.7	-2.6	-23.6
Saxony	948	1,576	381	969	1,679	336	+2.2	+6.5	-11.8
Wurttemberg	876	1,548	281	1,178	2,141	301	+34.5	+38.3	+7.1
Baden	873	1,548	257	1,168	2,133	254	+33.8	+37.3	-1.2
Hessen	775	1,371	224	988	1,765	251	+27.5	+28.7	+12.1
Meckl-Schwerin	680	1,168	225	1,059	1,860	309	+55.7	+59.2	+37.3
Großhz.Sachsen	835	1,385	340	1,052	1,852	315	+26.0	+33.7	-7.4
Meckl-Strelitz	723	1,241	248	1,034	1,826	281	+43.0	+47.1	+13.3
Oldenburg	691	1,200	215	1,051	1,870	265	+52.1	+55.8	+23.3
Braunschweig	956	1,536	391	1,241	2,051	489	+29.8	+33.5	+25.1
Sachsen-Mein.	1,105	1,897	381	1,180	2,098	331	+6.8	+10.6	-13.1
Sachsen-Alt.	871	1,406	376	877	1,499	294	+0.7	+6.6	-21.8
Sach-Cob-Gotha	871	1,515	303	822	1,510	210	-5.6	-0.3	-30.7
Anhalt	1,050	1,683	453	1,213	2,018	451	+15.5	+20.0	-0.4
Schwz-Sondrz.	1,287	2,004	636	985	1,780	274	-23.5	-11.2	-56.9
Schwz-Rudofs.	1,473	2,477	561	1,187	2,120	340	-19.4	-14.4	-39.4
Waldeck	478	890	139	429	815	90	-10.3	-8.4	-35.3
Schaum-Lippe	411	706	129	414	772	80	+0.7	+9.3	-38.0
Lippe	538	895	207	630	1,180	143	+17.3	+31.8	-30.9
Lubeck	936	1,695	268	1,043	1,827	323	+11.4	+7.8	+20.5
Bremen	1,564	2,859	436	2,131	3,793	503	+36.3	+32.7	+15.4
Hamburg	1,270	2,165	438	1,501	2,585	456	+18.2	+19.4	+4.1
Alsace-Lorr.	758	1,337	242	966	1,702	259	+27.4	+27.3	+7.0
German Reich	1,029	1,746	375	1,220	2,128	378	+18.6	+21.9	+0.8

Note: The figures represent the total number of convictions per 100,000 legally liable population of the appropriate gender.

Sources: Unless otherwise indicated, all figures in this and the following tables in this chapter come from *Statistik des Deutschen Reichs* and *Preußische Statistik*. Most of the criminal justice data are from the former series, particularly in yearly volumes entitled *Kriminalstatistik.*

Table 4.2 *Crime and Population Figures for the 57 Largest German Cities (Listed Alphabetically)*

City	LLPop.85	LLPop.05	TCR 83-87	A&B 83-87	Theft 83-87	TCR 03-07	A&B 03-07	Theft 03-07
Aachen	68,097	108,349	901	96 *	232 *	1,215	165	260
Altona	86,468	124,495	1,257	87	345	1,585	141	294
Augsburg	49,286	70,912	1,360	172	400	1,595	287	405
Barmen	69,750	112,897	850	155	182	966	163	204
Berlin	977,802	1,609,527	1,213	78	329	1,522	131	335
Bielefeld	23,645	51,802	1,157 *	228	253 *	1,415	192	239
Bochum	25,647	72,370	1,460 *	254	333	1,603	305	385
Bonn	?	57,485	?	?	?	1,525	224	288
Braunschweig	88,896	132,824	1,010	103	309	1,489	126	302
Bremen	83,521	159,558	1,170	123	330	1,897	283	395
Breslau	220,744	350,079	2,138	195	520	1,857	197	340
Chemnitz	79,997	176,745	1,511	79	460	1,188	75	294
Colmar	57,873	66,997	626	109	164	1,131	208	161
Danzig	80,291	112,412	2,016	202	700	1,732	256	370
Darmstadt	58,879	91,167	854	153	214	905	124	173
Dessau	41,069	62,499	1,008	88	318	1,324	164	366
Dortmund	51,286	121,551	1,232 *	203	301	1,628	242	396
Dresden	182,339	379,493	1,039	36	332	1,251	56	208
Düsseldorf	78,796	181,579	989	185	255	1,838	235	462
Duisburg	30,656	106,385	1,335 *	215	389	1,543	251	375
Elberfeld	72,756	119,097	888	144	235	1,639	202	364
Erfurt	40,739	71,294	1,526 *	97 *	416	1,447	83	369
Essen	43,211	149,782	1,151 *	197	306	1,884	323	435
Frankfurt	?	257,666	?	?	?	1,432	143	301
Freiburg	52,489	78,631	1,366	181	394	1,274	286	288
Gelsenkirchen	?	89,760	?	?	?	1,595	352	326
Giesen	50,286	63,887	787	121	171	757	166	119
Görlitz	41,007	63,399	1,339	96	360	1,543	133	326
Hagen	?	53,086	?	?	?	1,667	303	349
Halle	41,339	50,028	1,637	170	411	1,272	114	300
Hamburg	227,414	608,267	1,658	133	490	1,468	66	326
Hannover	99,265	187,853	1,270	124	326	1,964	174	381
Karlsruhe	64,283	108,864	985	148	300	1,437	277	257
Kassel	45,069	91,632	1,204 *	100 *	362	1,591	183	325
Kiel	34,051	102,066	1,701 *	101 *	525	2,079	160	442
Köln	113,859	311,332	931	112	244	2,446	322	384
Königsberg	109,693	156,445	2,066	150	529	2,017	262	402
Krefeld	62,128	85,004	850	149 *	170 *	998	102	196
Leipzig	128,084	382,529	1,373	52	455	1,335	83	292
Lübeck	39,559	66,546	959	84 *	276	984	72	266
Magdeburg	110,689	176,127	1,461	149	359	1,400	123	313

Table 4.2 (cont.)

City	LLPop.85	LLPop.05	TCR 83-87	A&B 83-87	Theft 83-87	TCR 03-07	A&B 03-07	Theft 03-07
Mainz	73,167	104,928	1,054	**183**	303	1,740	**347**	**321**
Mannheim	61,772	138,048	1,332	**215**	**439**	2,209	**576**	**402**
München	200,493	410,012	1,430	**210**	**397**	1,300	189	**302**
Münster	30,624	57,882	**1,069**	131 *	252 *	**1,163**	132	**261**
Mülhausen	103,465	130,880	1,152	**255**	**290**	**1,180**	**275**	201
Nürnberg	84,264	213,752	1,445	**191**	**422**	1,651	**361**	**344**
Posen	47,211	94,788	2,252 *	**293**	**645**	2,241	**370**	**497**
Rostock	46,926	66,809	**721**	83	217	**1,256**	154	**275**
Schwerin	46,056	54,519	**673**	72	195	**839**	103	191
Stettin	71,983	162,958	1,501 *	**161**	**342**	2,258	**278**	**381**
Strassburg	75,282	117,444	**1,000**	**185**	**296**	1,272	187	**254**
Stuttgart	92,842	178,163	1,005	73	**339**	1,307	132	**284**
Weimar	61,840	77,789	**949**	68	**323**	**1,135**	150	**300**
Wiesbaden	41,299	78,373	1,506 *	122 *	**371**	1,410	158	**314**
Worms	45,693	61,174	**930**	**190**	223	1,372	**360**	208
Würzburg	40,386	58,761	1,191 *	**165**	**317**	1,231	199	**286**
Averages	93,567	167,734	1,219	147	339	1,492	215	311
Averages for all Kreise in Reich			1,001	153	282	1,195	228	239

Note: Figures are in boldface if they exceed the national average for all Kreise in assault and battery and theft offenses, or if they are less than the average in the total crime category.

Key: * = Figures for 1883-97 substituted for unavailable 1883-7 period.
LLPop.85 = Legally liable population (age twelve and over) for 1885.
LLPop.05 = Legally liable population (age twelve and over) for the period 1905.
TCR = Total crime rate (convictions per 100,000 legally liable population).
A&B = Assault and battery rate (convictions for serious bodily harm per 100,000 legally liable population).
Theft = Theft rate (convictions for simple and grand theft per 100,000 legally liable population).

whole had grown by nearly 20 percent from the 1880s to the 1900s, but, as was discussed in the last chapter, this apparent increase in crime was more fabricated than genuine; it was due primarily to vigorous prosecution in the 1890s of certain political offenses that obviously were not common among some large components of the general population, such as women, whose overall crime rate held rather steady (see Chapter 5). This caveat notwithstanding, the westward expansion of crime was anything but illusory.

Numerous cities, towns, and villages of the Rhine, the Ruhr, and other western regions recorded huge increases in common offenses like theft, assault and battery, and murder, which had no obvious political roots. In the same period, many northeastern communities actually had declining crime rates. In Table 4.2, one finds an alphabetical listing of the fifty-seven largest

German cities (all with a legally liable population of over 50,000 by 1905) and information that helps one compare changes in their population with changes in their rates of crime from a five-year period in the 1880s to a five-year period in the early 1900s. The Rhineland cities of Cologne and Düsseldorf, for example, which in the 1880s had very low crime rates, recorded such huge increases in their overall crime totals and in individual offenses like assault and battery and theft that they ranked among the most crime-infested cities of Germany after the turn of the century. In the Prussian northeast, on the other hand, many cities like Königsberg, Breslau, and Posen actually recorded modest decreases in most types of crime over these years. These urban examples are not extraordinary. Many rural as well as urban districts in the west experienced dramatic increases in crime rates, while many rural as well as urban northeastern districts witnessed drops in their crime rates.[6]

Hence, by the turn of the century, there was no longer a clear geographic pattern in the distribution of crime rates across the map of Germany. This was true for both women and men and for most types of criminal offenses, though more so for property offenses and less so for crimes of violence, which, with some exceptions, remained most highly concentrated in northeastern Prussia and in Bavaria. This breakdown of the old regional distribution of criminality should lead one immediately to question the hypothesis that crime is primarily a learned behavior with fixed geocultural roots. This is not meant to dispute that some criminal activities, especially crimes of violence like assault, rape, and murder, do seem to have cultural components in Germany and in other societies.[7] However, it is meant to suggest there must have been other factors at work that would explain the considerable changes that took place in the regional bases of criminality. Developing a theory that accounts for the changes is no simple task. Several possibilities come quickly to mind, however, most of which hinge on theories stressing the importance of the processes of migration, population growth, and ur-

---

6 The average yearly crime rate grew between the periods of 1883–7 and 1903–7 in Düsseldorf *Stadtkreis* from 989 to 1,838 and in Cologne *Stadtkreis* from 931 to 2,446. At the same time, it grew in Düsseldorf *Landkreis* from 732 to 1,504, and in Cologne *Landkreis* from 851 to 1,534. In the same period, it declined in the almost completely rural districts of Labiau in Königsberg from 2,512 to 2,132, in Oletzko in Gumbinnen from 2,115 to 1,311, and Obornik in Posen from 2,131 to 1,527.
7 In a previous study, I found that there was a strong correlation between the violent crime rates of Prussian *Regierungsbezirke* in the 1880s and the 1900s (r = greater than .6), but not between property crime rates and other types of crime rates, like crimes against the state. Other scholars like Howard Zehr have noted this as well, though I think that Zehr's statement that "the biggest single cause of variance in assault rates" was regional tradition was perhaps overstating the case. See Zehr, *Crime and the Development of Modern Society: Patterns of Criminality in Nineteenth-Century Germany and France* (London, 1976), pp. 105 ff.

banization that were popular in Germany at the time and that remain popular in many countries today.[8]

All students of modern German history are aware that the last decades of the nineteenth century were characterized by sharp rises in population and urban growth, especially in the industrializing communities in the Rhine–Ruhr region. Given the huge *Landflucht* (flight) of eastern rural migrants into many of the western boom towns during the 1880s, 1890s, and early 1900s, would not the classical *Gemeinschaft* (community) to *Gesellschaft* (society) and anomie theories of Tönnies and Durkheim serve well enough to explain the perceived changes in the geographic loci of criminal behavior?[9] Could we not expect the uprooted immigrants who swelled the western cities and towns to have experienced alienation and anomie in their strange and new surroundings?

Pregnant with possibility as such theories might appear, in reality they are extremely questionable. Recent studies of the social impact of nineteenth- and twentieth-century German migrations by American scholars like Steve Hochstadt, James Jackson, and Walter Kampfhoefner, and by German scholars like Klaus Bade have found neither the migrants' experiences nor the process of migration itself to have been especially unsettling.[10] Furthermore, alienation, anomie, urbanization, and population growth arguments do not apply when one considers that cities like Munich, Hamburg, and Leipzig had declining crime rates even though they too had huge migrant populations and tremendous population growth. Part of the explanation for the changing regional bases of criminality may still have something to do

---

8   For discussions of these theories in German society, see Andrew Lees, "Critics of Urban Society in Germany, 1854–1914," *Journal of the History of Ideas*, 40 (1979): 61–83; and Lees, "Debates about the Big City in Germany, 1890–1914," *Societas* 5 (1975): 31–47. For a general discussion of these theories as they apply to criminological research, see Mannheim, *Comparative Criminology*, pp. 533–51.

9   For a discussion of the *Landflucht*, especially how it applied to the Poles of northeastern Prussia who moved into the Ruhr, see Christoph Klessmann, *Polnische Bergarbeiter im Ruhrgebiet 1870–1945: Soziale Integration und nationale Subkultur einer Minderheit in der deutschen Industriegesellschaft* (Göttingen, 1978). For a discussion more centered on economic conditions, see Frank B. Tipton, *Regional Variations in the Economic Development of Germany During the Nineteenth Century* (Middletown, Conn., 1976).

10 Walter D. Kamphoefner, "The Social Consequences of Rural–Urban Migration in Imperial Germany: The 'Floating Proletariat' Thesis Reconsidered" (Social Science Working Paper, California Institute of Technology, 1982); James H. Jackson, "Migration in Duisburg, 1867–1890: Occupational and Familial Contexts," *Journal of Urban History*, 8 (1982): 235–70; Klaus J. Bade, ed., *Auswanderer-Wanderarbeiter-Gastarbeiter: Bevölkerung, Arbeitsmarkt, und Wanderung in Deutschland seit der Mitte des 19. Jahrhunderts* (Ostfildern, 1984); Steve L. Hochstadt, "Migration in Germany: An Historical Study" (Ph.D. diss., Brown University, 1983); Hochstadt, "Migration and Industrialization in Germany," *Social Science History* 5 (1981): 445–68; David F. Crew, *Town in the Ruhr: A Social History of Bochum 1860–1914* (New York, 1979). For an excellent review of recent migration research, see James H. Jackson and Leslie Page Moch, "Migration and the Social History of Modern Europe," *Historical Methods* 22 (1989): 27–36.

with migration. I will labor to prove, however, that migration per se was of little or no importance. What was of importance was who exactly the migrants were and whether they were received as unwanted *Ausländer* (foreigners) and met with discrimination and hardship, as was the experience of many eastern Poles and Lithuanians, or whether they were more readily accepted, as was more often the case for western Europeans such as the Danes, Dutch, Belgians, and French.[11] But before discussing the significance of hardship and ethnic discrimination in more detail, it is first necessary to sort out and lay to rest for good the tired hypotheses that urbanization, population growth, and cities themselves cause crime.

URBAN-RURAL DIFFERENCES AND URBANIZATION

The notion that urban growth and big cities engender crime is a long-standing and well-articulated myth. This myth has also been widely shared, and Germans have done their part to perpetuate it. Based largely on belief, the myth has been very hard to shake, all the more so because it has often been propagated by the most respected guardians of the people's trust, from pious pastors to prominent politicians. By pointing the finger of blame at the city for generating crime and other social ills, theologians like Christian Rugge in the Kaiserreich, and political leaders like Adolf Hitler some years later, hoped to mobilize support for their own ideological aims and mobilize opposition against their enemies.[12] As the home of Jews, workers, socialists, and democrats, the city has been a logical target for conservative ideologues.

The city has also been a convenient and logical target for presumably less biased trustees of the truth. In Germany, perhaps the first "coherent [anti-urban] intellectual position" was worked out by Wilhelm Heinrich Riehl, a Bavarian journalist and university professor who wrote a four-volume treatise published between 1854 and 1869 depicting cities as symbols and sources of the worst aspects of the modern world: ruthlessness, declining

---

11 Kamphoefner found that Berlin immigrants from the east did much worse than immigrants from the west in Imperial Germany. Kamphoefner, "The Social Consequences of Rural-Urban Migration." Discrimination against the eastern immigrants is discussed at length in Klessmann, *Polnische Bergarbeiter,* esp. pp. 83–93; and in Richard Charles Murphy, *Guestworkers in the German Reich: A Polish Community in Wilhelmian Germany* (Boulder, Colo., 1983).

12 Rugge, a Protestant clergyman, argued that sharply increased rates of crime and vice resulted from the loss of communal controls and the emergence of self-centered personalities in cities: "It [the big city] becomes the dwelling place for masses of criminals. . . . An army of prostitutes and pimps eats away at its foundations." C. Rugge, "Die Bedeutung der Grossstädte für das Volksleben," *Die Reformation: Deutsche evang. Kirchenzeitung für die Gemeinde* 8 (1909): 389–90 (cited in Lees, "Critics of Urban Society," p. 70).

national identity, cosmopolitanism, godlessness, social disorder, and crime.[13] Of course, his arguments would find resounding echoes among other conservative-in-the-extreme thinkers and publicists, some of whom, like Walter Classen in the Kaiserreich, and Nazi theorists in Weimar and the Third Reich, even had racist biases against the metropolis.[14] But the anti-urban critique became all the more powerful when it was taken up by leading reform-minded thinkers of a less ideological bent, like the economist Karl Bücher, the intellectual historian Julius Langbehn, and the demographer Adolf Weber. As the American historian Andrew Lees, who has studied these anti-urban critics in German history perhaps more than anyone else, wrote: "It is clear . . . that by the early twentieth century criticism of cities was rampant in Germany. . . . Much of this criticism was hostile in the extreme. Conservative clergymen, social theorists, demographers, and publicists painted a dark picture of the urban scene."[15]

But, for our purposes, the Germans who have perhaps contributed most significantly to the long-standing myth that cities promote crime and disorder are among the founding fathers of modern sociology and criminology: especially Ferdinand Tönnies and Gustav Aschaffenburg. Their works stand alongside those of their French contemporary Emile Durkheim as classical bulwarks protecting the anti-urban mythos. Only very recently has their dogma been seriously challenged, largely by empirical-minded sociologists and historians finally armed with methodogical weaponry powerful enough to penetrate the fortresslike theories that they and their countless descendants have erected.[16]

Despite the mounting attacks of modern empiricists, the canon still sounds good. Cities cause crime because they are centers of prostitution and vice, which eat away at their foundations. People in cities do not know their neighbors and do not go to church, so the social and moral control supposedly characteristic of small-town and village life breaks down. It is easier to steal from or get into a fight with people one does not know. The population pressure makes one irritable and violent. The grime and pollution make one less respectful of public property. There is more to steal, more people to assault, and less risk of being caught. Cities are centers of bars,

13 Lees, "Critics of Urban Society," p. 62. Wilhelm Heinrich Riehl, *Die Naturgeschichte des Volkes als Grundlage einer deutschen Social-Politik*, 4 vols. (Stuttgart, 1854–69); vol. 1, "Land und Leute," contains his most extensive criticisms.
14 Walther Classen, *Das stadtgeborene Geschlecht und seine Zukunft* (Leipzig, 1914).
15 Lees, "Critics of Urban Society," p. 82. Karl Bücher, *Die wirtschaftliche Aufgaben der modernen Stadtgemeinde* (Leipzig, 1898); Julius Langbehn, *Rembrandt als Erzieher* (Leipzig, 1890); Adolf Weber, *Die Grosstadt, und ihrer sozialen Probleme* (Leipzig, 1908).
16 See, for example, Charles Tilly, *As Sociology Meets History* (New York, 1981), esp. his chapter on "Useless Durkheim."

gambling, and nightlife, which attract thieves, rapists, and murderers. They are purveyors of alcohol and drugs. Criminal-prone youths and gangs control the streets, and otherwise honest adolescents are pressed into lives of crime. Inhabitants of cities suffer from anomie and alienation and turn to crime to alleviate their anxieties. The mental life of the metropolis is disturbed. As behavior, crime is more acceptable. The possible arguments are endless.[17] Despite the common sense these arguments appear to make, cities, and for that matter all forms of settlement, are what society makes of them. Of course they can be filthy and stinking, swollen with the homeless and the jobless, the politically disenfranchised and the racially discriminated against, and, if so, they would logically be breeding grounds for criminality and other antisocial behavior. But they do not have to be, and they have not always been.

The data in Table 4.2 in fact show that German cities in the late nineteenth and early twentieth centuries were not particularly crime-ridden despite the fact that, according to classical sociological logic and the strength of the anti-urban political and moral forces lodged against them and their inhabitants at the time, they should have been. If the cities of Imperial Germany, which underwent growth at least equal to that of any other sizable European or North American land (see Table 4.2), can be shown to have been relatively safe and lawful, then no general theory accusing urban growth and urban environments of being crime-inducing is tenable.[18]

But perhaps German cities were exceptional, as indeed some American visitors, like the publicist Ray Stannard Baker and the police expert Raymond Fosdick, thought them to be. We recall how at the turn of the century Baker found German cities to be uncomfortably overregulated but, possibly as a result, "safer for strangers, perhaps, than any other in the world." And Fosdick, in 1909, while making a comparative study of crime and police practices in various European countries, was told by the Dresden police commissioner that there was not much crime in his city because "we have no real poverty here." On the other hand, the head constable of Liverpool,

---

17 For a further discussion, see Hans H. Burchardt, *Kriminalität in Stadt und Land* (Berlin, 1935); Denis Szabo, *Crimes et villes* (Paris, 1960); Johnson and McHale, "Socioeconomic Aspects of the Delinquency Rate," pp. 384–5; and Mannheim, *Comparative Criminology*, pp. 532–62.
18 In 1871, Germany had eight cities with over 100,000 inhabitants, fourteen in 1880, twenty-six in 1890, thirty-three in 1900, and forty-one in 1905. Gerd Hohorst, Jürgen Kocka, and Gerhard A. Ritter, *Sozialgeschichtliches Arbeitsbuch: Materialien zur Statistik des Kaiserreichs 1870–1914* (Munich, 1978). See also Adna Weber, *The Growth of Cities in the Nineteenth Century* (Ithaca, N.Y., 1899); Andrew Lees and Lynn Lees, eds., *The Urbanization of European Society in the Nineteenth Century* (Boston, 1976); N. L. Tranter, *Population and Society 1750–1940* (London, 1985); and H. J. Teuteberg, ed., *Urbanisierung im 19. und 20. Jahrhundert: Historische und Geographische Aspekte* (Cologne, 1983).

England, a city of about the same size, told Fosdick that "by far the greater part of the crime of Liverpool is due to poverty."[19] Certainly these American observers were not alone in noting the order, cleanliness, and relative lack of poverty that prevailed in German cities. For example, in the 1870s, a British visitor, Henry Vizetelly, though complaining about nearly everything under the German sun, as perhaps only a Briton can, from "dully paved roads" to the terrible odor he thought he smelled, was struck by the comparative lack of poverty in Berlin, which "with all its misery has nothing comparing to our London Rookeries."[20]

Although these observations are less than scientific, they can be supported by computer-analyzed data showing that measures of relative wealth like taxation, school spending, and literacy correlated positively, and measures of hardship and poverty such as infant and adult mortality correlated negatively, with the size of urban population in administrative districts in Imperial Germany.[21] This does not mean, of course, that many German cities were never centers of poverty and criminality, as indeed many were. It does demonstrate, however, that German cities were certainly not generally to be assumed to be sites of dirt and despair when compared with cities in other countries or with other types of communities in Germany at the time.[22]

Germans might have been particularly adept at handling the huge population and urban growth they experienced in the late nineteenth and early twentieth centuries, and perhaps largely for this reason there was no great surge in criminality in Germany over these years, as we know from the discussion in the previous chapter. But in recent studies of other countries like France, Great Britain, Sweden, and the United States there is much evidence that the second half of the nineteenth century, despite the growth of cities that prevailed everywhere, did not witness a general growth of

---

19 Both Baker and Fosdick begin their accounts with comments on the cleanliness and orderliness of German cities. Ray Stannard Baker, *Seen in Germany* (New York, 1901), p. 8; Raymond B. Fosdick, *European Police Systems* (New York, 1915), p. 5. See also William Harbutt Dawson, *German Life in Town and Country* (New York, 1901), pp. 273ff.
20 Henry Vizetelly, *Berlin: Under the New Empire* (New York, 1968: orig. London, 1879), 2:25.
21 Regression analysis, path analysis, and factor analysis are used to demonstrate this in Vincent E. McHale and Eric A. Johnson, "Urbanization, Industrialization, and Crime in Imperial Germany: Part I," *Social Science History* 1 (1976): 45–78. For a good general discussion of studies of health, hardship, and social inequality in nineteenth-century Germany, see Hartmut Kaelble, *Industrialization and Social Inequality in 19th-Century Europe* (Leamington Spa, 1983); and Richard J. Evans, *Death in Hamburg: Society and Politics in Hamburg During the Cholera Years 1830–1910* (Oxford, 1987).
22 For graphic portraits, often based on literary evidence, of urban conditions and criminality in Britain and France, see J. J. Tobias, *Urban Crime in Victorian England* (New York, 1972); Louis Chevalier, *Laboring Classes and Dangerous Classes in Paris During the First Half of the Nineteenth Century* (Princeton, N.J., 1981); and Gordon Wright, *Between the Guillotine and Liberty* (New York, 1983).

crime, however it is measured. In fact, the opposite was often the case. Crime rates appear to have actually declined in many societies.[23]

Nevertheless, it is generally rather dubious to speak of "the crime rate" as declining or growing or staying the same. The concept of the crime rate is in reality a kind of grab bag, sewn together from such myriad individual offenses, which go in and out of fashion with the whims of citizens and justice officials as rapidly as clothing styles, that it has almost no meaning except as a broad measure of the statistically reported operations of police and justice official machinery. Remembering the findings reported in the last chapter, the perceived growth in the "total" crime rate in the last decades of the nineteenth century in Germany was primarily a function of the authorities' efforts to curb the power and growth of the workers' movement. When this was controlled for, there was in fact no general increase whatsoever. Prudent scholars now recognize that if one wants to do anything more than merely discuss the ebb and flow of reported criminal activity in a particular society at a particular time, and especially if one wants to develop a theory about the causes of crime that has even a modicum of cross-cultural and cross-temporal validity, one must disaggregate the crime rate into its individual components and focus only on those acts, like theft, murder, and assault and battery, that all societies agree are criminal offenses.

Even though several scholars in several societies are now doing this, no one has been able successfully to weave together the individual threads of the finest scholarly craftsmanship into a generally accepted theoretical fabric. So politicians and ideologues and classroom teachers have been free to fabricate policy and consciousness out of the old yarn that cities cause crime.

From all the studies of which I am aware, and from the data that I have to present here, there is just one small strand of evidence that could support this

---

[23] Great Britain is a classic example. Tobias, using literary sources and fulminating against statistical evidence, nevertheless argued this to be true in his *Urban Crime in Victorian England*. For a defense of the statistical approach, see V. A. C. Gatrell and T. B. Hadden, "Criminal Statistics and Their Interpretation," in E. A. Wrigley, ed., *Nineteenth Century Society* (London, 1972), 336–96; and Gatrell, "The Decline of Theft and Violence in Victorian and Edwardian England," in V. A. C. Gatrell, B. Lehman, and G. Parker, eds., *Crime and Law since 1850* (London, 1980), pp. 238–38. Crime rates also appeared to decline in Sweden, Finland, and the United States. For Sweden, see Ted Robert Gurr, Peter N. Grabosky, and Richard C. Hula, *The Politics of Crime and Conflict: A Comparative History of Four Cities* (London, 1977); Jan Sundin, "Theft and Penury in Sweden 1830–1920: A Comparative Study at the County Level," *Scandinavian Journal of History*, 1 (1976): 265–92; Björn Horgby, *Den Disciplinerade Arbetaren: Brottslighet och social förändring i Norrköping 1850–1910* (Stockholm, 1986); and Hanns v. Hofer, *Brott och straff i Sverige: Historisk kriminalstatistik 1750–1984* (Örebro, 1985). For Finland, see Heikki Ylikangas, *Knivjunkarna: Valdskriminaliteten i Sydösterbotten 1790–1825* (Borga, 1985); and also his "Valdsbrottslighetens utveckling i Finland," *Tidskrift utgiven av Juridiska Föreningen i Finland* (1974). For the United States, see Roger Lane, *Violent Death in the City: Suicide, Accident and Murder in Nineteenth-Century Philadelphia* (Cambridge, Mass., 1979); and Eric H. Monkkonen, *Hands Up: Police in Urban America, 1860–1920* (New York, 1980).

concept. And the strand is a weak one. It relies primarily on what Lodhi and Tilly, Stinchcombe, and others have called a "structural theory," whereby certain types of crime are apt to be most prominent in certain types of social environment. According to this theory, property crimes like theft can be expected to have a higher frequency in urban than in rural settings because of the greater abundance of goods to steal and the more materialistic ethos of the city population, which means more people desire to accumulate goods, by stealing if they have to.[24] This theory does seem to make some sense, and it makes even more sense when we consider that cities usually have higher concentrations of young adult males (who, as will be demonstrated in Chapter 5, are particularly prone to property offenses) than rural settings, whose demographic makeup usually comprises a larger proportion of older people.

Even admitting all this, the structural theory is rendered rather limp and questionable when one considers that it is also possible for the more materialistic urban ethos to lead to statistically overcounted property crime rates, as, conceivably, urban inhabitants are more concerned with reporting property offenses and urging the criminal justice authorities to prosecute property offenders with more alacrity. (Remember, for example, how Dirk Blasius and others showed that theft offenses skyrocketed in the early 1800s owing to the new practice of vigorously prosecuting people for stealing wood from the forest of the now more materialistically minded German property owners.) Indeed, as conceded openly by its own authors, a limited and not thoroughly successful attempt to test this proposition was carried out a few years ago by Charles Tilly et al., who studied police activity in several societies in Europe and North America in the nineteenth century (though Germany was not one of them). Their findings led them to argue that with the growth of professional police forces, which occurred everywhere, "the intensification of policing undoubtedly tended to raise the proportion of all violations of the law which came to the attention of crime control specialists and thereby became visible," and that "at least part of the widespread increase" in reported crime in the first half of the nineteenth century in many societies "results from a rise in crime's visibility."[25] Since they found that the growth of police forces was generally faster in urban than

---

24 Arthur L. Stinchcombe, "Institutions of Privacy in the Determination of Police Administrative Practices," *American Journal of Sociology* 69 (1963): 150–60; Abdul Qaiyum Lodhi and Charles Tilly, "Urbanization, Crime and Collective Violence in Nineteenth-Century France," *American Journal of Sociology* 79 (1973): 196–218.
25 Charles Tilly, Allan Levett, A. Q. Lodhi, and Frank Munger, "How Policing Affected the Visibility of Crime in Nineteenth-Century Europe and America" (unpublished MS, University of Michigan Center for Social Research, 1982). On the growth of German and other European police systems, see Fosdick, *European Police Systems*, and the discussion in Chapter 1 on the police.

in rural communities, and since they expect that there were greater incentives both to steal and to report stealing in the city than in the village, the crime rates, particularly property crime rates, can be expected to have been overestimated in cities and underestimated in rural areas.

Some final problems I have with the structural theory are that it says nothing at all about the size, growth rate, or ethnic and economic makeup of the urban population. Furthermore, it tells us nothing about violent acts, which are what politicians and ideologues are most likely to condemn cities for and which most normal citizens probably fear the most (only extremely property-minded people can be expected to fear the loss of a pocketbook as much as they fear the loss of an eye, the breaking of a limb, or the loss of life).

The data presented below show that urban and population growth and urban settings themselves have very little to do with explaining crime patterns in Imperial Germany. What is of importance in explaining why some communities had more crime than others at particular times is not whether they were large, small, growing quickly, or even depopulating, but what the living conditions of their inhabitants were and often who these inhabitants were. What too many people have long overlooked is that hardship and discrimination, which, along with pure irrationality, should be accepted as being the real causes of criminality, are not confined within city walls. Just as cities can be infested dumping grounds for the wretched and the oppressed, so they can also be centers of hope and opportunity. The "smiling countryside," as Holmes called it, can easily be the domicile of downtrodden citizens frowning at the violence and criminality that their misery engenders.[26]

There are many ways in which this point can be illustrated. To begin with, we might take the example of Berlin, which was by far the largest German city, and whose population growth rate was one of the highest of all German cities (see Table 4.2). In Table 4.3 we find that, in comparison with other German cities, Berlin also had some of the lowest crime rates. Of the

26 In a recent essay on rural society in Imperial Germany, Cathleen S. Catt argues that, in Germany "the study of rural society has been largely neglected." This neglect, however, has been partially rectified by her essay, "Farmers and Factory Workers: Rural Society in Imperial Germany: The Example of Maudach," and by other essays in Richard J. Evans and W. R. Lee, eds., *The German Peasantry: Conflict and Community in Rural Society from the Eighteenth to the Twentieth Centuries* (New York, 1986). Crime and misery in the German countryside have received some treatment of late, however, especially in the works of Dirk Blasius, which deal primarily with the first half of the nineteenth century. See his *Bürgerliche Gesellschaft und Kriminalität: Zur Sozialgeschichte Preussens im Vormärz* (Göttingen, 1975), and *Kriminalität und Alltag: Zur Konfliktgeschichte des Alltagslebens im 19. Jahrundert* (Göttingen, 1978). See also Carsthen Küther, *Räuber und Gauner in Deutschland: Das organisierte Bandenwesen im 18. und frühen 19. Jahrhundert* (Göttingen, 1976); H. Reif, ed., *Räuber, Volk und Obrigkeit: Studien zur Geschichte der Kriminalität in Deutschland seit dem 18. Jahrhundert* (Frankfurt, 1984); and Richard J. Evans, ed., *The German Underworld*.

Table 4.3 *Crime, Population Density, Mortality, and Ethnicity in the 25 Largest Prussian Cities (Highest to Lowest Crime Rate)*

City	TCR0307	TCR8387	Pop.1906	Pop.Den	Death Rate 06	% Ethnic Pop. 00	Type
Köln	2,446	931	429,343	3,868	19	1.0	mixed
Stettin	2,258	1,501 *	224,423	3,350	22	1.0	Polish
Posen	2,241	2,252 *	137,006	4,152	23	56.0	Polish
Kiel	2,079	1,701 *	164,009	7,130	16	2.2	mixed
Königsberg	2,017	2,966	223,928	11,196	20	0.6	Lithuanian
Hannover	1,964	1,270	250,201	6,255	16	1.0	mixed
Essen	1,884	1,151	231,991	23,199	17	3.4	Polish
Breslau	1,857	2,138	471,921	13,096	22	1.6	Polish
Düsseldorf	1,838	989	253,700	5,178	17	1.8	mixed
Danzig	1,732	2,016	159,838	7,992	21	2.6	Polish
Elberfeld	1,639	888	163,052	5,260	14	0.9	mixed
Dortmund	1,628	1,232 *	175,897	6,282	21	3.7	Polish
Bochum	1,603	1,460	118,696	19,783	21	4.0	Polish
Gelsenkirchen	1,595	?	147,459	12,214	20	8.1	Polish
Kassel	1,591	1,204 *	120,583	5,481	14	0.5	mixed
Altona	1,585	1,257	168,445	7,657	16	1.4	mixed
Duisburg	1,543	1,335 *	192,754	5,210	19	6.3	Dutch
Berlin	1,522	1,213	2,041,590	32,406	16	1.6	Polish
Frankfurt	1,432	?	335,348	3,567	15	1.1	mixed
Wiesbaden	1,410	1,506 *	101,038	2,807	16	2.2	mixed
Magdeburg	1,400	1,461	240,845	4,379	17	0.5	mixed
Halle	1,272	1,637	170,167	4,254	21	0.6	mixed
Aachen	1,215	901 *	144,232	3,698	19	2.2	Dutch
Krefeld	998	850 *	110,463	5,260	14	1.0	Dutch
Barmen	966	850	156,289	7,104	13	0.4	mixed

Key: * = The crime rate for 1883-97 is substituted for 1883-7 as 1883-7 is missing.
TCR0307 = Total Crime Rate for 1903-7.
TCR8387 = Total Crime Rate for 1883-7.
Pop.Den. = Population Density.
Death Rate 06 = Deaths per 1,000 inhabitants in 1906.
Type = Dominant non-German-speaking, ethnic minority. "Mixed" means that no dominant ethnic minority prevailed.
Pop. 00 = Population in 1900.

twenty-five largest cities of Prussia, all with over 100,000 inhabitants in 1906, Berlin ranked eighteenth in the overall crime rate in the five-year period between 1903 and 1907, even though its population was over ten times that of ten of the cities that had a higher overall crime rate, and roughly five times that of its nearest rival in size, Cologne, which had the highest overall crime rate among major Prussian cities in this period.

These omnibus crime figures could, of course, be misleading; they might camouflage some much higher rates of individual offenses that would be more trustworthy than the overall crime rate. But they are not. In Table 4.4 one notes that in various five-year and longer periods from 1883 until 1912, Berlin had rates of assault and battery far lower than the average for all communities in Germany, whether they were rural *Landkreise* or urban *Stadtkreise*. This was also true in homicide offenses, both according to coroners' and court records (see Table 3.4). Furthermore, between 1883 and 1897, Berlin had a slightly lower rate of theft than was the average for all German cities and a modestly higher rate of theft than was the average for German *Landkreise*. Only after the turn of the century did Berlin's overall and theft crime rates exceed the average both for other city districts and for rural districts, and it was at this time that Berlin's crime rate ranked eighteenth of the largest twenty-five Prussian cities.

Many other figures can be brought forward to show that Berlin was not an exceptional case. The figures in Table 4.4 show that throughout the years of Imperial Germany violent criminality like assault and battery was more characteristic of the village and the countryside than of the city, but that property offenses like theft were somewhat more prevalent in cities than in rural communities throughout the 1880s and the 1890s, and were considerably more prevalent in cities after the turn of the century. But the growth of the overall population and the urban population in these years certainly did not bring about more property offenses, as the rate of theft declined in both city and rural districts after the turn of the century, though the decline was much more noticeable in the countryside. Why this was the case is open to speculation, but one suspects that it had to do with relative prosperity and hardship. The decline of theft rates in the rural communities probably reflected their improved conditions, as agricultural wages certainly improved around the turn of the century with the end of the "Long Depression" and the draining off of excess rural populations by the great *Landflucht* of the 1880s and 1890s. Furthermore, the theft rates of the urban population may have been retarded in the 1880s and 1890s as their wages steadily improved vis-à-vis declining agricultural prices.[27]

Whereas these figures lend some support to the structural theory, despite its weaknesses noted above, they strengthen the argument that neither popu-

---

27 On conditions in the northeast leading to the *Landflucht*, see Klessmann, *Polnische Bergarbeiter*, pp. 23–43; and William W. Hagen, *Germans, Poles, and Jews: The Nationality Conflict in the Prussian East, 1772–1914* (Chicago, 1980). And for an American contemporary's account, see Dawson, *German Life in Town and Country*, esp. pp. 68–92, and Dawson, *The Evolution of Modern Germany* (New York, n.d.). On the improvement in urban conditions and wages, see W. Masur, *Imperial Berlin* (New York, 1970), pp. 243ff.; Gerhard Bry, *Wages in Germany, 1871–1945* (Princeton, N.J., 1960); and Ashok V. Desai, *Real Wages in Germany* (Oxford, 1968). For the relationship among wages, prices, and crime, see Edward Renger, *Kriminalität, Preis und Lohn. Eine Kriminalstatistische Untersuchung für Sachsen von 1882 bis 1929* (Leipzig, 1933).

Table 4.4 *Average Yearly Rates of Crime in Selected Periods*

Period	Total Crime Rate			
	Entire Reich	Berlin	All[c] Stadtkreise	All[d] Landkreise
1883–7	1,001	1,216	—	—
1888–92	1,044	1,259	—	—
1893–7	1,177	1,682	—	—
1898–1902	—	—	—	—
1903–7	1,195	1,522	—	—
1908–12	1,184	1,682	—	—
1883–1897	1,075	1,346	1,428	951
1903–1912	1,190	1,602	1,461	1,015

	Assault and Battery[a]			
Period	ER	B	S	L
1883–7	153	94	—	—
1888–92	173	106	—	—
1893–7	219	137	—	—
1898–1902	—	—	—	—
1903–7	228	131	—	—
1908–12	204	122	—	—
1883–1897	183	104	177	190
1903–1912	216	127	207	240

	Theft[b]			
Period	ER	B	S	L
1883–7	282	338	—	—
1888–92	274	292	—	—
1893–7	—	—	—	—
1898–1902	—	—	—	—
1903–7	239	335	—	—
1908–12	249	421	—	—
1883–1897	269	341	345	299
1903–1912	244	378	323	191

Note: All crime rates are convictions per 100,000 population.

[a] *Gefährliche Körperverletzung.*
[b] *Einfacher und Schwerer Diebstahl.*
[c] The figures represent the computed means for all *Stadtkreise* in the Reich for which data are available. Only a few cases are missing. In the later period, 1903–12, there were many more *Stadtkreise* than there were in the earlier one, 1883–97 (151 versus 89).
[d] The figures are computed means for *Landkreise* in the Reich. Again, only a few cases (18) are missing. $N = 878$.

Table 4.5 Zero-Order Correlations Between Crime Rates and Socioeconomic Variables in All Kreise of the Entire Reich, 1883-1912

Dependent Variable	% Urban Pop.[a]	Pop. Density	% Ethnic Pop.	Death Rate
Total crime rate				
1883-7	-.02	.15	.43	.67
1883-97	.17	.24	.29	.50
1903-7	.31	.25	.27	.42
1908-12	.34	.28	.25	.40
Assault and battery rate				
1883-7	-.13	-.04	.23	.53
1883-97	-.12	-.05	.17	.53
1903-7	-.11	-.03	.20	.50
1908-12	-.15	-.04	.23	.52
Theft rate				
1883-7	-.03	.12	.51	.69
1883-97	.15	.20	.45	.66
1903-7	.37	.28	.39	.45
1908-12	.46	.35	.31	.38
Murder rate[b]				
1904-6	.25	.27	.04	.27

Note: N = 1,047 Kreise.

[a] % Urban Pop. = Percentage of people per Kreise living in communities of more than 2,000 population.
[b] Murder Rate = Per capita rate of murders and manslaughters (from coroners' records) in Prussian Kreise only.

lation growth, urban growth, nor city size had any significant impact on crime rates. This statement is supported by the results from several correlation analyses reported in Tables 4.5, 4.6, and 4.7. In the first of these tables, correlation coefficients between crime rates and several socioeconomic variables for all Kreise in the Reich (1,047 communities) are reported for several periods spanning the years of Imperial Germany. The low and sometimes negative (as in the case of assault and battery) coefficients between crime rates and measures of population and urban concentration demonstrate my point. Only in the case of theft, and only after the turn of the century, did any meaningful correlations emerge. But these are rather spurious correlations. The percentage of variance (R squared) that even the highest of these

Table 4.6 Zero-Order Correlations Between Crime Rates and Socioeconomic Variables for All Prussian Stadtkreise, 1903–1912

Dependent Variable	Urban Population	Pop. Density	Pop. Growth 1895–1910	% Ethnic[a] Pop. 1900	Death Rate 1904–1906
Murder rate, 1904–6	-.07	.31	—	.31	.33
Total crime rate, 1903–7	.07	.12	.20	.61	.48
Total crime rate, 1908–12	.10	.17	.19	.57	.47
Assault and battery rate, 1903–7	-.09	.14	-.06	.68	.56
Assault and battery rate, 1908–12	-.07	.14	-.15	.71	.58
Theft rate, 1903–7	.01	.16	.24	.65	.51
Theft rate, 1908–12	.07	.15	.28	.61	.47

Note: N = 78.

[a] % Ethnic Pop. 1900 = The percentage of Germans in each *Stadtkreis* listing their mother tongue as other than German in the 1900 census.

Table 4.7 Zero-Order Correlations between Crime Rates and Socioeconomic Variables for All Prussian Landkreise, 1903–1912

Dependent Variable	Urban Population	Pop. Density	% Ethnic Pop. 1900	Death Rate 1904–1906
Murder rate, 1904–6	.10	.15	.05	.29
Total crime rate, 1903–7	.15	.32	.55	.55
Total crime rate, 1908–12	.20	.37	.51	.53
Assault and battery rate, 1903–7	.11	.34	.54	.50
Assault and battery rate, 1908–12	.07	.31	.55	.52
Theft rate, 1903–7	.05	.15	.61	.58
Theft rate, 1908-12	.19	.25	.53	.53

Note: N = 462.

correlations renders is very low, and really all this shows is that after the turn of the century theft was more highly concentrated in cities than in the countryside, but that the size of the city did not make any difference.

This is demonstrated more clearly in Table 4.6, where correlation coefficients are presented for the socioeconomic variables and the crime variables in just the city districts of the Reich after the turn of the century, when the city–theft relationship was at its highest. Here we see that, if we consider just the individual cities, without the clouding caused by adding the rural districts into the calculation, the relationship between city size or population density and the crime rates disappears altogether. Furthermore, no significant relationships are found with the introduction of a measure of the growth rate of the urban population. The correlation coefficients for just the rural districts, without the city districts added (Table 4.7), show the same trends. The inclusion of a measure of the murder rate in all of these tables – especially because it, unlike the other crime variables, is based on coroners' records instead of the more dubious court records – adds confidence to the assertion that urban–rural differences and urban and population growth had very little impact on crime trends.

Before proceeding to a discussion of the social and economic conditions that one should indict for causing crime, it would be only fair to credit those cities that had consistently low rates of crime and to point out those cities that had exceptionally high rates. Returning to Table 4.2, which presents crime rates in two periods, one in the 1880s and one in the early 1900s, for the fifty-seven largest cities in Germany (all of which had a legally liable population greater than 50,000 in 1905), one finds that in the 1880s only eighteen cities had an average overall crime rate lower than the national average for all rural and city districts (namely, all *Kreise*); and in the period 1903–7 only ten of these cities continued to have lower crime rates than was average for all districts (note the boldface). This trend did not hold for assault and battery, however. In the earlier period only a third, or nineteen cities, had higher-than-average rates, and in the later period the total increased by only three cities, to twenty-two, with higher-than-average rates for all districts. The overall crime trends in the German cities were, on the other hand, directly in line with the patterns of theft, as in the earlier period forty had higher-than-average theft rates and in the later period the total increased to forty-six (one needs to keep in mind, however, that figures for three of the cities, Bonn, Frankfurt am Main, and Gelsenkirchen, are missing from the first period, so that actually very little change transpired between the two periods).

Not much can be said, with the information presented here, about the reasons why some of these cities had exceptionally low crime rates. The ten cities that continually had exceptionally low rates (Barmen, Colmar, Darmstadt, Giessen, Krefeld, Lübeck, Münster, Mulhausen, Schwerin, and Weimar) were, however, all relatively small or moderate-sized cities, though all experienced some growth, and half of them grew by upward of about 50 percent between the census years 1885 and 1905. Otherwise, there is not much to set these cities apart. They were not concentrated in any geographical region; some had a clear Protestant or Catholic majority, others were religiously mixed; some were made up of almost totally German-speaking inhabitants, others comprised large non-German-speaking minorities, as in the case of the French-speaking citizens of Colmar and Mulhausen. Little also can be said about the eight cities that once were in this low-crime group but no longer were after the turn of the century (Aachen, Cologne, Düsseldorf, Dessau, Elberfeld, Karlsruhe, Rostock, and Worms). All, with the exception of Cologne, were either small or moderate-sized cities, and all had increasing populations as well; though some of them, like Rostock and Worms, had quite low rates of population growth. Again, there was no noteworthy geographic or religious pattern. What might be mildly interesting, however, is that only a few cities had exceptionally low rates of one kind of crime and exceptionally high rates of another. Although only three (Hamburg, Leipzig, and Chemnitz) consistently demonstrated this disparity, and only Berlin could possibly be added from the earlier period, all but moderate-sized Chemnitz were very large cities by German standards. And all of them had low rates of assault and battery and high rates of theft.

One can say a bit more, however, about the cities that had exceptionally high crime rates. To begin with, many of them were located in the Prussian northeast. Table 4.3 shows that half of the ten Prussian cities with the highest crime rates in the 1903–7 period are today part of either Poland or Russia (Stettin, Posen, Breslau, Danzig, and Königsberg). And since only two cities from the rest of Germany, Bremen and Mannheim, had crime rates among the top ten, it is clear that most non-Prussian cities and cities south of the Main had generally modest crime rates. In addition, the vast majority of the leading crime cities were ports, which probably comes as little surprise. Finally, as I will soon argue, what really set many of the cities and other communities with high crime rates apart from the rest is that they housed a relatively great amount of human hardship.

HARDSHIP AND ETHNICITY

If the many Germans who considered the city to be crime-inducing were wrong, the many who considered ethnicity and poverty to be determining factors in causing crime were nearer the mark, as these two factors were often of prime importance in distinguishing high-crime from low-crime communities in Imperial Germany. Of course, ethnicity and poverty have also been found to figure heavily in criminal activity in many other societies,[28] especially because they often go hand in hand. But one must, nonetheless, be careful in using these terms. Although poverty, which is usually a relative concept, is often more difficult to measure than ethnicity, which is more concrete, there is probably not as much danger that its impact will be misunderstood or misused. Whereas few people would expect all poor or relatively poor people to be criminals and would not damn the poor for simply being poor, even though many of them may have turned to criminality, many people in many societies are often not so hesitant to stigmatize certain ethnic groups if some of their members can be shown to be guilty of wrongful behavior (Poles, for example, were often stigmatized as habitual and biologically inclined criminals in Imperial Germany).[29] Accordingly, one must be wary of making statements that can be confused with or turned into sociobiological pronouncements.

Hence I wish to stress from the start that even though certain ethnic minorities in Imperial Germany will be shown to have been associated with a high level of criminality, this does not mean that these same ethnic minorities were in any way criminally prone, for their crime rates in other lands, under other social, economic, and political conditions, have often been very low.[30] Indeed, it will become clear that the strong association between ethnicity and criminality that is so often found is mostly a spurious correlation brought about by intervening variables such as social stigmatization, political repression, and economic hardship.[31]

The examination of popular opinion in Chapter 2 demonstrated that

---

28 Historians of crime in America often point to ethnicity and race (or racism) as being perhaps the key factor in determining crime rates and criminal patterns. Roger Lane, for example, argues that the perceived increase in homicide in post–World War II America is almost totally a function of a huge increase in black homicide rates, some twenty times that of white rates, which have not changed at all. The black rates are explained, of course, in relation to their immiseration. Roger Lane, "Urban Homicide in the Nineteenth Century: Some Lessons for the Twentieth," in Inciardi and Faupel, *History and Crime*, pp. 91–109. For a fuller discussion of ethnicity and homicide in the nineteenth century, see Lane's *Violent Death in the City*. For the importance of ethnicity in colonial America, see Douglas Greenberg, *Crime and Law Enforcement in the Colony of New York, 1691–1776* (Ithaca, N.Y., 1976), pp. 25 ff. And for a discussion of the impact of race and racism throughout American history, see Samuel Walker, *Popular Justice. A History of American Criminal Justice* (New York, 1980). On the impact of ethnicity and poverty upon nineteenth-century French criminality, see David Cohen and Eric A. Johnson, "French Criminality: Urban–Rural Differences in the Nineteenth Century," *Journal of Interdisciplinary History* 12 (1982): 477–501. The classic statement of the importance of poverty is Willem Bonger, *Crime and Economic Conditions* (Bloomington, Ind., 1969; originally published 1905).
29 Klessmann, *Polnische Bergarbeiter*, p. 79.
30 Roger Lane, for example, found that the homicide rates of Poles in nineteenth-century America were very low. See his "Urban Homicide in the Nineteenth Century," p. 99.
31 On the stigmatization and miserable economic conditions of Poles, see Klessmann, *Polnische Bergarbeiter*.

many Germans believed crime to be a kind of foreign phenomenon, and that two ethnic groups in particular, Poles and Lithuanians, were frequently singled out as criminals, both in journalistic and in literary accounts. Evidence of the pervasive ethnic bias against these Slavic minorities is easy to find in other places as well, and not just among conservatives, theologians, and others with a political program or an ideological axe to grind. Even leading criminologists like Gustav Aschaffenburg, who aimed at unbaised and dispassionate analyses of the crime problem and who tried to argue against the notion that the Slavs were congenital criminals by pointing to their poverty as the real cause of their illegal activity, were nonetheless, if unwittingly, often guilty of adding to the racial stereotyping and stigmatization of these peoples. For example, Aschaffenburg stated in his leading text that the persistence of high crime rates in the Prussian northeast was at least in part due to the fact that these districts were "partly inhabited by a Slavic population," which was "culturally not so highly developed."[32]

To many, it appeared that the bias against these groups, the poverty in which many of them lived, and the hostility between them and the government were nearly all pervasive, especially in the case of the Poles. In 1913, the editor of a Polish newspaper in the Westphalian city of Herne wrote that the cause of much recent criminality in his area should be "blamed in the first instance on the anti-Polish system, which the Germans learn . . . the Poles are [constantly] insulted and ridiculed. . . . Taunts like 'damned Polacks' and other such are heard daily on the street."[33] Indeed, the anti-Polish sentiment was so widespread that even foreign visitors seldom failed to notice it and frequently made it a subject of their commentary.

In the 1870s the British visitor Vizetelly, reporting on the poor public image of the Slavs in Berlin, wrote that "the girls who come from Prussian Poland are credited with being exceedingly untidy and lazy."[34] And, at the turn of the century, William Dawson put the whole Polish question into perspective for his American readership with the words: "And today, as for the last hundred years, there still goes on between the Prussian Government and its administrative officials in the Polish districts, on the one hand, and the Polish people on the other, an unceasing feud, an unchanging contest for ascendancy, maintained with equal resolution on both sides, the one seeking

---

32 Gustav Aschaffenburg, *Crime and Its Repression* (Montclair, N.J., 1968; originally published 1913), p. 58. It should be noted, however, that Aschaffenburg was also quick to point to the economic hardships of these people as the major cause of their high crime rates. See also P. Frauenstädt, "Die preussischen Ostprovinzen in kriminal-geographischer Beleuchtung," *Zeitschrift für Sozialwissenschaft* 9 (1906): 570–83.
33 Cited in Klessman, *Polnische Bergarbeiter*, p. 81.
34 Vizetelly, *Berlin Under the New Republic*, 1:31.

to assert German influence, ideas, culture, language, the other tenaciously, unwearyingly, and desperately resisting the onslaught with all the strength and bitterness which pride of race and of history can generate. . . . The present position of the Polish question, then, is this – on the Prussian side repression, on the Polish side embitterment, on both sides suspicion and antagonism."[35] Surely the large Polish minority (roughly three million at the turn of the century) and the small but significant Lithuanian population both had a bad image and, often, a bad time in Imperial Germany; both groups were held in low repute, were often compelled by their poverty to take on the worst kinds of labor, were confronted with such strict Germanizing policies that they could not educate their children or even represent themselves in court in their native tongue.[36] It is no wonder that these "guestworkers in Imperial Germany," as they have been referred to in a recent book by that title, often found themselves on the wrong side of the law.[37]

As the experience of other ethnic minorities in the Reich shows, however, to be of non-German ethnic origin was not necessarily to be persona non grata, in dire economic straits, and consequently involved frequently in criminal activity. The German Reich also had sizable Danish, Dutch, Belgian, and French minorities, but these western peoples appeared to fare much better than the downtrodden Slavs.

There is much evidence to support these points. One might start by looking back at the correlation coefficients shown in Tables 4.5 through 4.7. In Table 4.5 we find that, with the exception of the murder rate, there is a positive, consistent, and often quite strong correlation between various crime measures in different periods and the percentage of the population of a community that was of non-German ethnic origin (that is, that did not list German as its mother tongue in the 1900 census). There are even higher correlations in the more than a thousand communities for which figures are available between crime rates and death rates, which here are used as measures of the relative poverty or wealth of a community. Even though these measures of ethnicity and poverty correlate more strongly with the crime variables than do measures of population concentration – which makes it clear that they are of greater consequence – they are still artificially low.

---

35 Dawson, *The Evolution of Modern Germany*, pp. 490, 496.
36 Klessmann, *Polnische Bergarbeiter;* Murphy, *Guestworkers in Imperial Germany*. For other discussions of the conditions, image, and treatment of Poles in Germany, see Barrington Moore, Jr., *Injustice: The Social Bases of Obedience and Revolt* (White Plains, N.Y., 1978), pp. 119–274; Elizabeth Wiskemann, *Germany's Eastern Neighbours* (New York, 1956), chaps. 1 and 2; and Piotr S. Wandycz, *The Lands of Partitioned Poland, 1795–1918* (Seattle, Wash., 1974).
37 Murphy, *Guestworkers in Imperial Germany*.

By using figures for all *Kreise* in the Reich, roughly half of which had almost no "ethnic" inhabitants, the correlation coefficients are necessarily reduced. Furthermore, by including all ethnic minorities in one lump-sum variable, the relatively low crime rates of some ethnic populations attenuate the effect of the high crime rates of other minorities. If it were possible to use a more exact measure of poverty than the rather crude death rate, it is very likely that the correlation between poverty and criminality would become even more pronounced. In some previous studies, I have in fact used other measures of the relative poverty or wealth of a community, from doctors and taxes per capita to illiteracy rates, and have found higher correlations. But these studies are all based on a much higher level of aggregated data (the Prussian *Regierungsbezirke*) and are thus less reliable.[38] Unfortunately, if, as in this case, one wants to gain more reliability by using much smaller and more numerous units of analysis, one may have to sacrifice some accuracy in the measurement of a concept like poverty, because these other measures are just not available for the smaller districts. But even if the strength of the correlation coefficients is not as great as I believe, it is still very high, and it is certainly indicative of a close relationship between poverty and criminality. There are several reasons why one should accept the death rate as a decent, though far from perfect, measure of poverty. Not only have many other scholars studying Germany and other lands demonstrated, often mathematically, the strong link between poverty and death,[39] but in my other studies I have found a very strong correlation between the death rate and other measures of well-being and hardship at other levels of analysis, and quite similar correlations between crime variables and the death rate and other measures of well-being and hardship.[40]

The significance of the poverty and ethnicity variables is even more evident in Tables 4.6 and 4.7, where Prussian *Stadtkreise* and *Landkreise* are treated separately. Whereas the size of the urban population, the population density, and population growth had very low and sometimes even negative correlations with the crime variables, the correlations between the crime

38 Using data from the thirty-six Prussian *Regierungsbezirke,* McHale and I found, for example, that the correlation between a crude rate of literacy and the overall level of crime was −.86 in the 1880s. McHale and Johnson, "Urbanization, Industrialization, and Crime," p. 236.
39 For a mathematical treatment in German history, see R. Spree, *Wealth and Social Class in Imperial Germany* (Leamington Spa, Eng., 1987); for a nonquantitative treatment in British history, see E. P. Thompson, *The Making of the English Working Class* (New Yrk, 1966), pp. 314–50. For an intriguing analysis of post–World War II USSR, see Nick Eberstadt, "The Health Crisis in the U.S.S.R.," *New York Review of Books*, vol. 23, Feb. 19, 1981, pp. 23–31. For a further discussion on the usefulness of mortality rates as a measure of poverty, see my "The Roots of Crime in Imperial Germany," *Central European History* 15 (1982): 370.
40 Johnson and McHale, "Socioeconomic Aspects of the Delinquency Rate," and McHale and Johnson, "Urbanization, Industrialization, and Crime."

variables and ethnicity and death/poverty are positive and quite strong. Note, for instance, how the correlations between ethnicity and all but the murder rate jump from the mild coefficients hovering between roughly $r = .2$ to $.5$ in Table 4.5 to a range of $r = .5$ to $.7$ in these two tables. What these figures show is that larger cities, and quickly growing cities, did not have levels of criminality any higher than did smaller cities or medium-sized cities that may have been growing rapidly or not experiencing much growth. But if population pressure accounted for little, hardship and ethnicity counted for a lot. In both cities and rural districts, taken separately, crime rates varied directly with a kind of final measure of "un-well-being" (death) and with the relative size of the non-German ethnic population.

A way of further illustrating the importance of these two variables is to juxtapose the data presented in Tables 4.8 and 4.9, which treat the twelve districts with the highest and lowest overall levels of criminality in the five-year period between 1903 and 1907 (out of the more than one thousand districts in the entire Reich). We see that the districts in the first table had a crime rate roughly eight times that of the districts in the second table. The death rate of the high-crime districts was about 50 percent higher than that of the low-crime districts, and the percentage of ethnic inhabitants was over a hundred times higher in the high-crime districts. Although half of the high-crime districts were cities and all of the low-crime districts were composed mainly of rural communities, which accounts for the higher average population and population density of the high-crime districts, only one truly large city, Cologne, is to be found in either table.

Cologne's exceptionally high rates of crime after the turn of the century deserve special comment. First of all, they need to be contrasted with the city's rather low rates in the 1880s (see Table 4.3). Although Cologne experienced rapid urban growth in these years, it was not urban growth per se that caused its apparent increases in crime; rather, it was the type of growth that Cologne experienced. From the figures in Table 4.2, one notes that the city's population grew by almost three times between 1885 and 1905. This was certainly a huge increase; but it was not the likely cause of the explosion of Cologne's crime rate (note that other cities like Leipzig and Hamburg also tripled in size but actually experienced declining crime rates in the same period). More significant is the fact that in 1888 Cologne experienced the greatest territorial expansion in its entire history. Until this time, Cologne had been very small in physical size (about six square kilometers); its city limits housed mainly well-off burghers and relatively few working-class people or socialist-party supporters; even the various harbor areas serving the city were outside the city proper (in nearby Deutz, Riehl, Bayenthal, and

Table 4.8 *Twelve* Kreise *with Highest Crime Rates, 1903-1907*

Kreis	Type	Location	TCR0307	Pop.06	Pop.Den. 1906	Death Rate	%Ethnic 1900	Type Ethnic
Königshütte	S	Silesia	3,391	66,192	11,032	28	44	Polish
Kattowitz	S	Silesia	3,167	35,167	8,953	19	23	Polish
Beuthen	L	Silesia	3,094	168,821	1,723	26	73	Polish
Zabrze	L	Silesia	3,019	139,832	1,165	23	69	Polish
Bremen[a]	L	Bremen	3,000	61,585	267	?	0.5	mixed
Gleiwitz	S	Silesia	2,716	61,441	2,194	21	26	Polish
Ludwigshafen[a]	L	Pfalz	2,702	90,474	768	?	0.5	mixed
Heydekrug	L	E. Prussia	2,647	43,307	54	26	57	Lithuanian
Niederung	L	E. Prussia	2,386	55,174	62	25	15	Lithuanian
Neidenburg	L	E. Prussia	2,358	57,426	35	21	25	Polish
Oberhausen	S	Westphalia	2,447	52,305	4,023	20	?	?
Cologne	S	Rhineland	2,446	429,343	3,868	19	1	mixed
Averages			2,781	105,143	2,845	23	30	

Key: [a] = Figures for death rates are missing for these two non-Prussian districts. Type = S is *Stadtkreis* (city district); L is *Landkreis* (rural district). Death Rate = Deaths per 1,000 population in 1906. Type Ethnic = Dominant non-German speaking ethnic minority. TCR0307 = Total Crime Rate for the period 1903-1907.

Table 4.9 *Twelve* Kreise *with Lowest Crime Rates, 1903-1907*

Kreis	Type	Location	TCR0307	Pop.06	Pop.Den. 1906	Death Rate	%Ethnic 1900	Type Ethnic
Lübbecke	L	Minden	224	50,879	90	15	.02	PG
Wittlage	L	Osnabrück	262	17,998	57	16	.08	PG
Gammertingen	L	Sigmaringen	287	12,836	39	23	.12	PG
Hümmling	L	Osnabrück	305	17,098	21	16	.25	PG
Mühlhausen	L	Erfurt	352	35,906	91	18	.06	PG
Warendorf	L	Münster	359	30,986	55	16	.18	PG
Tondern	L	Schleswig	369	57,149	32	14	69.00	Danish
Montjoie	L	Aachen	369	17,647	49	19	.24	PG
Melle	L	Osnabrück	372	26,586	105	15	.09	PG
Husum	L	Schleswig	372	39,741	47	15	13.00	Danish
Lingen	L	Osnabrück	375	34,218	43	17	.66	PG
Zeven	L	Stade	394	16,388	25	15	.07	PG
Averages			337	29,776	55	16.6	.18[a]	

Key: PG = almost all native pure German-speaking population.

[a] = the two districts with large Danish populations not included. See key to preceding table for all other notes.

Mülheim – all at that time in the *Landkreis* of Cologne, and not in the Cologne *Stadtkreis*). By the incorporation (*Eingemeindung*) in 1888 of these harbor areas and of several hard-core working-class sections such as Nippes and Ehrenfeld (most of which were within a few kilometers at most from the Cologne cathedral in the small, old, medieval inner city), Cologne grew in a single stroke by 85,000 inhabitants, and its entire nature changed.[41] In short, as a result of the changing of the territorial boundaries of the city, Cologne officially became a poorer, tougher, more radical, and more crime-infested place. In addition to this territorial change, one could also explain the rising crime rates in terms of Cologne's growing status in the late decades of the nineteenth century as the major railway and entertainment center for the burgeoning Rhine–Ruhr area. With greatly improved transportation possibilities, many people residing in nearby cities and towns had the opportunity to visit Cologne for a night on the town and ended up as easy prey for thieves and confidence men or becoming involved in a fistfight or brawl.

With the exception of Cologne, the most significant differences between communities with high as opposed to low crime rates were not, therefore, usually found in their size, but in their death rates and the size of their minority populations. The type of ethnic minority population was also of great importance, however, as Poles and Lithuanians were the predominant minority population in all the communities with high crime rates and large ethnic minority populations. In the low-crime districts, on the other hand, most were made up of purely German-speaking populations, though two had large Danish-speaking populations (Tondern and Hufum, both in Schleswig). If we return for a moment to Table 4.3, where the twenty-five largest Prussian cities are presented in ranked order from the city with the highest level of crime in this period, Cologne, to the city with the lowest level, Barmen, we find similar trends, though not quite as pronounced. The death rate and the size of the ethnic population was usually much higher in the cities with higher levels of crime than in those with lower levels of crime, and Polish and Lithuanian minorities predominated in the former but were seldom to be found in the latter, though in this case the low-crime communities often had significant Dutch populations.

These figures show clearly that, whereas hardship was nearly always a major determining factor in the crime rate of a community, ethnicity only

---

41 Hermann Kellenbenz, "Chronologie Kölner Stadterweiterungen und Eingemeindungen vom Mittelalter bis 1975," in his edited volume, *Zwei Jahrtausende Kölner Wirtschaft* (Cologne, 1975), 2:534–5; and Friedrich-Wilhelm Henning, "Die Stadterweiterung unter dem Einfluß der Industrialisierung (1871 bis 1914)," in ibid., pp. 359–473. Among other things, Henning explains that the 1888 city expansion led to an increase of 50 percent in the Social Democratic Party's vote in Cologne between 1887 and 1890 (from 20 to 30%).

mattered in the case of Poles and Lithuanians, for communities with other ethnic minorities had either unremarkable or low rates of crime. But the reason why the Slavic minorities had such high crime rates was that they were socially stigmatized, politically repressed, and usually at the bottom of the economic ladder. Their economic woes and the close relationship among them between poverty and criminality is perhaps most sharply demonstrated in Tables 4.10 and Table 4.11. In the first table, we find that communities with large Polish minorities almost always had greater-than-average crime rates (only a quarter of the 173 communities did not), and that all of the communities with significant Lithuanian minorities had high crime rates (though there were only nine of them). The vast majority of the communities with predominantly French-, Dutch-, or Danish-speaking minorities had lower-than-average crime rates, and in the case of the Dutch and the Danish very low crime rates. The communities without any significant minority population (less than 1 percent foreign speakers) were distributed evenly in the high-, moderate-, and low-crime categories. The "other" group, which was made up of a wide variety of ethnic minorities, from tiny groups like the Wends to Masurians and Italians, usually had lower-than-average crime rates, and the "Mixed" group had higher than average rates (Poles were usually the largest ethnic minority in these communities, but they were not classified as Polish, as the Poles did not make up a clear majority).

Table 4.11 makes plain the strong association between well-being or the lack of it and the different ethnic minority populations. Whereas communities made up of purely German speakers or communities with sizable western European minority populations had low death rates, and the Danes and Dutch had very low death rates, the Polish and Lithuanian minorities nearly always resided in communities where people lived hard lives and died young. Crime, poverty, and death haunted the Polish and Lithuanian peoples in Imperial Germany. It did not matter if they lived in the city, the town, or the countryside, and it did not matter if they stayed in their often hard-pressed ancestral homelands in the Prussian northeast or moved away to the booming industrial "Wild West."

Crime, in its many forms, and independently of how it was measured, from the reasonably reliable coroners' records of homicide[42] to the more suspect court records of theft and assault and battery, was not caused by the industrial revolution, the growth of cities, the size of cities, population

---

42 In his excellent overview of historical studies of English crime rates, Lawrence Stone argues that homicide is the "one crime about which the evidence is most reliable," as "homicide is the most difficult crime to conceal." Stone, "Homicide and Violence," pp. 295–6.

Table 4.10 Cross-tabulation of Total Crime Rate and Ethnic Grouping of All Kreise in the Entire Reich, 1908–1912

	Lowest Crime Rates	Low-Medium	Medium-High	Highest Crime Rates	N
Purely German–speaking (less than 1% foreign)	30%	27%	25%	18%	678
Lithuanian	0%	0%	22%	78%	9
Polish	7%	20%	27%	46%	173
French	19%	50%	19%	12%	16
Dutch	52%	9%	22%	17%	23
Danish	63%	25%	12%	0%	8
Mixed	9%	20%	17%	54%	35
Other	28%	33%	19%	19%	36
				Total	978

Note: Each Crime Rate category represents 25% of all Kreise in the Reich.

Table 4.11 Cross-tabulation of Death Rates and Ethnic Groupings in All Prussian Kreise, 1904–1906

	Lowest Death Rates	Low-Medium	Medium-High	Highest Death Rates	N
Purely German–Speaking	35%	29%	24%	12%	309
Lithuanian	0%	0%	22%	78%	9
Polish	5%	12%	32%	51%	169
French	—	—	—	—	0
Dutch	9%	61%	26%	4%	23
Danish	100%	0%	0%	0%	8
Mixed	—	—	—	—	24
Other	21%	36%	7%	36%	14
				Total	556

Note: Each Death Rate category represents 25% of all Prussian Kreise.

density, anomie, or other intangible and impersonal factors, as many inhabitants of Bismarckian and Wilhelmian Germany and many other societies often liked to think. Moreover, the lack of a meaningful city–crime association in Imperial Germany is all the more noteworthy considering that so many of the government's political enemies, such as socialist workers and Jews, whom the justice authorities relished throwing in the dock at the most minor provocation, lived in the cities. Violent crimes such as murder, manslaughter, and assault and battery may have become more prevalent over the years, but they had roots just as deep in the countryside as in the city.

Property offenses like theft generally declined in both urban and rural settings, but more quickly in the countryside, after the turn of the century. As the death rate was the only consistent correlate with all crime rates, in all periods, and in all settings, the only sensible conclusion is that the best way for society to reduce crime is to reduce human hardship.

5

Criminals and Victims: The Crucial Importance of Gender

The information presented in the preceding two chapters demonstrated that business-cycle downturns and economic hardship, the political repression of certain stigmatized ethnic groups, and the implementation of new and the more vigorous application of old laws to check the rise of political enemies did more than sociological modernization and urbanization theories to explain national-level, time-series trends and regional and cross-sectional patterns of criminality in nineteenth- and early-twentieth-century Germany. Furthermore, one's confidence in these assertions is increased by the fact that the statistical evidence jibes with the qualitative evidence to show that the combined weight of a repressive government, legal system, and biased public opinion frequently worked to bring foreigners and outsiders like Poles, Lithuanians, and socialist workers to the dock.[1] But what about the rest of the population? How often, for example, were women, youth, Protestants, farmers, and common married people involved in criminal acts? How were their patterns of behavior affected, if at all, by the processes of urban and industrial growth and change? Was their role really, as often depicted by opinion makers, confined to that of the victim in the criminal drama?[2]

This chapter, then, completes the analysis of criminal activity in the Kaiserreich by disaggregating the national- and cross-sectional data to treat the demographic characteristics of both criminals and victims. In particular, it stresses the crucial role of women, which, though always of interest to the public and commonly figuring in sensationalist treatments of criminal activity, too often has been overlooked in both theoretical and empirical

---

1 On the importance of combining qualitative with quantitative evidence in historical studies on criminal justice, see the essays by J. A. Sharpe and Jan Sundin, in Eric A. Johnson, ed., *Quantification and Criminal Justice History,* special issue of *Historical Social Research/Historische Sozialforschung* 15 (1990).
2 For extended discussions of some of the most notorious cases, see Hugo Friedlaender, *Interessante Kriminal-Prozesse von Kulturhistorischer Bedeutung: Darstellung merkwürdiger Strafrechtsfälle aus Gegenwart und Jüngstvergangenheit,* 3 vols. (Berlin, 1911).

sociological study. Because the changing status of women is one of the most significant aspects of societal modernization,[3] a theoretically relevant explanation of criminal trends can profit greatly from systematically counting in women's activity as part of the modernization equation.

Part I: Criminals

GENDER

Whereas much scholarly attention has been focused on the important role of youth in criminal activity,[4] there is considerable truth to the lament of the criminologist Doris Klein that "the criminality of women has long been a neglected subject area of criminology." This she finds partly understandable because of "women's low official rate of crime . . . [and] the preponderance of male theorists in the field,"[5] but not at all excusable, because women are and always have been important social actors and they deserve to be studied with the same vigor and scholarly dispassion as men and youth. But Klein argues that to the extent that female criminality has been studied at all, it has been studied without reference to women's social, economic, and political roles. In an article reviewing the literature on female criminality from the turn-of-the-century works of Cesare Lombroso through Sigmund Freud,

---

3 For a relevant bibliography on the history of women, see note 5 below.
4 For bibliography, see Eric A. Johnson and Vincent E. McHale, "Socioeconomic Aspects of the Delinquency Rate in Imperial Germany, 1882–1914," *Journal of Social History* 13 (1980): 384–402.
5 Doris Klein, "The Etiology of Female Crime: A Review of the Literature," in Laura Crites, ed., *The Female Offender* (Lexington, Mass., 1976), p. 5. With the obvious exception of the voluminous literature on prostitution, Klein's complaint about the almost total lack of scholarly studies of female criminality still applies. Dirk Blasius, for example, has argued this recently in his review essay on criminology and historical social science. Dirk Blasius, "Kriminologie und Geschichtswissenschaft: Bilanz und Perspektiven interdisziplinärer Forschung," *Geschichte und Gesellschaft* 14 (1988): 136–49. In German history, my own article, "Women as Victims and Criminals: Female Homicide and Criminality in Imperial Germany, 1873–1914," *Criminal Justice History* 6 (1985): 151–75, has only begun to fill this scholarly void. For prostitution in German history, see Richard J. Evans, "Prostitution, State and Society in Imperial Germany," *Past and Present* 70 (1976): 106–29; Regina Schulte, *Sperrbezirke: Tugendhaftigkeit und Prostitution in der bürgerlichen Welt* (Frankfurt am Main, 1979); and Karin Walser, "Prostitutionsverdacht und Geschlechterforschung. Das Beispiel der Dienstmaädchen um 1900," *Geschichte und Gesellschaft* 11 (1985): 99–111. For an excellent bibliography on the history of German women from early times to the present, see John C. Fout, ed., *German Women in the Nineteenth Century: A Social History* (New York, 1984), pp. 385–95. See also Fout's useful review published in the same volume on some recent research on German women in the nineteenth century (Fout, "Current Research on German Women's History in the Nineteenth Century," pp. 3–54). For some other literature that Fout's bibliography missed, see the special issues in *Geschichte und Gesellschaft* on women's history: "Frauen in der Geschichte des 19. und 20. Jahrhunderts" 7 (1981) and "Frauenleben" 10 (1985). More recent bibliography can be found in Ute Frevert's intriguing first general treatment of German women in the past two centuries, *Woman in German History: From Bourgeois Emancipation to Sexual Liberation* (New York, 1989).

Otto Pollack, and on up to recent writers, Klein finds that "the road from Lombroso to the present is surprisingly straight."[6] She and several other feminist writers believe that almost all of the past work done on female criminality is "classist, racist, and sexist" and based nearly completely on preconceived notions about women's particular psychological and physical character, which is supposedly greatly different from men's. A graphic example Klein uses is Otto Pollack's argument that women really do have as high a level of criminality as men but are better at concealing their crimes just as they are at faking their orgasms.[7]

One of the most important concerns of feminist criminologists is to debunk the myth that the rise of the social, economic, and political status of women has led to a "new, violent, and aggressive female animal."[8] In an article examining postwar U.S. crime rates, Laura Crites concedes that the overall arrest rate of American females according to *FBI Uniform Crime Reports* grew by 108 percent between 1960 and 1974, whereas the men's rate grew only by 23 percent. She also concedes that this means that women's share in the crime rate grew from 10.7 percent of the total to 16.9 percent. But, these figures notwithstanding, she argues that if one examines the crimes that women committed, and which women committed the crimes, one finds that women continued to participate in a very small proportion of violent crimes (their share of the total in this period for all violent crimes remained at about 10 percent), and that the vast majority of female offenders continued to come from poor and minority backgrounds.[9] Hence she concludes that neither the emancipated woman nor the emancipation of women is to be feared, as most crimes committed by women remain "distinctly nonviolent and nonaggressive" and are committed by the unemancipated, not the emancipated, female. Finally, she suggests that the women's movement may be proving a negative benefit to women, as the overall rise in women's arrest rates may be due mostly to "a changing attitude within the criminal justice system toward females."[10]

The feminists' arguments are well worth considering. Although they have possibly overstated the case, there are others who agree, among them the noted British criminologist Hermann Mannheim, that it is not clear from the evidence compiled from many countries that industrialization and the rise of women in economic, social, and political life have led to more female

6   Klein, "The Etiology of Female Crime," p. 8.
7   Ibid., pp. 21–3.
8   Laura Crites, "Women Offenders: Myth vs. Reality," in Crites, *Female Offender*, p. 35.
9   At the time Crites was writing, she said that 64 percent of female prisoners in the United States were from minority groups. Ibid., pp. 35–7.
10 Ibid., p. 39.

criminality and a narrowing of the gap between men's and women's crime rates.[11] Indeed, in his own studies, Mannheim found that industrialization has probably led to more crimes committed against women than it has to more crimes committed by women.[12] As will soon be demonstrated, this appeared to be true in Imperial Germany. Women were becoming increasingly involved in the work life of the nation (both in and outside the home), but their crime rates, with few exceptions, remained quite steady and far below that of men. On the other hand, their new employment status may not have helped them escape criminal misdeeds, as their chances of becoming victims of homicide were increasing much more rapidly than those of men.

The occupational census figures appear to show that German women were taking an ever more active role in economic life. During the two and one-half decades between the occupational census years of 1882 and 1907, the German economy underwent a tremendous expansion, especially in both heavy and light industry, and a tremendous population explosion occurred as well.[13] Many new jobs were created for both sexes, and the total number of employed grew from nearly 18 million to 27 million (a growth of circa 52 percent). For males, however, the employment growth rate was slower than for females. Between 1882 and 1907, the number of employed males grew from 13.4 million to 18.6 million, thus representing a growth rate of about 39 percent. For females, on the other hand, the growth rate was about 93 percent in this period, as the number of employed females rose from about 4.3 million in 1882 to about 8.2 million in 1907. By 1907, women made up about one-third of the entire work force, whereas in 1882 they had made up only about one-quarter.

Not only was there a massive growth in the numbers of women employed, the growth was not confined to a circumscribed area of the econ-

---

11 Hermann Mannheim, *Comparative Criminology* (Boston, 1965), 676–98.
12 Hermann Mannheim, *War and Crime* (London, 1941), pp. 116–20.
13 Not all observers believe that the occupational statistics clearly demonstrate that women's work changed dramatically in the last decades of Imperial Germany. Barbara Franzoi argues, for example, that "contemporaries accepted without question an apparent increase of 35 percent in the number of women working . . . between 1895 and 1907." In her view, these figures overestimate the number of women working outside the home and have led to the faulty conclusion that a great many women became involved in factory production. Much of women's work "outside the home" was done inside the home on an outwork basis, and many of the new female factory workers were employed only for brief periods. "Whatever increase was apparent did not mean permanent transition into factory work." Barbara Franzoi, *At the Very Least She Pays the Rent: Women and German Industrialization 1871–1914* (Westport, Conn., 1985), p. 17. For a useful, conventional summary of occupation, population, and other statistics, see Gerd Hohorst, Jürgen Kocka, and Gerhard A. Ritter, *Sozialgeschichtliches Arbeitsbuch: Materialien zur Statistik des Kaiserreiches 1870–1914* (Munich, 1978).

omy. To be sure, the agricultural sector remained the greatest employer of women throughout the period, and by 1907 women almost equaled men in that sector of the economy;[14] but, by 1907, women had become active and important laborers in many other areas of the economy as well, especially in manufacturing, commerce, and finance. In the manufacturing industry, for example, women had held only about 995,000 jobs in 1882, but that total grew to about 1.9 million by 1907. Thus women more than doubled their representation in this important and expanding part of the economy. More men also found higher employment opportunities in manufacturing, as the growth in male manufacturing jobs grew by more than two million in this period. But, since there were about four men for every one woman working in the manufacturing industry in 1882 and only about three men for every one woman in 1907, it is clear that the men's growth rate was far surpassed by the women's, even in some of the most important branches of industrial employment.[15]

Although it is debatable whether the rise in female employment led to a corresponding rise in the social and political status of women in Imperial Germany – for some have argued that German women continued to be far more traditional-minded and resigned to the status quo than women from Britain, France, and other countries, and they did not make many serious gains in political rights until the Weimar period[16] – one would expect that their changes in economic role would have an influence on their social behavior. As feminists charge, many people expect that *any* changes in women's roles are likely to lead to negative results in their social behavior. Many of the Germans of the time, especially those of a conservative cast, did indeed expect such negative repercussions from the new economic roles of

---

14 See Table 5.9.
15 For these and other figures, see Brian Mitchell, *European Historical Statistics 1750–1975* (London, 1981). For literature on women and work, see U. Knapp, "Frauenarbeit in Deutschland zwischen 1850 und 1933," *Historical Social Research/Historische Sozialforschung* 29 (1984): 3–42.
16 The fullest treatment of women's work and its consequences for women's lives and status in Imperial Germany is Barbara Franzoi's *At Least She Pays the Rent*. For briefer treatments, see Eda Sagarra, *A Social History of Germany 1648–1914* (London, 1977), pp. 405–24; and Gordon A. Craig, *The Germans* (New York, 1982), esp. chap. 7 on "Women," pp. 147–69. Craig explains that the difficult plight of women was "of course, not a solely German phenomenon. Women were victims in all bourgeois societies, and their plight was no better in Victorian England than in Bismarckian Germany. What was unique to Germany was that the subordination of women was more stubborn and protracted than in the advanced western societies" (p. 147). Ute Frevert argues that German women were so poorly off under the kaisers and in the Weimar Republic that they actually fared better in some ways under the Nazis. See her *Women in German History*, esp. pp. 205–52. Peter Stearns compared British with French and German women and found that British women were worse off in the late nineteenth century, though French and German women were "newer to the cities" and "preserved more traditional resignation." Stearns, "Working-Class Women in Britain, 1890–1914," in Martha Vicinus, ed., *Suffer and Be Still: Women in the Victorian Age* (Bloomington, Ind., 1972), p. 119.

women. In an article cited in Chapter 2,[17] the editorial staff of the *Kreuzzeitung* wrote in 1914 that they were astounded by the recent finding of the criminal justice bureau that the women's crime rate was not increasing. But, bothered as many were about the possible unfortunate outcome of the changing economic status of women, their worries proved to be unfounded, at least in regard to the criminal behavior of German women.

The figures in Table 5.1 show clearly that German women were far less prone to crime than German men and that their patterns of criminal behavior did not change much throughout all the years of Imperial Germany, and certainly well into the Weimar period as well. More than this, it appears that earlier trends were the same. The studies of Wilhelm Starke and Dirk Blasius show that Prussian women in the first three-quarters of the nineteenth century did not manifest any marked trend toward increases in criminal behavior. Starke, for example, found that, between 1854 and 1878, the women's share in criminal activity dropped from 23 percent to 17 percent of the men's crime rate, but by 1881 it had returned to roughly 22 percent.[18] Blasius, whose work is roughly one hundred years more recent than Starke's but is focused on an even earlier time period, found that, in 1833, the crime rate of women was only 25.6 percent that of men.[19] Both scholars conclude that, with the exception of particularly hard economic periods like the late 1840s when women's crime rates rose dramatically (especially in theft offenses), the overall trend in the women's crime rate vis-à-vis men's was probably downward from the early part of the nineteenth century. The finding that women's rates are most volatile in times of economic stress is supported by studies in several other countries. Everywhere it seems that women are much more likely to be involved in property crimes than in crimes of violence, and, like men, they are much more likely to commit property crimes during hard economic times than during good times.[20]

Table 5.1 shows that the overall crime rate of German women actually declined as a percentage of the men's overall rate from 1882 to 1914. The fact that it started at a level almost identical to that reported by Starke for

17 *Kreuzzeitung*, July 4, 1914.
18 W. Starke, *Verbrechen und Verbrecher in Preussen 1854–1878. Eine kulturgeschichtliche Studie* (Berlin, 1884), p. 205.
19 Dirk Blasius, *Kriminalität und Alltag: Zur Konfliktgeschichte des Alltagslebens im 19. Jahrhundert* (Göttingen, 1978), p. 80.
20 Many scholars have linked theft rates to economic trends in Germany (ibid., p. 82); W. Woytinsky, "Lebensmittelpreise, Beschäftigungsgrad und Kriminalität," *Archiv für Sozialwissenschaft und Sozialpolitik* 61 (1929): 21–62; L. Fuld, *Der Einfluss der Lebensmittelpreise auf die Bewegung der strafbaren Handlungen* (Mainz, 1881); and Howard Zehr, *Crime and the Development of Modern Society: Patterns of Criminality in Nineteenth-Century Germany and France* (London, 1976). For other societies, see also Willem Bonger's classic study, *Criminality and Economic Conditions* (Bloomington, Ind., 1969, originally published 1905).

Table 5.1 *Women's and Youth's Crime Rates as Percentage of Men's Crime Rates, 1882–1927*

Period/Year	All Crimes		Simple Theft		Assault and Battery[a]		Homicide[b]	
	Women	Youth	Women	Youth	Women	Youth	Women	Youth
1882–85	22	33	40	80	7	18	26	14
1886–90	21	34	40	92	8	19	22	17
1891–95	20	35	39	96	9	21	23	20
1896–1900	18	35	37	104	8	22	23	26
1901–5	18	34	35	104	8	22	18	25
1906–10	18	33	31	104	8	21	14	32
1911–13	18	32	30	103	8	20	14	23
1914	19	35	30	108	9	23	14	24
1915–18	—	—	—	—	—	—	—	—
1919	29	68	40	120	21	30	19	20
1920–24	20	40	25	80	12	14	16	18
1925–27	17	21	28	79	7	18	16	13

Note: These figures are adapted from *STDR*, 370, 39–61. All rates are average yearly conviction rates per 100,000 legally liable population.

[a] Assault and battery includes both *leichte Körperverletzung* and *gefährlicher Körperverletzung*.
[b] Homicide includes both *Mord* and *Totschlag*.

Prussian women in the early 1880s heightens one's confidence that Starke's and Blasius's studies of Prussian women in the early and middle years of the nineteenth century were representative of women throughout Germany in these years. In Table 5.1, the women's rate vis-à-vis the men's rate was always much higher in property offenses like simple theft than in violent offenses like homicide and assault and battery. Perhaps the most striking finding, however, is that the women's rate of simple theft underwent such a dramatic decline during these years. As was noted previously and is demonstrated in Table 5.2, the rate of simple theft declined for the entire German population, and thus for men as well as for women. But the rate did not decline nearly as rapidly for men. Between 1882 and 1914, the women's theft rate dropped from 40 percent of the men's rate steadily downward to a low of 30 percent on the eve of the First World War. In assault and battery offenses, the women's rate showed some tendency to increase, as did the men's, over the years of Imperial Germany, but the women's increase was just about in step with the men's. In homicide offenses, which, as explained earlier, were going down for all Germans in the conviction figures but possibly not in reality, as coroners' figures point out entirely different trends (though with these figures we unfortunately cannot determine who did the killing), the women's rate vis-à-vis the men's fell even lower than in simple theft offenses; hence the women's rate fell by almost 50 percent as compared with the men's

Table 5.2 *Men, Women, and Youth Crime Rates, 1882–1927*

Period/Year	All Crimes				Simple Theft			
	Total	Men	Women	Youth	Total	Men	Women	Youth
1882–5	1,003	1,685	377	564	234	341	136	272
1886–90	1,021	1,738	365	596	204	295	117	270
1891–5	1,155	1,978	401	701	209	305	118	292
1896–1900	1,197	2,084	382	725	185	272	100	283
1901–5	1,220	2,128	380	731	183	273	95	284
1906–10	1,210	2,114	371	708	181	278	87	289
1911–13	1,191	2,074	370	661	171	270	80	278
1914	940	1,618	311	565	139	218	66	235
1915–18	—	—	—	—	—	—	—	—
1919	736	1,186	340	803	222	327	130	393
1920–4	1,430	2,476	487	979	423	689	171	550
1925–7	1,232	2,182	365	467	147	231	66	183

	Assault and Battery				Homicide			
1882-1885	196	378	28	272	.94	1.52	.40	.22
1886-1890	228	432	34	84	.78	1.28	.28	.22
1891-1895	270	512	44	108	.80	1.30	.30	.26
1896-1900	308	580	48	126	.70	1.14	.26	.30
1901-1905	306	576	46	128	.66	1.12	.20	.28
1906-1910	278	520	42	110	.64	1.14	.16	.36
1911-1913	248	472	40	94	.72	1.30	.18	.30
1914	180	344	32	78	.66	1.16	.16	.28
1915-1918	—	—	—	—	—	—	—	—
1919	66	112	24	34	.92	1.58	.30	.32
1920-1924	84	162	20	22	1.16	2.04	.32	.36
1925-1927	94	168	12	30	1.14	2.02	.32	.26

Note: See Table 5.1 for source and notes.

rate. And, in Table 5.2, we find that the female conviction rate in homicide offenses dropped, between the periods of 1882–5 and 1911–13, by more than 50 percent, from 0.40 to 0.18.

Thus the foregoing figures might well be used to support the arguments of the feminist criminologists of present-day America. Although German women became more active in the German economy, they did not become "violent and aggressive female animals." On the contrary, it appears that they became even more upright and law-abiding. Their crime rates in most offenses either remained stable or even decreased, as was the case in both homicide and theft. The feminists' argument that women are not likely to become more crime-prone with their emancipation is buttressed further by what happened in the Weimar years. Weimar women continued to become ever more active in the German economy, and even gained political enfranchisement, but their crime rates, with only some minor exceptions, sank by the mid-twenties to a level even lower than in the nineteenth century.[21]

Because these figures show that women's role in criminal activity was not increasing in Imperial Germany but the overall rate of crime did show some increase, whatever increase did take place obviously has to be attributed to men. But, as explained earlier, the overall increase in crime was in large degree "manufactured" by the discriminatory enforcement of political offenses.[22] Hence, with the exception of some ordinary crimes such as assault and battery, which did appear to show an increase, the pattern of both female and male criminality did not change significantly in Imperial Germany despite the massive economic and social changes that took place there. The numbers of crimes committed by both women and men always remained in approximately the same proportion to one another. Violent offenses appeared to be almost the sole preserve of men. Women, for example, never accounted for even as much as 10 percent of assault and battery offenses, and they also accounted for a small and apparently rapidly declining proportion of homicide offenses. Again, however, one must be extemely cautious in placing too much trust in these figures. It was only in property offenses that women appeared to commit a sizable amount of misdeeds, and here, too, the women's rate was declining vis-à-vis the men's rate.[23]

AGE

If gender was more or less a constant in the criminal activity of Bismarckian and Wilhelmian Germany, age appears to be more of a variable. In Table 5.2, it is apparent that the overall crime rate of German youth increased consid-

---

21 For the struggle for women's rights, see Richard J. Evans, *The Feminist Movement in Germany 1894–1933* (London, 1976); Ute Frevert, *Women in German History;* and Evans, "Liberalism and Society: The Feminist Movement and Social Change," chap. 7 in his *Rethinking German History: Nineteenth-Century Gernmany and the Origins of the Third Reich* (London, 1987). See also Claudia Koonz, *Mothers in the Fatherland: Women, the Family and Nazi Politics* (London, 1986), esp. chap. 2 on "Weimar Emancipation."
22 See the discussion in Chapter 3.
23 Of course, the women's crime rate might have been considerably higher had prostitution been counted in the German crime statistics. But it makes sense not to include prostitution in crime rates, as not only is it impossible to measure prostitution offenses with any kind of objectivity, but prostitution itself hardly compares with real crimes. Aschaffenburg explained: "Many a young girl would resort to stealing and embezzlement in order to gratify her desire for pleasure and dress, if prostitution did not afford her an easier and more profitable means of satisfying her wishes." Nevertheless, he went on to explain that he does not "believe that it is the male thief, street robber, or forger that corresponds to the prostitute, but the beggar and the vagrant." Thus, "I can see no reason for regarding prostitution as a kind of criminal safety valve." Aschaffenburg, *Crime and Its Repression,* trans. Adalbert Albrecht (Montclair, N.J., 1968; originally published in 1913).

erably throughout much of this period, with the most dramatic increase occurring in the 1880s, and 1906 standing as the peak year.[24] Not only did the rate of juvenile delinquency appear to show a significant increase, the actual volume of juvenile delinquency (that is, of youths between twelve and eighteen years of age) always represented a significant fraction of most criminal activity. Like women, youths were far more prone to commit crimes against property than crimes against persons. But their criminal patterns in this period differed from those of women in that they registered an increase in almost all major types of criminal activity (note in Table 5.2 that homicide rates of German youth increased in these years even though the homicide rates of both women and men decreased). Furthermore, the juvenile share of criminal activity sometimes even surpassed that of men. (For example, this was especially true in simple theft offenses, as here again both women's and men's rates declined, but the juvenile rate registered a mild increase, and by the late 1890s, the youth rate was even higher than the men's.)

There is considerable debate about whether this apparent upward trend in juvenile delinquency had been going on throughout the nineteenth century and if it was attributable to the unsettling effects of the processes of urbanization and industrialization, which, again, really took off in the years of Imperial Germany. In his important study of Prussian crime trends from the mid-nineteenth century until the early 1880s, Wilhelm Starke commented on the common perception that German youth had been becoming increasingly lawless throughout these years. His data and his argument, however, showed that Prussian youth were in fact not becoming more prone to crime. Rather, he explained that the marked rise recorded in the official figures after 1871 was occasioned by a change in the upper age limit when youths were prosecuted as juveniles as opposed to as adults. Prior to 1871, Prussian youth between the ages of twelve and sixteen were considered juveniles. But after 1871 the upper age limit was extended to eighteen. Once this was controlled for, argued Starke, there was no increase in the juvenile crime rate from mid-century until the early 1880s.[25]

Hence, if juvenile delinquency actually remained quite stable during the period prior to 1880 but appeared to increase thereafter, and this increase appeared to coincide with Germany's real urban and industrial take-off, which began in the 1880s, the argument that the rise in delinquency during the years of Imperial Germany was occasioned, at least in part, by urbanization and industrialization would seem to make sense. Many of Germany's

---

24 See the government's commentary on periodic trends in juvenile delinquency in *Kriminalstatistik für das Jahr 1927, Statistik des Deutschen Reichs* 370 (Berlin, 1930): 33.
25 Starke, *Verbrechen und Verbrecher in Preussen,* pp. 208–9.

leading contemporary criminologists such as Friedrich von Liszt and Gustav Aschaffenburg did make this argument in the late nineteenth century, and it has remained a common thesis of criminologists and sociologists in most countries for at least the past one hundred years.[26] The argument is reasoned as follows: urbanization and industrialization produce normlessness, anomie, and unsettled home environments; overcrowded urban centers make it easier for delinquents to avoid police surveillance; and greater opportunities exist for delinquents to commit their misdeeds (especially property offenses).[27] In that youth in all societies have been shown to be particularly prone to theft offenses,[28] and that German youth by our own statistics seem no different, the argument that delinquency should rise in direct proportion to industrial development and its concomitant urban growth appears to make sense, especially as cities provide more goods to steal than more rustic environments. As William D. Morrison explained in 1896: "The strongest temptation of the ordinary juvenile is the impulse to steal: in the towns, this impulse is stimulated in every street by interminable lines of shops and warehouses exhibiting all kinds of merchandise in a half-protected state."[29]

But, curiously perhaps, Aschaffenburg, Liszt, and other German criminologists began to turn away from the urbanization and industrialization theory around the turn of the century, and there are many reasons why we should too. In the main, the contemporary Germans' change of view was occasioned by an apparent decline in some categories of juvenile offenses, which led them to question if in fact industrialization might not have a civilizing effect on most people, and especially on youth. Hence, Aschaffenburg: "Now, as industrial life has made a tremendous advance . . . the whole number of workmen employed, and also the number in proportion to minors, must have grown, it might almost appear as if crime was rather prevented than furthered by the entrance of young people into industrial life."[30] And Liszt hypothesized: "Under favorable economic conditions, and when the demand for workmen is high, a number of youths are employed in factories as substitutes for grown workmen. There their situation is assured to a certain extent by legislation for the protection of workmen, much more,

---

26 See, for example, the review of works on juvenile delinquency in Imperial Germany in the *Kreuzzeitung*, November 22, 1902. For other societies, see, for example, Joseph M. Hawes, *Children in Urban Society* (New York, 1971); and William Douglas Morrison, *Juvenile Offenders* (London, 1896).
27 See, for example, Louise I. Shelley, *Crime and Modernization: The Impact of Industrialization and Urbanization on Crime* (Carbondale, Ill., 1981); and Marshall B. Clinard and Daniel J. Abbott, *Crime in Developing Countries* (New York, 1973).
28 Mannheim, *Comparative Criminology*, pp. 682–3.
29 Morrison, *Juvenile Offenders*, p. 172.
30 Aschaffenburg, *Crime and Its Repression*, pp. 148–9.

indeed, than it would be today at least, if they were engaged in home industries."[31]

Both Aschaffenburg's and Liszt's optimism was countered, however, by their belief that this positive impact of industrial employment would only hold true during favorable economic times. Thus Liszt warned: "When the economic situation becomes less favorable, the boys employed in the factories are the first to be dismissed and turned into the street. They then have lost the means of earning their livelihood and are no longer able to satisfy the new tastes and habits they have formed, so that social shipwreck is bound to occur."[32] And Aschaffenburg echoed: "But what may happen if hard times again succeed the present prosperous period? . . . It is always dangerous to prophesy, but, still, I consider it necessary to prognosticate the coming years. If it should come true, it may be considered as a test of the correctness of the views I have just advanced. The industrial crises will bring about a drop in wages and a greater number of dismissals. These dismissals will first affect the youthful workmen and those who are physically and mentally inferior. A part of them will seek to obtain by dishonesty what their lack of employment prevents their obtaining otherwise."[33]

Thus, contemporary German theorists like Aschaffenburg and Liszt appeared to waffle on whether industrialization and urbanization occasioned more or less delinquency. But there is no reason for us to waffle. Industrialization, urbanization, and modernization did not cause delinquency, just as they did not cause adult criminality. Had Liszt and Aschaffenburg not concluded their observations at the beginning of the twentieth century (Aschaffenburg's go up until 1906, and Liszt's stopped at 1900), they might indeed have had a chance to test their hypotheses. The figures in Tables 5.1 and 5.2 allow us to do that for them.

Although the figures for all criminal offenses listed in Table 5.2 show that convictions for German youths increased from a rate of 564 in the years between 1882 and 1885 to a rate of 661 in the years between 1911 and 1913, this does not necessarily mean that German youths were actually becoming more crime prone, and it certainly does not mean that industrialization and urbanization engendered more delinquency. Aside from the fact, which always bears repeating, that conviction statistics are always to be viewed with caution, and that any generalizations based on broad categories such as convictions for "all crimes" have already been proven to be dubious (espe-

---

31 Friedrich von Liszt, "Die Kriminalität der Jugendlichen," lecture delivered to the Rheinisch-Westfälischen Gefängnisgesellschaft in 1900, cited in Aschaffenburg, *Crime and Its Repression*, p. 149.
32 Aschaffenburg, *Crime and Its Repression*, p. 149.
33 Ibid., pp. 151–2.

cially as they often conceal "manufactured crimes" and new offenses that account for the bulk of any apparent increases), it makes no sense to argue that juvenile delinquency was increasing in this period if we do not admit that adult criminality was increasing as well, for the juvenile rate (as shown in Table 5.1) actually *declined* over these years vis-à-vis the men's rate. Hence, in the years between 1882 and 1885, the juvenile rate for all crimes stood at 33 percent of the rate for adult men, and throughout the period it continued to hover around that same percentage and even declined to 32 percent in the years between 1911 and 1913, on the eve of the First World War. And just as was the case for adults, the juvenile delinquency rate reached a peak in the early 1900s and was declining in the decade prior to the war. As these years continued to be marked by urban and industrial growth, and delinquency was actually declining, it can hardly be said that modernization caused delinquency.

If modernization did cause delinquency, then one would have to expect that there would be a consistent rise in property offenses. Although Table 5.1 indicates that in simple theft offenses (which represented the most significant amount of delinquency in general, in fact roughly 50 percent of all juvenile offenses were of this type) the youth rate increased in these years vis-à-vis the adult men's rate, this really means nothing. The figures in Table 5.2 show that there was no appreciable increase in simple theft offenses for German youth (in the period 1882–5, the simple theft rate stood at 272, and in the period 1911–13, it was almost exactly the same, 278). All that happened, and what accounts for the increased proportion of youthful theft offenses, was that the adult rate declined while the youth rate held steady. Although juveniles did appear to register higher rates of personal offenses (see the figures in Table 5.2 for assault and battery and homicide), these were still rather infrequent offenses for youths to commit, their trend was going downward in the decade prior to the war, and modernization theorists do not expect urbanization and industrialization to occasion more crimes of violence, rather the opposite.[34]

As Aschaffenburg and Liszt suspected, then, what really had an impact on delinquency was economic hardship, not urbanization, or industrialization, or modernization. In an essay written some years ago, Vincent McHale and I demonstrated, by using correlation analysis for time-series and cross-sectional data, that the rate of juvenile delinquency in Imperial Germany varied directly with food prices;[35] the rate went up when food prices rose,

---

34 See, for example, Helmut Thome, "Gesellschaftliche Modernisierung und Kriminalität. Zum Stand der sozialhistorischen Kriminalitätsforschung," *Zeitschrift für Soziologie* 21 (1992): 212–28.
35 Johnson and McHale, "Socioeconomic Aspects of the Delinquency Rate," p. 390.

Table 5.3 *Zero-Order Correlations between Juvenile Delinquency Rates and Measures of Education, Illegitimacy, and Mortality in 36 Prussian Regierungsbezirken, 1883–1912*

Period	Illiteracy	Students	Sch. Spending	Illegitimacy	Mortality
1883–7	.74	-.58	-.33	.46	.64
1888–92	.68	-.65	-.31	.45	.66
1893–7	.48	-.75	-.32	.53	.61
1898–1902	.49	-.66	-.35	.46	.63
1903–7	.46	-.51	-.46	.34	.47
1908–12	.53	-.44	-.42	.21	.50

Key: Illiteracy = Number of individuals who could neither read nor write per 1,000 inhabitants.
Students = Number of children attending school per 1,000 school-age population.
Sch. Spending = Amount of public expenditure per student.
Illegitimacy = Rate of illegitimate births per legitimate births.
Mortality = Deaths per 1,000 inhabitants.

and went down when they declined; the rate was generally unrelated to urban growth, population density, or measures of industrial concentration;[36] but it was highly related to measures of poverty, as is shown in Table 5.3.

Although poverty and economic hardship are difficult to measure, the five variables listed in Table 5.3, when taken collectively, represent an indication of these problems, if still an imperfect one. Certainly it is not outlandish to argue that districts with high rates of illiteracy, illegitimacy, and mortality, and low amounts of students and school spending per capita, are beset by economic difficulties. Thus, in that the juvenile delinquency rate consistently had a high correlation with all of these measures in each of the six five-year periods under scrutiny, one must conclude that delinquency was in large part exacerbated by economic woes in Imperial Germany.

One final argument against the notion that juvenile delinquency was in any way caused by urban-industrial development and for the fact that it was indeed mostly related to economic difficulties is that, after the war, the rate of juvenile delinquency, especially in property offenses, soared during Weimar's first five, extremely troubled years; but after the stupendous inflation and huge wave of strike activity abated during the Weimar Republic's more prosperous and settled middle years, the juvenile delinquency rate returned to levels below the rate registered at any time during the Kaiserreich. Thus, in Table 5.2, one notes that the overall delinquency rate rose in the period between 1920 and 1924 to a level that was nearly double the rate

---

36 Ibid., 393.

Table 5.4 *Age Differences in Male and Female Criminality, 1886–1895*

	All Crimes		Simple Theft		Grand Theft		Receiving Stolen Goods		Embezzlement	
	M	F	M	F	M	F	M	F	M	F
12–18	1,034	230	418	152	89	10	29	4	47	11
18–21	3,291	444	627	233	150	15	40	9	133	28
21–25	3,327	444	515	185	108	12	36	12	143	26
15–30	2,928	482	455	161	72	9	34	17	135	25
30–40	2,259	523	365	141	44	7	33	26	106	24
40–50	1,651	489	272	118	25	5	28	31	72	21
50–60	1,068	315	184	76	13	2	21	20	42	12
60–70	572	153	110	40	5	1	12	8	21	f
70 and over	227	58	46	15	1	.1	4	3	7	2
Average	1,847	380	352	132	58	7	28	16	81	18

	Fraud		Simple A&B		Aggravated A&B		Libel		Resistance to Authorities	
	M	F	M	F	M	F	M	F	M	F
12–18	34	18	30	2	149	6	23	7	8	0.8
18–21	135	40	198	7	1,013	20	127	31	121	5
21–25	165	33	244	12	958	28	198	53	174	8
15–30	156	26	230	20	646	38	265	84	162	9
30–40	119	21	165	23	339	43	324	114	111	9.3
40–50	83	17	102	19	194	38	316	119	68	8.9
50–60	50	10	54	11	117	24	235	82	36	5
60–70	24	5	25	5	57	11	132	41	16	2
70 and over	9	2	9	2	22	4	52	16	5	1
Average	88	20	118	13	357	26	204	69	77	6

Note: All figures are average yearly conviction rates per 100,000 legally liable population. Maximum values in each category are underlined.

of the period between 1882 and 1885 but dropped by half in the more prosperous years immediately following. Also, the changes were the most dramatic in theft offenses, as the juvenile theft rate dropped in the mid-Weimar years to a level barely a third of what it had been in the troubled years just before that time.

Although the intention of the foregoing discussion is to show that modernization did not change gender-specific or age-specific patterns of criminality, it is certainly not to discount the importance of gender and age in criminal activity. That they were indeed two extremely important, demographic determinants of wrongdoing is brought into bolder relief by the information contained in Table 5.4, where the age and gender of offenders for nine different types of offenses are computed for a ten-year time period between 1886 and 1895.

What strikes one immediately is that criminality of almost all types was predominantly the preserve of men, and in particular young men between the ages of eighteen and thirty. For the sum of all offenses in this period, the most crime-prone group was men between the ages of twenty-one and twenty-five, with the second-highest group being men between eighteen and twenty-one years of age, and the third-highest men between twenty-five and thirty. Young adult males were in fact the most likely people to commit all of the nine types of offenses listed here except libel, where the men were slightly older. On the other hand, women of all ages were rarely criminal offenders, and a woman's age did not seem to make much difference. Whereas the younger a male was, usually the more likely he was to commit a crime, this cannot be said of women. The highest prone age group for female criminals was between thirty and forty, and women in their forties were even slightly more likely to commit crimes than women in their twenties. Only in theft, and some other property offenses such as embezzlement and fraud, were young women more likely to be offenders than women of their middle to somewhat older years.

MARITAL STATUS

Age and gender differences were not only important in and of themselves, they also often acted as mediating influences on the impact that other demographic characteristics such as marital status had on criminality. In Table 5.5, figures are presented for the period 1882–93 which demonstrate that the relationship between marital status and the propensity to commit a crime was often quite different for women than it was for men, and that age at marriage was important for both sexes in determining the likelihood that one would commit a crime.[37] For both sexes, people who married exceptionally early or were divorced or widowed, particularly those who lost their partners at a young age, were far more likely to commit crimes than those who waited until a normal age to marry and stayed married or never married at all. The reason early marriages were so crime-inducing was probably because of poverty. As Gustav Aschaffenburg explained near the time that

---

37 For a nineteenth-century contemporary's discussion of the impact of marriage on criminal activity, see Prinzing, "Der Einfluss der Ehe auf die Kriminalität des Mannes," *Zeitschrift für Sozialwissenschaft* 2 (1989); and Prinzing, "Die Erhöhung der Kriminalität des Weibes durch die Ehe," *Zeitschrift für Sozialwissensshaft* 3 (1900). Both of Prinzing's articles are used heavily in Aschaffenburg's own contemporary discussion of marital status, *Crime and Its Repression*, pp. 162–8.

Table 5.5 *Marital Status and Age of Male and Female Offenders, 1882–1893*

Age	All Crimes					
	SM	SF	MM	MF	DWM	DWF
12–15	661	150	?	?	?	?
15–18	1,319	321	?	?	?	?
18–21	2,995	415	6,413	603	?	?
21–25	3,107	418	3,566	470	?	1,339
25–30	2,951	441	2,505	455	4,274	1,149
30–40	2,881	446	1,961	500	3,798	1,030
40–50	2,206	335	1,489	468	2,626	710
50–60	1,242	222	1,010	300	1,268	369
60 and over	495	102	490	133	343	111

Age	Simple Theft					
	SM	SF	MM	MF	DWM	DWF
12–15	?	?	?	?	?	?
15–18	?	?	?	?	?	?
18–21	552	210	1,418	209	?	?
21–25	428	177	685	148	627	386
25–30	383	159	412	132	572	319
30–40	412	137	297	127	550	266
40–50	365	92	216	104	420	176
50–60	233	61	152	64	231	89
60 and over	109	32	84	31	67	28

Age	Assault and Battery					
	SM	SF	MM	MF	DWM	DWF
12–15	?	?	?	?	?	?
15–18	?	?	?	?	?	?
18–21	961	21	1,309	68	?	?
21–25	949	25	808	61	1,102	96
25–30	730	30	519	59	736	89
30–40	425	30	298	61	412	70
40–50	203	21	181	55	226	47
50–60	92	14	115	34	108	26
60 and over	32	7	49	14	30	9

Note: All figures are convictions per 100,000 legally liable population of each category. These figures are adapted from Gustav Aschaffenburg, *Crime and Its Repression*, pp. 164–65. Maximum values in each category are underlined.

these figures were first generated: "One of the external causes [of this phenomenon] is undoubtedly the poverty that so often accompanies early, heedless marriages."[38] That this was not the case in just Imperial Germany but has held true in many societies in more recent times as well, has been noted by many people. In his classic text, *Comparative Criminology*, published in 1965, Hermann Mannheim explained that "this can easily be explained by the probability for young men [that] marriage often means financial and moral responsibilities with which they cannot well cope, especially as very early marriages are more frequent among the poorer classes.[39] Although Aschaffenburg said that he could not explain why widowed or divorced women or men had such high crime rates, and Mannheim only stated that this was a normal occurrence in most societies, it would certainly be easy to demonstrate that poverty also was often the cause here as well, especially for women.[40]

But for the majority of German women and men who adhered more closely to society's norms – by marrying sometime in their twenties, as most people did, or by holding off a bit to a later age, as many did, and by never getting divorced or only losing their partner through death at a late age – it is curious, perhaps, why marriage itself had such a different effect on women than it did on men. With the exception of the youngly married population of both sexes, married men of all ages were considerably less likely to commit crimes than single men, but the opposite was usually the case for women; for marriage did not retard criminality for German women, it appeared to increase it. Aschaffenburg opined that marriage was generally a good thing for both sexes, and that the reason why married women were more likely to be criminals than single women was because of the bad influence that their always more crime-prone men had on them. Noting that, in theft offenses, single women were more often criminals than married women, however, Aschaffenburg stated that "when a mature married woman transgresses it is generally as an accessory, a receiver of stolen goods, or an offender against trade regulations."[41] But this cannot be accepted as a valid explanation, for in assault and battery cases the difference between a married woman's propensity to commit a crime was even more pronounced than it was for the run of all offenses. Mannheim is not very useful here either, as he tells us, without citing any supportive evidence, that it is normal

38 Ibid., p. 162.
39 Mannheim, *Comparative Criminology*, p. 626.
40 See the review article on the impact of divorce in historical perspective by Lawrence Stone, in the *New York Review of Books*, 36 (1989).
41 Aschaffenburg, *Crime and Its Repression*, p. 166.

in most societies, except for the most heinous of crimes, for married women to have higher crime rates than unmarried women. Hence, he argues that "if criminality is weighed, not merely counted, married women are therefore in a more favourable position than single ones."[42]

Unfortunately, I do not have an explanation for this phenomenon either. I can suggest that some of this evidence seems to jibe, though somewhat indirectly, with a rash of sociological and psychological studies in various western societies suggesting that marriage today seems to be much more salubrious for men than it is for women, and that perhaps this was always the case. But in the nearly total absence of historical work on women's crime patterns in general and on the differential psychological and sociological impact of marriage on women and men, one can only speculate that psychological factors must have played an important role in these matters. It is hoped that answers will soon emerge as gender history becomes more developed and advanced.[43] Clearly, much more needs to be done on the criminality of women and youth in all societies, as standard arguments about the impact of urbanization and industrialization seem to have little utility in explaining why youth and women were so different from men, and economic arguments take us only part of the way. Empirically based historical studies that somehow tap the psychological and emotional motivations and differences among men, women, and youth are badly needed.

RELIGION

Religion is another demographic factor that highlights the importance of cultural differences as opposed to urban-industrial growth and change in the etiology of criminality. Although it is easy to demonstrate that there were considerable differences among the three major religious groups in Germany (Protestants, Catholics, and Jews) in their recorded rates of crime (see Tables 5.6 and 5.7), it is no simple task to explain these differences. Certainly many German scholars of the period took a serious interest in this task, as many books, articles, and parts of books were devoted to the influence of religion on criminality, and especially to explaining why Catholics seemed to have such high crime rates and Jews did not.[44] By attempting to explain away the

---

42   Mannheim, *Comparative Criminology*, p. 626.
43   A recent master's thesis by Mary Orr Johnson uses quantitative evidence to show that marriage had a differential impact on the emotional lives of women and men in Victorian Britain. Mary Orr Johnson, "Gender and Insanity in Nineteenth-Century Scotland" (M.A. thesis, University of Strathclyde, 1994).
44   See, for example, Ludwig Fuld, *Das jüdische Verbrecherthum: Eine Studie über den Zusammenhang zwischen Religion und Kriminalität* (Leipzig, 1885); and Rudolf Wassermann, *Beruf, Konfession und Verbrechen* (Munich, 1907).

Table 5.6 *Religion and Crime, 1892-1901*

Type of Offense	Protestants	Catholics	Jews
All Crimes	1,122	<u>1,361</u>	1,030
All Crimes against the State, Public Order, and Religion	169	164	<u>234</u>
All Crimes against Persons	461	<u>634</u>	382
All Crimes against Property	489	559	<u>410</u>
Individual Offenses			
Resisting officers	42	<u>48</u>	13
Violation of Lord's Day regulations	21	13	<u>127</u>
Aggravated assault and battery	185	<u>314</u>	75
Libel	140	148	<u>200</u>
Rape	11	<u>13</u>	9
Simple theft	219	<u>254</u>	80
Grand theft	32	<u>36</u>	10
Embezzlement	<u>53</u>	52	48
Fraud	46	52	<u>94</u>
Bankruptcy	2	1	<u>26</u>
Perjury	2	2	<u>3</u>

Note: All figures are convictions per 100,000 legally liable population of the respective religious denomination. The figures are adapted from data presented in Gustav Aschaffenburg, *Crime and Its Repression*, p. 54. Maximum values in each category are underlined.

differences in crime rates as attributable to the varying economic standings of the religious groups, many of these scholars were no doubt trying both to be objective and to do their best to promote social harmony. But noble as this aim was, the fact that they had to try so hard to do it demonstrates that, either explicitly or implicitly, they recognized that their society had serious biases regarding religious issues and that these biases had much to do with the recorded rates of criminality for the different religious groups.

In the foreword to his study of Jewish criminal trends, written in 1885, Ludwig Fuld stated that it was his duty to consider objectively what he said was the "trite anti-Semitic fable of Jewish criminality," which was a "burning issue of the day."[45] And in commenting not infrequently on the issue of religion and criminality, the government itself clearly demonstrated that racial bias was not limited to anti-Semitism. Shortly after the turn of the century, the Imperial Criminal Bureau (*Reichkriminalamt*) stated in the official statistical series *Statistik des Deutschen Reichs* that "the fact that crimi-

---

45 Fuld, *Das jüdische Verbrecherthum*, p. v.

Table 5.7 *Religion and Homicide Convictions in Two Periods, 1882–1886 and 1903–1907*

Year	Protestants	Catholics	Jews[a]
1882	194	125	0
1883	160	157	0
1884	153	117	0
1885	89	76	2
1886	108	73	0
Totals 1882–6	704	548	2
1903	139	141	1
1904	81	87	1
1905	147	122	1
1906	126	133	0
1907	140	131	1
Totals 1903–7	633	614	4

Note: Total number of convictions for both premeditated murder *(Mord)* and unpremeditated murder *(Totschlag).*

[a] All Jewish homicide convictions were for unpremeditated murder.

Source: Appropriate yearly *Kriminalstatistik* volumes of the governmental series *Statistik des Deutschen Reichs.*

nality among Catholics is greater is largely due to the preponderance of Catholicism in those districts of the Empire lying on its eastern border, which are partly inhabited by a Slavic population and are culturally not so highly developed, and where the greatest number of convictions occurs."[46] Obviously, if scholars like Fuld felt compelled to demonstrate that Jews were not necessarily criminals and the government's criminal justice bureau explained the Catholic rate in terms of racist comments about Slavs, then one can hardly place much faith in the recorded figures that seemed to indicate great differences among the criminal propensities of different religious groups. Clearly the biases of both the population and the officials must have had much to do with manufacturing the criminal trends.[47]

---

46 Cited in Aschaffenburg, *Crime and Its Repression,* p. 58.
47 For discussions of the bias against Slavs in Imperial Germany, see Richard Charles Murphy, *Guestworkers in the German Reich: A Polish Community in Wilhelmian Germany* (Boulder, Colo., 1983); Piotr S. Wandycz, *The Lands of Partitioned Poland 1795–1918* (Seattle, 1979); and William W. Hagen, *Germans, Poles, and Jews: The Nationality Conflict in the Prussian East, 1772–1914* (Chicago, 1980). For a discussion of Polish criminality, see Christoph Klessman, *Polnische Bergarbeiter im Ruhrgebiet 1870–1945* (Göttingen, 1978), pp. 78–83.

All this once said, the criminal trends of the different major religious groups in Imperial Germany are still interesting to note. Although they cannot be taken at face value, they probably do point out some differences in the unlawful behavior of the various criminal groups. The cause for these differences may have been largely ethnic bias, but they probably are also related to some economic and cultural differences as well, for it is well established that there were indeed considerable differences in the economic standing of these religious groups, and the German patterns corresponded rather closely to those of other societies in the same and in different time periods.[48]

Perhaps what is most striking about the figures themselves are the very low rates of Jewish criminality. As Fuld labored to show in the 1880s, these were far below those of the dominant Christian majority in all but a few offenses, such as bankruptcy and fraud, which are clearly associated with the bourgeois occupations in which Jews were so highly represented. That Jews were also convicted more often than either Protestants or Catholics for offenses such as libel and perjury is somewhat more difficult to explain, though one suspects that part of the reason was that the justice and court officials were probably more likely to prosecute and convict these people, whom many Germans considered dishonorable and untrustworthy, for these crimes of honor.[49] And, clearly, the only other offense for which Jews had higher conviction rates than Protestants and Catholics, "Violation of the Lord's Day Regulations" (which made up a sizable proportion of the overall Jewish crime rate but hardly a fraction of the crime rate of other religious groups), was almost by definition a "trumped-up offense."

Jews had very low rates for all other types of offenses, and perhaps one might add for all offenses that were not of the utmost sensitivity to political and cultural bias. Table 5.6 demonstrates that Jews had roughly one-third the crime rate of Protestants and Catholics in theft offenses, and in violent crimes such as assault and battery and homicide the Jewish rate was even comparatively lower. The homicide figures in Table 5.7 are particularly worth noticing here, as these raw figures for two five-year periods, one in the early 1880s and the other in the early 1900s, demonstrate that Jews were almost never murderers, and, of the total of six Jewish homicide convictions in these two periods, none was for first-degree murder (*Mord*), all were for

---

48 Mannheim, *Comparative Criminology*, pp. 567–70; Hans von Hentig, *The Criminal and His Victim: Studies in the Sociobiology of Crime* (New York, 1979), pp. 329–42.
49 See the discussion in Chapter 2 of the conservative bias against Jews as being untrustworthy. The literature on anti-Semitism in German history is immense, but one especially thought-provoking discussion of Jews in German society is Gordon A. Craig's chapter on "Jews and Germans," in his *The Germans*.

unpremeditated murder (*Totschlag*). Furthermore, if we adjust for the size of the population, we find that Jews had only about one-third the rate of Protestant murder convictions and about one-fifth that of Catholics, as Protestants outnumbered Jews by about sixty to one and Catholics outnumbered Jews by about thirty to one in the general population. Although we have already argued that homicide conviction figures are not to be highly trusted, especially as they do not jibe well with the more reliable coroners' figures for homicide, in this instance we can place some trust in the trends that these figures show even if we cannot trust the absolute figures. As will be demonstrated later in the section on victims in this chapter, the proportion of Jewish to Protestant and Catholic homicide victims stood at just about the same level as the proportion of Jewish homicide convictions to Protestant and Catholic convictions. And this fact should help one to trust the trends displayed in Table 5.7, as it is well established that the largest proportion of all murders in most countries is attributable to friends and family. Thus, most Jewish murder victims were probably murdered by Jewish murderers, and most Jewish murderers probably murdered Jewish victims.

So if Fuld was correct in pointing out that the "fable of Jewish criminality" was indeed largely an anti-Semitic myth, what can be said about the criminal activity of the two preponderant religious groups in Germany: the Protestants, who made up roughly two-thirds of the population, and the Catholics, who accounted for most of the remaining population? Certainly the figures in Tables 5.6 and 5.7 point out that, for most offenses, the Catholic crime rate was significantly higher than the Protestant rate. For all crimes and misdemeanors in the ten-year period between 1892 and 1901, the Catholic rate stood at 1,361 versus 1,122 for the Protestants. And, considering the individual offenses, the Protestant rate only exceeded the Catholic rate by a narrow margin in embezzlement and by a slightly higher margin in "Violation of the Lord's Day Regulations." Although Catholics appeared to be more likely to commit a crime than Protestants in all other types of offenses, it was in violent offenses such as assault and battery and homicide that the Catholic preponderance was most striking. In Table 5.6, the Catholic rate of assault and battery was nearly twice that of Protestants; and, in Table 5.7, once we adjust for the roughly two-to-one majority of Protestants to Catholics, we find that the Catholics once again had about twice the rate of the Protestants in homicide offenses, a ratio that will be sustained in the victimological figures presented later in this chapter.

Though some of the difference between the two religious groups might be explained by the contemporary criminologist Gustav Aschaffenburg's contention that it was because "the material circumstances of Catholics in general are less than those of Protestants,"[50] not all of it is explained by pointing to material circumstances alone. One suspects that the government's biased view of the Slavic population, which composed a considerable amount of the Catholic population in Germany, especially in the notoriously high-crime areas of the Prussian northeast, may have accounted for much of this difference. Although one cannot help bristling at the racist conception of these people being labeled "culturally not so highly developed," there does seem to be some cultural component to criminality.[51] Indeed, scholars from Durkheim to modern-day criminologists like Marvin Wolfgang have argued that criminality is at least in part a learned behavior, and that "cultures of violence" do indeed exist.[52] In that the Catholic rate of crime was also somewhat higher than the Protestant rate in areas like Bavaria, which did not have high concentrations of non-German ethnic populations, and that the differences were most notable in violent offenses, one must recognize that religion was indeed a significant factor in differentiating criminal offenders from law-abiding citizens. But with so many ethnic biases, racial stereotypes, political divisions, and social and economic factors at work in a society like Imperial Germany, one certainly cannot point the finger of blame at any one religious group. In sum, one would do well to agree with the prudent criminologist Hermann Mannheim that "it is not the denomination as such but certain socio-economic and cultural factors, possibly associated with it, which influence criminality."[53]

SOCIAL STANDING/OCCUPATION

Germans did not hesitate to point the finger of blame, however, and this was especially true in regard to social standing, the last demographic factor to be considered before turning to a discussion of the victims of criminal activity. Although it will be of some interest to determine to what extent the conservative upper classes or the socialist working classes were correct in pointing the finger of blame at each other, what is of most concern here is to see to what extent the urban and industrial advances of Imperial Germany were

---

50 Aschaffenburg, *Crime and Its Repression*, p. 58.
51 For a quantitative treatment of the relationship among poverty, ethnicity, and criminality in Imperial Germany, see Eric A. Johnson, "The Roots of Crime in Imperial Germany," *Central European History* 15 (1982), esp. 366–73.
52 See, for example, the by now classic study of Marvin Wolfgang, *Patterns in Criminal Homicide* (New York, 1966).
53 Mannheim, *Comparative Criminology*, p. 572.

Table 5.8 *Occupational Classifications of German Workers, 1882–1907 (In Thousands)*

Year	Agriculture, Forestry, Husbandry, and Fishing			Industry, Mining, and Construction		
	M	F	T	M	F	T
1882	5,702	2,535	8,237	5,230	1,023	6,253
1895	5,540	2,753	8,293	6,694	1,397	8,091
1907	5,284	4,599	9,883	9,043	1,942	10,985
Year	Trade and Commerce			Services			Other		
	M	F	T	M	F	T	M	F	T
1882	1,101	190	1,291	1,173	443	1,616	168	67	235
1895	1,598	318	1,916	1,596	745	2,341	150	51	210
1907	2,234	592	2,826	1,907	1,069	2,976	114	42	156

Note: These figures are adapted from Brian Mitchell, *European Historical Statistics,* p. 164.

accompanied by changes in the social class and occupational standing of criminals.

Table 5.8 provides information that enables us to determine the percentage of criminal convictions for "All Crimes" and for six important individual offenses that were attributable to seven different occupational classifications of German citizens. By comparing these figures with the respective percentage of the population that fell into each of these occupational classifications (listed at the bottom of the table), it is possible to make some statements both about what kinds of workers were likely to commit (or at least to be prosecuted for) what types of crimes, and about whether or not urban–industrial growth and change had anything to do with the criminal trends. One must be warned, however, always to bear in mind the changes in the work force over time and the male to female ratio in each occupational category. These important considerations are treated in the subsequent Table 5.9, which breaks down the work force by major occupational category for the three occupational census years of Imperial Germany: 1882, 1895, and 1907.

Simply by looking at the figures for "All Crimes," one immediately sees that the largest amount of criminal activity in Imperial Germany might be attributed to the working classes, not only in absolute, but also in relative terms. Workers, or rather assistants, as they were classified by the German occupational census takers, in the major job categories, and workmen in unspecified trades were the only ones to account for a proportion of crimes that significantly exceeded their proportion in the general population. Furthermore, industrial workers were markedly more crime-prone, it appears,

Table 5.9 *Occupations and Crime in Two Periods, 1890-1894, 1904-1906*

Type	Agriculture, Forestry, Hunting, and Fishing			Industry, Mining, and Construction			Trade and Commerce		
	I	A	R	I	A	R	I	A	R
All crimes									
1890–4	4.7	18.4	2.3	6.9	30.4	4.4	5.7	5.8	1.2
1904–6	3.7	14.5	1.6	6.4	36.2	4.7	7.7	8.7	1.3
Theft									
1990–4	2.4	23.4	3.4	2.3	28.8	6.4	1.4	5.4	1.1
1904–6	2.1	17.7	2.4	1.6	32.9	8.1	1.4	8.5	1.3
Embezzlement									
1890–4	2.3	15.4	1.4	6.7	31.8	3.9	4.6	12.8	.82
1904–6	1.5	10.6	.70	4.6	36.8	4.4	4.5	19.6	1.0
Fraud									
1890–4	2.4	19.0	1.2	6.2	31.6	2.8	8.4	10.1	.78
1904–6	1.7	11.9	.84	4.3	31.5	2.8	6.9	13.8	.80
Resisting officers									
1890–4	2.9	11.9	.89	5.2	46.3	1.4	3.8	7.2	.39
1904–6	1.6	8.0	.44	3.2	51.9	1.1	3.4	10.5	.32
Aggravated assault and battery									
1890–4	5.1	25.9	1.4	5.2	41.3	2.3	2.9	3.9	.52
1904–6	4.4	21.8	1.2	4.1	48.3	2.8	3.1	5.2	.50
Homicide[a]									
1882–4	6.1	22.5	2.2	6.4	32.0	2.5	1.9	3.3	.33
1904–6	2.2	20.8	1.1	3.4	49.5	2.5	.37	3.9	.25
% of Adult Population in 1895 Census	7.0	15.6	1.2	5.6	17.0	14.5	2.3	4.1	4.6

Note: All figures represent percentages of convicted persons in each respective category. The 1890–4 figures are adapted from Gustav Aschaffenburg, *Crime and Its Repression*, p. 66; the 1904–6 figures have been computed from figures in *STDR*, vol. 164, 176, and 189.

[a] Homicide includes both *Mord* and *Totschlag*. The 1882–4 figures come from *STDR*, vol. NF8, NF13, and NF18.

Key: I = Independents, A = Assistants, R = Relatives, AE = Actively Engaged.

than agricultural workers; and workers in heavy industry, mining, and the building trades were the most crime-prone of all. The exception were workmen in unspecified trades, whose crime rates were not just twice what one would expect from their percentage of the population, as was the case with the industrial workers, but who were actually closer to twenty times as likely to commit a crime, or at least to be caught and convicted for a crime, than the rest of the population. Aschaffenburg, who originally compiled

Public Service and Professions		Domestic Servants		Workmen, without Specification		Trade, Unspecified	
AE	R	AE	R	AE	R	AE	R
1.3	.17	1.6	.02	10.4	1.8	4.6	.27
1.4	.14	1.5	.01	9.0	1.2	3.6	.35
.54	.15	4.3	.04	15.0	3.5	1.3	.45
.69	.17	4.9	.01	11.1	2.7	1.1	.43
1.7	.15	2.3	.01	12.7	1.7	1.5	.20
2.0	.11	1.8	.01	10.5	1.3	1.5	.19
2.1	.13	3.1	.01	9.6	.01	1.4	.16
2.1	.15	2.5	.01	7.2	.51	1.4	.17
.96	.07	.30	.003	15.8	.54	2.2	.11
.97	.05	.25	—	15.7	.37	2.1	.11
.62	.07	.22	.02	8.6	.91	.9	.13
.40	.07	.23	—	7.7	.66	1.2	.15
1.2	—	5.5	—	10.8	.88	3.3	.22
.99	—	2.1	—	.83	.25	1.5	.25
2.2	1.8	4.3	.2	.6	.4	5.8	1.9

much of this information, took pains to point out that there was obviously a great deal of tension between the authorities and the workers.[54] This is made

---

[54] Aschaffenburg, p. 65. Blasius treats this theme in depth throughout his *Kriminalität und Alltag* and also in several of his other works. See his *Bürgerliche Gesellschaft und Kriminalität: Zur Sozialgeschichte Preussens in Vormärz* (Göttingen, 1976) and *Geschichte der politischen Kriminalität in Deutschland (1800–1980)* (Frankfurt am Main, 1983). The struggle of the workers against the authorities in nineteenth-century Germany has been the subject of a great deal of historical writing in recent years. For some examples, see Klaus Saul, *Staat, Industrie, Arbeiterbewegung im Kaiserreich* (Düsseldorf, 1974); Richard Tilly, *Kapital, Staat and Sozialer Protest in der deutschen Industrialisierung* (Göttingen, 1980); R. Witz, "*Widersetzlichkeiten, Excesse, Crawalle, Tumulte und Skandale*": *Soziale Bewegung und gewalthafter sozialer Protest in Baden 1815–1848* (Frankfurt am Main, 1981); and J. Bergmann and H. Volkmann, eds., *Sozialer Protest: Studien zu traditionaler Resistenz und Kollektiver Gewalt in Deutschland vom Vormärz bis zur Reichsgründung* (Opladen, 1984). A useful English-language survey of much of this writing is found in Richard J. Evans, "In Pursuit of the *Untertanengeist*: Crime, Law and Social Order in German History," in Evans, ed., *Rethinking German History*, pp. 156–87. For an intriguing documentary history of many instances of working-class hostility toward the police and justice authorities, see Richard J. Evans, ed., *Kneipengespräche im Kaiserreich: Stimmungsberichte der Hamburger Politischen Polizei 1892–1914* (Hamburg, 1989), esp. pp. 182–242.

evident by the figures for the offense of resisting officers, in which the workers had their highest rates of criminality, though this tension must have been greatest among industrial workers and workers without a trade, for they accounted for approximately two-thirds of the convictions even though they comprised only about one-sixth of the working population. Although tension between the authorities and the workers might account for some of the high crime rate of the German workers, it seems a bit implausible that it would account for all or even most of it. Hence, before one concludes too quickly that workers were by nature prone to crime, or that they had high crime rates because they often ran afoul of the police and other authorities, one might better look at an even more convincing explanation for their high crime rates, which is based on gender.

One ascertains in Table 5.9 that women always made up a sizable proportion of the agricultural work force, and by 1907 this proportion almost equaled that of men. But in the prime working-class occupations of industry, mining and construction, women made up a maximum of less than 20 percent of the work force. Given that it has already been established that women committed only a small fraction of all crimes, the major reason urban and industrial workers appear to have had higher crime rates than rural and agricultural workers was not because of their urban or industrial employment but because of the fact that men dominated in urban and industrial jobs and not in agricultural ones. Although we do not have optimal figures to prove this, as the German census materials make such figures well-nigh impossible to obtain and compute, it seems logical to conclude that industrial workers were probably not significantly more crime-prone than most other German workers, even though the government was particularly keen to use the justice system to keep them in check. To be sure, well-to-do owners in industry and farming and members of the liberal professions had lower crime rates on average than the less well-to-do run of agricultural and industrial laborers, but that is to be expected in any society. Nonetheless, these figures do appear to support the contention of the socialist newspaper *Vorwärts* that true socialists were not likely to be criminals.[55] Additional support for this argument found in these figures is that gender as an intervening variable could be used to explain away virtually all of the apparent differences in the crime rates of different occupational classifications except for workers without a specified trade, and these "lumpen proletarians" were generally people who were unlikely to be socialist party members.[56]

55   *Vorwärts*, May 29, 1878.
56   For a discussion of Marxist theory and criminality, see David Greenberg, ed., *Crime and Capitalism: Readings in Marxist Criminology* (Palo Alto, Calif., 1981).

The great importance of gender again comes into play when one considers the question of whether the advance of German industry had anything to do with causing criminal activity. At least some German contemporaries, like Wilhelm Starke, did not think it did. Starke argued in 1884, in his volume on German crime trends between 1855 and 1878, that his evidence showed there was actually a decline in criminality among the working class.[57] But his figures were based upon only the most serious crimes tried before jury courts; so it is indeed possible that workers' crime rates were increasing in lesser offenses. Furthermore, the greatest industrial advances in Germany took place after Starke wrote; so even if workers were not committing more crimes during the period he studied, they might have done so later. Our evidence, however, does not support such an eventuality. True, the percentage of all crimes committed by heavy industrial laborers increased from 30.4 in the early 1890s to 36.2 in the early 1900s, and this admittedly does represent a 19 percent growth in only slightly more than a decade of rapid urban and industrial expansion. But the industrial work force actually grew at a much more rapid rate during this period than the percentage of crimes for which it accounted. Between the census years of 1895 and 1907, the industrial work force grew from about 8.1 million to nearly 11 million employees, and this represented an increase of nearly 36 percent. Hence, on their face, these figures show that the working class did not become more crime-prone in Imperial Germany, and this squares with what the contemporary scholar Wilhelm Starke argued for the period immediately prior to it. And one of the most salient reasons for this was likely that women became ever more a part of the work force, a situation that was even more noticeable in agricultural labor than in heavy industry, and thus a plausible reason for the decline in the percentage of crimes committed by agricultural workers noted in Table 5.8 between the 1890s and the early 1900s.

What all of this demonstrates is that a more urban and industrialized Germany was not a more crime-ridden Germany. We know this already from our prior discussion of long-term trends and of urban–rural differences in the previous two chapters, but here we see that the growth of the working class which accompanied the urban-industrial advance did not bring in its wake higher amounts of criminal activity, even though the government frequently launched the criminal justice system against its socialist enemies. Just as the Socialist Party leaders and newspapers argued, solid members of the working class were no more apt to be criminals than other German

57 Starke, *Verbrechen und Verbrecher*, pp. 215–18.

citizens, and it was only lumpen proletarians who had extraordinarily high crime rates that demographic factors could not explain away.

Part II: The Demography of Murder Victims

Although the rate of different types of unlawful activity and much of the criminals' demographic patterns were not greatly affected by the urban and industrial changes, there may still be some reason not to consign all arguments concerning socioeconomic change to the dust heap of worn-out fads in modern historiography.[58] For, as has been shown, and will be dealt with more fully in the discussion of victimological trends, arguments that focus directly on the changing status of women in urbanizing and industrializing society, and how this affected criminological and victimological trends, can have explanatory power. Hence, the focus of the following discussion of victimological patterns in Imperial Germany will be on the differential impact that urban development and socioeconomic change had on females and males. Unfortunately, the only plentiful source of data pertaining to victims available comes from coroners' reports. So the discussion will only pertain directly to a circumscribed set of victims and, furthermore, will be limited both geographically to the state of Prussia and demographically to age, religion, and marital status.[59] Nonetheless, even with these limited data, though added to in part by some correlation analyses of social and economic variables provided by the census data, the picture that emerges is an ominous one for women. For if modernization usually entails the emancipation of women in the workplace, the family, and eventually in political life as well, it may also, as these German data show, entail some very grave risks to women's security.

Hence, if Germans had little need to worry about women as criminal offenders, this does not mean that they did not have to worry about them as the victims of criminal wrongdoing, particularly where heinous criminal activities such as homicide were involved. The record left by contemporary German writers and journalists, in fact, shows that Germans were particularly concerned about female homicide victims. Whereas the homicide of a man was usually given only a few scant lines in any German newspaper, it

---

58 Surveying the recent trends in historical writing, Konrad Jarausch states: "Hailed as brilliant insights a generation earlier, such terms as 'class struggle' or 'modernization' only evoke a tired smile in the late 1980s." Konrad H. Jarausch, "Towards a Social History of Experience: Postmodern Predicaments in Theory and Interdisciplinarity," *Central European History* 22 (1989): 432.
59 The coroners' data are found in yearly volumes of the Prussian government's series *Preussische Statistik* under the title of *Die Sterblichkeit*.

was not rare to see huge and lurid stories whenever a woman was killed.[60] German society's concern over the role females played as homicide victims seemed justified when the first empirical study of murder victims was published in 1938. In his "Mörder und ihre Opfer," E. Roesner examined all murder trials that ended in convictions in the years between 1928 and 1930.[61] In these trials the murderers were overwhelmingly male, but the victims were more often than not female. Thus, of 169 convicted murderers, 151, or 89.3 percent, were male and only eighteen, or 10.7 percent, were female; but of the 187 murder victims only 81, or 43.8 percent, were male, and 106, or 56.7 percent, were female. Thus it appeared that German women were much more likely than German men to become victims of homicide.

In 1948 a German criminologist, Hans von Hentig, was the first to put crime victims into theoretical perspective.[62] In his work *The Criminal and His Victim,* Hentig offered a general typology of people most likely to become victims and their psychological traits. Of the major types of people apt to become victims, "The Female" came second only after "The Young" and preceded "The Old," the "Mentally Defective and Other Mentally Deranged," and "Immigrants, Minorities, and Dull Normals."[63] According to Hentig, what related women to these other groups and made all these people especially good victims, specifically in homicide cases, was weakness. Although he admitted that women's physical weakness vis-à-vis men was not a real issue,[64] his discussion of the psychological traits of victims and his very limited statistical data made it apparent that he believed women were likely to become homicide victims because they were psychologically weak (of course, he has no meaningful data to support this assertion), and weaker than men in social and economic position.[65]

Although I do not dispute that German women were in a relatively weaker social and economic position than men,[66] and even though Hentig's argument that people in a weak position are easy prey makes some intuitive sense, the evidence to be put forward does not support him. In addition to

---

60 As explained in Chapter 2, the murder of women was a popular theme in literary treatments of criminal justice issues as well. Besides the works of Rudolf Schenda and Rolf Engelsing cited in that chapter, see, for example, H.-O. Hügel, *Untersuchungsrichter-Diebfänger-Detektive: Theorie und Geschichte der deutschen Detektiverzählung im 19. Jahrhundert* (Stuttgart, 1978).
61 E. Roesner, "Mörder und ihre Opfer," *Monatsschrift für Kriminalbiologie und Strafrechtreform* 29 (1938): 161–85, 209–28.
62 Hentig, *The Criminal and His Victim.*
63 Ibid., 404–19.
64 Ibid., 407.
65 Ibid., 390–404, 419–38.
66 See note 16 above.

disagreeing with his obvious sexist bias, I have to take issue with him at an even more basic level, for my data show that men were actually much more likely to be murder victims in Imperial Germany than women. Assuming that he would never allow that men were therefore weaker than women, how then could Hentig sustain the argument that weakness invited victimization and that women were more often victims than men? He was able to do this because he used a previous, supposedly pioneering, study written by the well-placed and highly informed Berlin justice official Roesner as his evidentiary base. But how could Roesner, whose study was presumably objective and unbiased even though it was written in 1938, have been so wrong as to not even get straight who the murderers and who the victims were in the more democratic Weimar years? The reason was not Nazi bias; rather, it was because he used the wrong figures.

By basing their arguments on court statistics, both Roesner and Hentig were on shaky ground. German courts in both Imperial Germany and Weimar only prosecuted a small minority of murderers, and hence in using court statistics they were dealing with a small percentage of homicide victims. Furthermore, it is very likely that their sample was an extremely biased one. Not only was it likely to be biased by *Klassenjustiz*, it probably suffered from gender bias as well. Given the great popular concern for female victims, it is reasonable to assume that the courts chose to prosecute cases of female homicides more vigorously than those of male homicides. For example, what if the victim died as a result of a heated dispute? Were it not highly likely that the courts would prosecute the murderer for a lesser charge if the victim was male than if she was female? Although I do not have direct evidence to prove conclusively that German courts acted in these ways, and this would make an excellent study in itself, several studies have shown that German courts in Imperial and Weimar Germany were increasingly trying people for milder offenses. The literary evidence in Chapter 2 adds to a considerable volume of works pointing toward the administration of class-based justice in both periods, and, most importantly, the coroners' records I prefer to use make it plain that more men were killed than women. So discriminatory justice had to have been employed.[67]

Clearly, coroners' records tell a very different story than do court records.

---

[67] For discussions of the sentencing practices of German courts and how there was a pronounced trend toward convicting people for lighter offenses, see Franz Exner, *Studien über die Strafzumessungspraxis der deutschen Gerichte* (Leipzig, 1931), and Rupert Rabl, *Strafzumessungspraxis und Kriminalitäts – bewegung* (Leipzig, 1936). The ideological and class-based practices of German judges in the Weimar period are well known. See, for example, Ralph Angermund, *Deutsche Richterschaft 1919–1945. Krisenerfahrung, Illusion, politische Rechtspechung* (Frankfurt am Main, 1990).

Table 5.10 *Homicide Deaths and Homicide Convictions in Prussia and Berlin, 1873–1913*

| | Homicide Deaths[a] | | | |
| | Average Yearly Total | | Average Yearly Rate (Per Million Population) | |
Period	Prussia	Berlin	Prussia	Berlin
1873–84	478	13	17.5	10.2
1885–94	419	16	14.0	10.1
1895–1904	596	30	17.0	16.4
1905–13	779	38	19.4	18.3

| | Homicide Convictions[b] | | | |
| | Average Yearly Total | | Average Yearly Rate (Per Million Population) | |
Period	Prussia	Berlin	Prussia	Berlin
1873–84	182	4	6.7	3.2
1885–94	150	5	5.0	3.1
1895–1904	139	4	4.0	2.1
1905–13	169	8	4.2	3.8

[a] Based on coroners' reports.
[b] Based on court statistics.

In the figures listed in Table 5.10, the number of homicide convictions in Prussia was a small and declining fraction of the number of homicide deaths reported by German coroners. In the period between 1873 and 1884, there was an average of 478 homicide deaths reported each year, but there was an average of only 182 court convictions for homicide. Of course, it is possible that 182 murderers could kill 478 victims, but this is not likely given Roesner's figures, which showed that 169 murderers in the years between 1928 and 1930 killed only 187 victims. In the period between 1905 and 1913, the number of homicide victims reported by German coroners had risen to 779 per year, whereas the number of people convicted of homicide had declined to 169. Thus, over these years it appears that the actual number of homicides increased but the number of homicide convictions decreased; in the earlier period there were about three times more homicide cases reported by the coroners than there were court convictions for homicide, and in the later period the ratio had grown to about five to one. If a control for the growth of the population is established, one finds that the coroners' reports recorded an increase in the actual rate of homicide but the courts showed a decline. So which was it? I think it was on the rise.

By basing the argument on coroners' reports instead of on court records, one observes in Table 5.11 that German women in every year throughout the entire period of Imperial Germany were far less likely to be murdered than men. In the years between 1873 and 1907 there were 12,767 Prussian men murdered and only 5,052 women; in other words, men were murdered about two and one-half times more often than women. These figures are sufficient proof to call into question Hentig's entire argument that women are particularly suitable murder victims. The evidence presented below calls into question his argument for why this is so. That is, it challenges his argument that female weakness leads to homicide.

The evidence also calls into question some more recent arguments about homicide victims. Although few empirical, theoretical, or historical studies on homicide victims exist that have treated women or gender differences explicitly,[68] the few that do exist (mostly sociological works on American women since World War II) seem to agree on the theoretical premise that the more women (and presumably, but less so, men) are involved in what Durkheim referred to as "collective life," the more likely they are to be murdered. As Margaret Zahn, the author of several of these studies, put it: "Long-standing theory and recent research suggest that as people become more involved in collective life, their risks of becoming a homicide victim increase."[69] Unfortunately, what she means by "collective life" is not entirely clear, but I take it to mean life that involves intimate and frequent contact with family and friends, which Durkheim thought was more characteristic of traditional village and rural society than of the more anomic life of the metropolis. After demonstrating that, in Philadelphia between 1969 and 1973, a much larger proportion of women than men were killed in their homes and by their spouses, relatives, and friends, an observation that confirmed the figures Hentig provided in his discussion of murder victims, Zahn concluded that "traditional domestic, especially marital contexts, then, still prove the most lethal for women."[70]

Although my evidence does not permit me to say anything about who actually killed the women listed in the coroners' reports, and although I do not doubt that one would probably find that most of the women were killed by family and friends, it can be argued that Zahn's theoretical argument was no more supported by my data than was Hentig's. The data demonstrate that, by and large, German women were not in great danger of being murdered if they lived in "traditional domestic, especially marital contexts."

68 The closest thing to a truly historical study of female victims is Nancy Tome's article on interfamilial violence in working-class families in Victorian England: "'A Torrent of Abuse': Crimes of Violence between Working Class Men and Women in London, 1840–1875," *Journal of Social History* 11 (1978): 328–45.
69 Margaret A. Zahn, "The Female Homicide Victim," *Criminology* 13 (1975): 3–23.
70 Ibid., 413.

On the contrary, I find that German women who lived in the city were more likely to be murdered than women who lived in the countryside. Since one would expect that urban women were probably less involved in traditional domestic life than rural women, and probably more likely to be standing on their own and, in accord with Durkheim's classical argument to be more likely to be involved in "anomic" instead of "collective life," then there is even less reason to support Zahn's, Durkheim's, or Hentig's theoretical positions.

Rather, what I find is that the more traditional the life circumstances of German females, the less likely they were to become murder victims. I also find that the patterns of female homicide victims were very different from the patterns of male homicide victims to whom the collective-life argument might possibly apply (Durkheim did not control for gender differences): Rural married women were in less danger than urban single women. As more women entered the work force in Imperial Germany, more of them moved into urban areas away from traditional domestic settings and probably became stronger, not weaker, in a social and economic sense.[71] But more women were also killed. Although the rate of men who were murdered showed some increase during this period of tremendous urban growth and industrial expansion, the male victim rate did not increase nearly as rapidly as the female rate, and the urban setting along with the growing urbanization of society did not seem to put men in more danger. Nevertheless, men were always in more danger than women. What seemed to make the most difference for men was the religious background from which they came; Catholic men were in greater jeopardy than Protestant or Jewish men. Religion, however, did not seem to make much difference for females.

URBANIZATION, ETHNICITY, AND RELIGION

One observes in Tables 5.11 and 5.12 that men were murdered far more often in Imperial Germany than women; but, with the passage of time, women represented a somewhat higher percentage of all people killed. In the 1870s and 1880s, women usually comprised about 25 percent of the total number of people murdered, but later, women often made up more than 30 percent. For both males and females there was no tremendous growth, however, in their victim rates until after the mid-1890s. After the mid-1880s especially, there was a rapid urban growth, and the changing ratio of women's to men's homicides seems to have been associated with the process

---

71 See Patricia Branca, *Women in Europe since 1870* (New York, 1978), esp. pp. 47–51.

Table 5.11 *Homicide Deaths by Gender in Prussia and Berlin, 1873-1914*

Year	Prussia					Berlin		
	Total	Male	%Male	Female	%Female	Total	Male	Female
1873	516	394	76	122	24	9	6	3
1874	556	424	76	132	24	2	1	1
1875	547	386	71	161	29	24	5	19
1876	471	357	76	114	24	10	6	4
1877	543	416	77	127	23	22	11	11
1878	471	354	75	117	25	9	6	3
1879	455	341	75	114	25	2	1	1
1880	470	340	72	130	28	7	2	5
1881	432	299	69	133	31	8	2	6
1882	444	328	74	116	26	21	11	10
1883	406	281	69	125	31	12	7	5
1884	419	298	71	121	29	13	6	7
1885	446	340	76	126	24	10	4	6
1886	432	307	71	124	29	12	4	8
1887	374	258	69	116	31	17	10	7
1888	377	264	70	113	30	23	15	8
1889	320	215	67	105	33	11	7	4
1890	275	191	69	84	31	20	9	11
1891	442	298	67	144	33	24	13	11
1892	485	365	75	121	25	17	9	8
1893	516	358	69	158	31	12	5	7
1894	517	374	72	143	28	18	10	8
1895	471	324	69	147	31	17	10	7
1896	587	429	73	158	27	27	13	14
1897	524	365	70	159	30	28	7	21
1898	534	381	71	153	29	17	7	10
1899	569	441	77	128	23	29	16	13
1900	684	493	72	191	28	27	15	12
1901	664	497	75	167	25	46	31	15
1902	580	410	71	170	29	27	14	13
1903	691	473	68	218	32	39	20	19
1904	708	524	74	185	26	38	21	17
1905	697	486	70	211	30	41	23	18
1906	696	491	71	205	29	33	11	22
1907	788	574	73	214	27	41	20	21
1908	?	?	?	?	?	?	?	?
1909	?	?	?	?	?	?	?	?
1910	800	570	71	230	29	?	?	?
1911	?	?	?	?	?	?	?	?
1912	804	533	66	271	34	?	?	?
1913	889	609	68	285	32	?	?	?
1914	1,459	1,094	75	365	25	?	?	?
Totals (through 1907)	17,819	12,767	72	5,052	28	713	358	355

Table 5.12 *Periodic Homicide Death Rates in Prussia and Berlin, 1873-1914*

	Prussia							
		Average Yearly Total					Average Yearly Total (Per Million)	
Period	Total	Male	%Male	Female	%Female		Male	Female
1873–82	460	333	72.4	127	27.6		26.2	9.7
1883–92	400	282	70.5	118	29.5		20.2	8.1
1893–1902	564	407	72.2	157	27.8		26.0	9.6
1903–14	836	594	71.1	242	28.9		32.2	12.8
	Berlin							
		Average Yearly Total					Average Yearly Total (Per Million)	
Period	Total	Male	%Male	Female	%Female		Male	Female
1873–82	11	5	45.5	6	54.5		10.2	12.4
1883–92	15	8	53.3	7	46.7		12.6	10.2
1893–1902	25	13	52.0	12	48.0		16.0	13.6
1903–14	38	19	50.0	19	50.0		19.2	18.3

of urbanization. The more urbanized Germany became, the more females vis-à-vis males were murdered. Why the victim rates of both males and females grew so dramatically after the mid-1890s, however, is certainly not clear. One possible explanation is that the murder rate corresponded with changes in the business cycle. After the mid-1890s, the long depression in agricultural prices ended and there was a rising trend in the prices of nearly all commodities. Although there are various arguments and counterarguments about what the impact of this was on people's real wages,[72] the inflationary price trend in the late 1890s and continuing on to the war must have hurt many people and this may have resulted in more murders. One thing is certain, the victim rate of females was rising much more rapidly than that of males. Whereas the male victim rate grew by only about 23 percent, the female victim rate grew by about 33 percent; this is true either when one compares the decade of the mid-1870s to the mid-1880s with the last decade of Imperial Germany, or when one compares this last decade with the one immediately preceding it (see Table 5.12). Therefore, these figures seem to show that women were more affected than men by the changes in the business cycle and by the process of urbanization.

---

72 For a discussion of many of these arguments, see Frank E. Tipton, *Regional Variations in the Economic Development of Germany During the Nineteenth Century* (Middletown, Conn., 1976), pp. 42–44. The most detailed discussion of prices and wages, though, is found in Gerhard Bry, *Wages in Germany, 1871–1945* (Princeton, N.J., 1960).

The figures in Tables 5.11 and 5.12 also demonstrate some marked differences between Berlin and the rest of Prussia in the patterns of male and female homicide deaths. Whereas Berlin females were in far greater danger than females in the rest of Prussia, Berlin males were actually much less likely to be murdered than males elsewhere. In all of Prussia, as was shown earlier, males were roughly two and one-half times as likely to be murdered as females; but, in Berlin, males and females had almost exactly the same chance of being murdered. Between 1873 and 1907, only three more males were murdered than females, 358 to 355. When one controls for the male and female population, the figures reveal that, in Berlin in the period between 1903 and 1914, the yearly male murder death rate was 19.2 per million males and the female rate was 18.3 per million females; in the rest of Prussia the male rate, however, was much higher and the female rate much lower (32.2 to 12.8). Therefore, as Berlin was the largest city in Prussia, these figures strongly suggest that the urban woman was in far more peril than her rural counterpart, but that urban environments were relatively safe for men.[73]

Another way to demonstrate the important differences between urban and rural settings in the homicide deaths of females and males is to employ the results of a correlation analysis (see Table 5.13). In this analysis, the rates of male and female homicide victims, in the period 1904–6, for each of Prussia's *Regierungsbezirke,* are correlated with various social and economic indicators.[74] With the exception of Berlin, all of these districts contained both rural and urban areas. For each district, a rate for urban population was computed by dividing the number of inhabitants in the district's cities of more than 20,000 by the total number of inhabitants of the district. Some districts, like those in the Prussian northeast, had urban rates that were less than 25 percent; but others, like Berlin, Cologne, and Düsseldorf, had rates higher than 50 percent. The remaining districts fell between these extremes. When one compares the correlations between the male and female victim

---

73 Though the coroners' data are not perfect for the task, additional support for this supposition is found by examining the breakdown of the female homicides by their or their family's chief occupation. In 1905 and 1906, for example, of a total of 416 female homicides in the state of Prussia, only 83 were of women who were listed as being involved in agriculture, forestry, husbandry, or fishing. This is considerably below what one would expect for women associated with such nonurban pursuits. Men involved in such occupations, however, had a greater chance of being murdered. Thus, of 977 male homicides in Prussia between 1905 and 1906, 248 were ascribed to these occupations. Hence over one-quarter of Prussian male homicides and only one-fifth of female homicides were of people in what can loosely be described as agricultural pursuits. These figures are found in *Preussische Statistik* 199 (1907): 206–8, and (1908): 208–10.

74 I use *Regierungsbezirke* as the level of analysis because there are so few female homicide deaths that correlation figures would be meaningless for lower levels of aggregation.

Table 5.13 *Zero-Order Correlations between Men's and Women's Homicide Rates and Socioeconomic Variables in Prussia, 1904–06*

Dependent Variable	Men's Rate	% Urban Population	Wealth (Income Tax)	Ethnicity	% Catholic
Women's Rate	.25	.36	.48	-.13	.10
Men's Rate	—	-.20	-.06	.29	.64

Note: The units of analysis are the 36 Prussian *Regierungsbezirke*.

% Urban Pop. = Number of inhabitants living in cities over 20,000 people per *Regierungsbezirk*.
Wealth = Income tax paid per capita.
Ethnicity = Percent of population listing their mother language as other than German.

rates and the rates of urban population, one finds a stark contrast. The rate of urban population showed a mild but still significant correlation with the female victim rate ($r = .36$), but a negative, though weaker, correlation with the male rate ($r = -.20$). These correlations are not terribly strong, but they do add support to the contention that the urban environment posed a greater danger to women than to men.

Other significant differences between the homicide deaths of males and females come into view when one considers wealth, ethnic, and religious factors relating to homicide deaths. The correlations show that women were more often murdered in wealthier districts ($r = .48$) than in poorer ones, but that the wealth of a district made no difference in the homicide patterns for males ($r = .06$). This, of course, does not mean that wealthy women were murdered more often than poor women; but it does mean that women who resided in relatively poor communities were probably in less danger of being murdered than women who lived in richer ones. Whereas communities with a large number of ethnic inhabitants in Germany (mainly Poles and Lithuanians) have been shown elsewhere to have had particularly high rates of crime, the ethnic homogeneity or heterogeneity had no significant influence on the homicide deaths of females.[75] The negative sign of the correlation coefficient even suggests that the greater the ethnic concentration of a community the less the danger of homicide for females. But the ethnicity of the community had a different effect on the homicide of males; the positive correlation ($r = .29$) between the male homicide rate and the percentage of ethnic inhabitants in a district demonstrates that the more ethnic the community was, the greater the number of homicide deaths of male inhabitants. Even more significant in differentiating female from male patterns is the

---

75 Johnson, "The Roots of Crime."

Table 5.14 *Homicide Victims by Religion and Gender in Prussia, 1904–06*

Religion	Male	Male Yearly Rate (Per Million Males)	Female	Female Yearly Rate (Per Million Females)	Female as % of Males
Protestant	704	21.5	320	9.8	.45
Catholic	682	37.5	188	10.3	.28
Jewish	10	17.0	3	5.1	.30
Unknown	105	——	90	——	.86

religion of the community. The strong positive correlation between the male rate and the percentage of Catholics in a district makes it plain that Catholic communities were often quite dangerous places for German males. The religion of the district did not, however, have much of an influence on female homicide deaths.

The importance of religious differences in the patterns of male and female homicide deaths comes into greater relief with the information presented in Table 5.14. In this table, all known homicide victims in Prussia between 1904 and 1906 are classified by gender and religion. Here one finds that slightly more Protestant males were murdered than Catholic males (704 to 682), and that many more Protestant females were murdered than Catholic ones (320 to 188). In the case of Jewish people, there were almost no murders of either males or females. When one considers that Protestants made up about two-thirds of all Prussians, and that Catholics made up almost all of the other third, with Jews and other religions comprising less than 2 percent of the Prussian population, one begins to appreciate the great differences that religion made for the male population. As the correlation figures suggest and these figures confirm, Catholic males were the most likely people to be murdered in German society.[76] With a yearly homicide death rate of 37.5 Catholic men per million, Catholic men were about twice as likely to be murdered as Protestant or Jewish men (their rates were 21.5 and 17.0, respectively), who were themselves between two and four times as likely to be murdered as any type of woman. Again, as the correlation figures suggest, Catholic and Protestant females were murdered in about the same

[76] Emile Durkheim argued that Catholics had higher homicide rates than Protestants in both Germany and other countries in the nineteenth century. Using conviction statistics, he pointed out that predominantly Catholic countries like Italy and Spain had homicide rates of approximately seventy per million inhabitants, but that Protestant-dominated countries like Germany, England, and Denmark had homicide rates of only about three per million inhabitants. Durkheim, *Suicide, A Study in Sociology*, trans. John A. Spaulding and George Simpson (New York, 1951), p. 353.

proportion to the total number of Catholic females or Protestant females in the country (the Catholic female rate was 10.3, the Protestant female rate 9.8). One also observes that Catholic women were in far less danger of being murdered than their men, as more than three times as many Catholic men were murdered than women. Protestant women, on the other hand, had more parity with their men, in that only about two Protestant men for every Protestant woman were murdered.[77]

AGE AND MARITAL STATUS

Age and marital status are other factors that had borne heavily upon homicide deaths. Table 5.15 compares the male and female homicide deaths of infants and people over age one in Prussia and Berlin in two separate five-year periods, 1887–91 and 1902–7. In both periods, both in Prussia and in Berlin, female infants made up a large but declining proportion of all female homicide deaths. In the years 1887–91, over half of all female homicide deaths in Berlin were infants (56.1 percent) and, in the same period, infants comprised nearly half of all female homicide deaths in Prussia (42.2 percent). But after the turn of the century, the percentage of female infant homicide deaths had dropped in Berlin to 40 percent and in Prussia to 34.8 percent. In that it has already been established that the overall female homicide rate had increased markedly in the later period, these figures demonstrate that German society was clearly becoming more dangerous for adult women as time went on. This was true also in the case of men, as the percentage of homicide deaths made up of infants in both Berlin and Prussia was declining over time as well. With the exception of Berlin, this was not quite so important a development for males as it was for females, however, as a much smaller proportion of male homicide deaths was made up of infants (22.6 percent in the earlier period and 15.7 percent in the later).

In Table 5.16, one can determine at which ages males and females were murdered, and how age made a major difference between the sexes. As children, males and females shared a nearly equal chance of being murdered; for very young children this danger was extremely great. Between the ages of five and fifteen, however, not many children of either sex were murdered.

77 When one compares the murder rates of females in different parts of Germany, it turns out that areas with mostly Catholic inhabitants had much higher male than female homicide rates. Between 1904 and 1906, there were 41 men murdered in Westphalia but only 9 women; in Posen there were 29 men murdered and 9 women. In Protestant areas, the rate of female homicide deaths was much closer to that of male homicide deaths. Thus, in Schleswig-Holstein in the years between 1904 and 1906, 16 males and 8 females were murdered. In Brandenburg, 20 males and 11 females were murdered; and in Saxony 21 males and 14 females were murdered.

Table 5.15 *Children under One Year Old as Percentage of Homicide Victims in Prussia and Berlin in Two Periods, 1887–1891 and 1902–1907*

	Total Number of Homicides		Homicides of Children		Children as % of Total Homicides	
	Male	Female	Male	Female	Male	Female
Prussia						
1887–91	1,226	562	277	237	22.6	42.2
1902–07	2,958	1,203	465	419	15.7	34.8
Berlin						
1887–91	54	41	28	23	51.8	56.1
1902–7	109	110	38	44	34.8	40.0

Table 5.16 *Homicide Deaths by Age and Gender in Prussia, 1904–06*

Age	Male	Female	Female as % of Male
0–5	291	234	80
5–10	27	28	104
10–15	14	18	129
15–20	120	44	37
20–25	223	58	26
25–30	230	39	17
30–40	268	49	18
40–50	170	52	31
50–60	85	33	39
60–70	44	19	43
70–80	14	14	100
Over 80	14	12	86

Between the ages of fifteen and forty, males were increasingly in more danger of being murdered than females, but after this age women started to catch up with men once again. It was not until truly old age, however, that women reached the parity with men that they had shared as children. These figures clearly show that, as young and middle-aged adults, women were far safer from being murdered than men, but that as infants and old people, women received no preferential treatment.

The figures in Table 5.17 relate to the influence that marriage had on the homicide death rate of Prussian females. They suggest that marriage was in fact not the type of lethal context for women that some people have argued. On the contrary, they demonstrate that marriage served to protect women from harm. Most women married sometime in their twenties: between the ages of twenty and twenty-five slightly more than a quarter of all women

Table 5.17 *Female Homicide Deaths, by Marital Status and Age in Prussia, 1904-1906*

Age	%Married	%Single	N of Homicides Married	N of Homicides Single	% of Homicides Married	Hom. Rate Married	Hom. Rate Single	Hom. Rate[a] All Women
15-20	0.7	99.3	6	38	13.6	77.6	4.0	4.6
20-25	28.4	71.6	11	47	19.0	8.1	13.8	12.4
25-30	64.5	35.5	20	19	51.3	7.5	13.0	9.4
Over 30	87.2	12.3	106	20	84.1	7.6	11.6	8.0

Note: The homicide rate for widowed or divorced women was 11.9.

[a] Homicide rates are per million women per year.

were married; between the ages of twenty-five and thirty over two-thirds of all women were married; and eventually almost all women married. With the exception of the fifteen-to-twenty age group, when very few women were married, married women had considerably lower homicide death rates than did single women. If we recall the figures presented in Table 5.12, which showed that women of any age in this period had a homicide rate of 12.8 per million women, it turns out that married women over the age of twenty had lower rates of homicide than women in general. Married women between the ages of twenty and twenty-five had a homicide death rate of 8.1, but single women of this age group had a rate of 13.8. Between the ages of twenty-five and thirty, when most women were married, the married women's homicide rate was again only about one-half that of the single women's rate (7.5 to 13.0). After the age of thirty, when nearly 90 percent of women were married, the married women's rate was 7.6, whereas the single women's rate was 11.6.

Why young married women between the ages of fifteen and twenty diverged from this pattern by having much higher homicide death rates than single women in this age group is uncertain. A possible explanation might be that women were acting in an unorthodox way by getting married, and that their youth may have increased the strains of marriage. And, as is often the case with exceptionally young couples today, their family economy may have been quite precarious. Of course this is only conjecture; as there were only six married women who were murdered in this age group in these years, the extremely high rate of murder might have been an aberration. But if we take all of these results into consideration, it appears that women who followed the traditional pattern of getting married at a "normal" age seemed to be in less danger of being murdered than if they broke with tradition, either by getting married at a young age or by not getting married at all.

MEANS OF DEATH

Before concluding, there are a few interesting observations to be made about the means by which the victims were killed. The figures in Table 5.18 show that women were usually murdered by different means than were men, except when they were children. Most children of both sexes were murdered either by drowning, smothering, or, to a lesser extent, by poisoning or beating. Adult men were most often murdered by being stabbed or beaten. Adult women, on the other hand, were more than twice as likely to be shot as to be murdered by any other means; and if the example of Berlin was at all representative, it appears that urban woman were in particular danger of being shot. Note that, of the twenty-two women over the age of fifteen, between 1904 and 1906 in Berlin, fourteen were shot, only three were beaten to death, two had their throats slit, and no other means of murder accounted for more than one death. Of the twenty-four men over fifteen who were murdered in Berlin, however, only six were shot. Although in Prussia as a whole, more men were shot than women, less than one-half as many men were murdered by being shot as by being beaten, and less than one-third as many men were shot as stabbed to death. These findings might suggest that men were often killed in the course of some kind of struggle, but there may have been more intention involved in the murder of women.

CONCLUSION

Some important and interesting observations emerge from the preceding discussion. Above all, there is no reason to believe that women are particularly vulnerable, either because they are weak or because they often accept traditional social roles. Quite the opposite. The evidence presented here demonstrates that women were always less likely to be murdered than men and that the more traditional their social role, the safer they were. In an interesting study that treats interfamilial violence in Victorian England, Nancy Tomes argues that "in 1890, working-class women were far less likely to experience physical violence at the hands of a man than they were in 1840."[78] Her argument is that English working-class women had actually by that time experienced a decline in their economic and social status; but that they worked less often, and more frequently resigned themselves to traditional roles, thus acting subserviently to their men and allowing men to act as their protectors. If Tomes is correct, it appears that English women were like

78   Tomes, "A Torrent of Abuse," p. 342.

Table 5.18 *Means of Homicide by Gender in Prussia and Berlin, 1904-1906*

Means	Prussia				Berlin			
	All Homicides		Over Age 15		All Homicides		Over Age 15	
	Male	Female	Male	Female	Male	Female	Male	Female
Hanged	16	16	3	3	0	3	0	0
Strangled	64	60	11	31	4	1	0	0
Smothered	60	70	3	5	1	7	0	1
Drowned	93	60	9	6	8	5	0	0
Shot	169	120	156	108	7	16	6	14
Stabbed	497	54	491	47	8	2	7	2
Throat slit	25	35	13	24	0	2	0	1
Burned	1	3	1	2	0	0	0	0
Poisoned	23	23	4	0	6	8	1	0
Pushed down stairs	10	7	6	4	2	1	0	1
Beaten	382	84	357	65	6	3	6	3
Buried alive	4	4	0	0	0	0	0	0
Other means	61	19	38	9	2	1	0	0
Unknown	96	46	87	17	5	0	4	0

German women, in that women who accepted a traditional role were less likely to be harmed than women who did not.

At the beginning of this section on victims, it was stated that recent sociological studies of American women show that in the postwar period women who have accepted traditional roles are in the most danger of being victimized. But, throughout this section, it has been argued that women in Imperial Germany who broke with tradition were the ones in danger. How can these contradictory findings be reconciled? The answer may lie in what can be considered "traditional," or rather "normal" at a particular point in time. In the nineteenth and early twentieth century, it was considered traditional, or normal, for women to be married and not to work outside the home. In modern America, some may still consider it traditional and normal for women to be married and not to work outside the home. But with the current American divorce rate exceeding 50 percent and with the majority of women now working outside the home, clearly what is normal for women has greatly changed.[79] Hence, the present-day American woman who stays at home and attends to the family may be acting outside of societal

---

[79] For a historical perspective on the changing sexual, familial, and occupational norms for both women and men, see Lawrence Stone's review articles on "The Children and the Family" and on "Sexuality" in his *The Past and the Present Revisited* (London, 1987), pp. 311–26 and 344–82.

norms and thus putting herself in danger, whereas the situation in Imperial Germany was very much the opposite.

The case of German women, then, shows that women who broke with the norms of society – either by marrying too young, by staying single too long, or by moving out of the protective family environment and seeking employment (particularly in the city) – placed themselves in danger of being victimized. Although the norms for men were not always the same as they were for women, being outside of the norm, in reality or in the perception of others, was also dangerous for them. Many male and female foreigners, socialists, Jews, and other outsiders in modern German history have learned this lesson.

6

Conclusion: Crime Rates, Crime Theories, and German Society

This study of crime and criminal justice in Germany's Second Empire contributes to both historical sociology and social history. As a work of historical sociology, it employs the abundant social and economic statistical data of nineteenth- and early-twentieth-century Germany, buttressed by qualitative data generated from an analysis of popular perceptions of criminal justice activity and unlawful behavior, to test several important theories about the effects of urban–industrial development and societal modernization on the incidence of criminal activity. As a study of social history, it investigates the nature and values of the German criminal justice system and the ways in which the law and criminal justice institutions and practices were applied to uphold the social and political order. Whereas it demonstrates that the law, police, attorneys, and judges all rated high marks for technical expertise and high educational standards, and that their efforts helped to ensure that German society remained quite orderly, the often discriminatory justice they dispensed exhibited some disturbing parallels between the Kaiserreich and the Third Reich.

Imperial Germany, despite a trend toward increasing violence around the turn of the century, was one of the safest societies in modern history, with some of the lowest rates of interpersonal violence. This statement can be made with some confidence: Foreign travelers often remarked on how secure they felt in German cities; the contemporary sociologist Emile Durkheim found Germany and Holland to have the lowest homicide rates in Europe in the last decades of the nineteenth century; and our own more detailed examination of Germany's homicide rates can now be shown to have compared favorably with the rates of other countries, which recently have been reconstructed painstakingly by other criminal justice historians for countries like Sweden, Holland, England, and the United States.

Although they, like all crime statistics, are not without problems, murder rates are generally regarded as the most trustworthy measures of criminal activity to use when comparing levels of crime among different countries, or even among different communities and time periods in the same country. In Germany's largest state of Prussia, the annual murder rate (including both premeditated and unpremeditated murder) fluctuated between circa four and six murders per million population between the 1880s and the eve of the world war, if one uses conviction statistics as a measure, and circa twelve and twenty, if one uses the more accurate measures based on coroners' statistics. And in Germany's largest city, Berlin, and in other major cities as well, there were years with no, or nearly no, convictions for homicide; and the annual homicide conviction rate, computed in five-year periods, fluctuated between circa two and five, usually slightly below the Prussian and the national average. The homicide rate based on coroners' inquests was also almost always lower in Berlin and other major cities than the Prussian or the national rate.

These German rates are in line with other comparatively nonviolent northern European countries and are considerably below American rates in the same period. In a recent article tracing Swedish crime rates from the fourteenth century to the present, the Swedish historian Eva Österberg argues, for example, that Sweden had an annual homicide conviction rate between six and nine per million inhabitants between the 1880s and 1920; and, in an essay analyzing Dutch homicide rates from the fifteenth century to the present, the Dutch historian Pieter Spierenburg argues that the Dutch rate hovered around five per million inhabitants in the same period.[1] Although there are no trustworthy national statistics for late-nineteenth-century America, the American historian Roger Lane, in his book on suicide, accident, and murder in nineteenth-century Philadelphia and in a subsequent article on the topic, found turn-of-the-century Philadelphia to have had an annual rate of twenty-seven, which is several times that of Berlin and the rest of Germany in the same period.[2]

Although neither the foregoing figures nor any crime figures are abso-

---

[1] Eva Österberg, "Criminality, Social Control, and the Early Modern State: Evidence and Interpretations in Scandinavian Historiography," *Social Science History* 16 (1992): 77. Pieter Spierenburg, "Long-Term Trends in Homicide: Theoretical Reflections and Dutch Evidence, 15th–20th Centuries," in Eric A. Johnson and Eric H. Monkkonen, eds., *Violent Crime in Town and Country since the Middle Ages* (forthcoming). For his calculation of the homicide rate in late-nineteenth-century Holland, Spierenburg relied upon evidence presented in a recent article by Herman Franke, "Geweldscriminaliteit in Nederland. Een historisch-sociologische analyse," *Amsterdams Sociologisch Tijdschrift* 18 (1991): 13–45. See Durkheim's classic work, *Suicide: A Study in Sociology* (London, 1952), p. 353; Durkheim found Germany and Holland to have the lowest rates of homicide in Europe.

[2] Roger Lane, *Violent Death in the City: Suicide, Accident and Murder in Nineteenth Century Philadelphia* (Cambridge, Mass., 1979). Roger Lane, "Urban Homicide in the Nineteenth Century: Some Lessons for the Twentieth," in James A. Inciardi and Charles E. Faupel, eds., *History and Crime: Implications for Criminal Justice Policy* (London, 1980), pp. 91–109.

lutely comparable, one can be quite sure that the amount and level of interpersonal violence in the Kaiserreich was far below that which was experienced in the more distant past or is presently being experienced in many societies today. Using the careful estimates of scholars like Ted Robert Gurr, Lawrence Stone, Eva Österberg, Pieter Spierenburg, and others, the German homicide rates in the decades around 1900, irrespective of how they are calculated, were up to one hundred to five hundred times lower than the rates of late medieval Europe.[3]

The recent effort to reconstruct historical homicide and other crime rates has been fueled by scholars' long-standing goal of trying to understand the causes of crime, which historians have always believed, and many sociologists now believe, can only be done by placing current problems in a historical perspective. It has also benefited from a renewed excitement over modernization and other socioeconomic and cultural theories of the genesis and significance of crime, which Norbert Elias first developed in the middle decades of this century, and which scholars like Michel Foucault, Gurr, Stone, and others have recently generated.[4] Whereas, until the last couple of years, the empirical evidence to test these theories was limited almost solely to England, a cluster of scholars organized loosely in the European-based International Association for the History of Crime and Criminal Justice, such as Österberg, Spierenburg, J. A. Sharpe, Jan Sundin, Herman Diederiks, and others, have added comparable data from several other national and regional contexts.[5] Their work demonstrates quite conclusively

---

3 Ted Robert Gurr, "Historical Trends in Violent Crime: A Critical Review of the Evidence, *Crime and Justice: An Annual Review of Research* 3 (1981): 295–353. Lawrence Stone, "Interpersonal Violence in English Society, 1300–1980," *Past and Present* 101 (1983): 22–33; and "Homicide and Violence," in his *The Past and the Present Revisited* (London, 1987), pp. 295–310; Österberg, "Criminality, Social Control, and the Early Modern State"; Spierenburg, "Long-Term Trends in Homicide." See also J. S. Cockburn, "Patterns of Violence in English Society: Homicide in Kent, 1560–1985," *Past and Present* 130 (1991): 70–106; J. A. Sharpe, "The History of Violence in England: Some Observations," *Past and Present* 108 (1985): 206–15; and Sharpe, "Crime in England: Long-Term Trends and the Problem of Modernization," in Johnson and Monkkonen, *Violent Crime in Town and Country since the Middle Ages.* Comparing Germany's homicide rates for 1991, computed by the Bundeskriminalamt, and published in a recent *Stern* magazine essay, with those of the period under study here, Germany's turn-of-the-century homicide rate was at least several times lower than it is today as well. See the somewhat sensational article in the popular *Stern* magazine on Germany's recent alarming crime figures: "Tatort Grossstadt," January 14, 1993, pp. 67–80.
4 Norbert Elias, *The Civilizing Process,* vols. 1 and 2 (Oxford, 1982); Michel Foucault, *Discipline and Punish: The Birth of the Prison* (New York, 1979). Elias's work, first published in the late 1930s and somewhat unheralded for several decades, has been rediscovered. Several papers communicated the importance of Elias's work for present scholarship at a lively session on modernization and crime at the November 1991 annual meeting of the Social Science History Association in New Orleans. The 1993 annual meeting in Baltimore has devoted two round-table sessions to Elias's work and the problem of modernization and crime.
5 For Österberg, Sharpe, and Spierenburg references, see note 3 above. Jan Sundin, *För Gud, Staten och Folket. Brott och rättskipning i Sverige 1600–1840* (Lund, 1992). Many of his findings are presented in

that, in every case studied, there was a long-term decline in homicidal and, likely, other forms of interpersonal violence dating from at least the late Middle Ages to the twentieth century.

Although this evidence appears to confirm some of Elias's arguments that a "civilizing process" took place over the long haul of European history, at least in terms of violent acts among citizens, and at least until the twentieth century, it does not prove Foucault's and others' theories about a modernization process in which patterns of crime shifted with the rise of bourgeois society from "violence to theft." Stone has perhaps stated the theory most clearly: the "sociologically based explanation for the decline of crimes of violence over the past five centuries would link it to a shift from a feudal to a bourgeois society. In the former, honor and status are the most prized attributes, and crimes are therefore directed against the person; in the latter, money and market relationships form the basis of social organization, and crimes are therefore directed against property; hence the progressive shift over the centuries from the one to the other as society modernizes."[6]

Although it sounds logical enough, the most recent evidence from the Dutch, Swedish, and English cases does not demonstrate a consistent, long-term increase in theft and other property offenses.[7] Furthermore, the theory does not account, as both Richard Evans and Helmut Thome have argued, for either twentieth-century political violence under the Nazis and Soviets or for the post–World War II upsurges of violent crime in many American and European cities.[8]

Most significantly, perhaps, the present study is one of the first to test

---

English-language form in his article, "For God, State and People: Crime and Local Justice in Preindustrial Sweden," in Johnson and Monkkonen, *Violent Crime in Town and Country since the Middle Ages*. Herman Diederiks, president of the International Association for the History of Crime and Criminal Justice, has written extensively on preindustrial Dutch criminality. See his new article in the above volume, "Urban and Rural Criminal Justice and Criminality in the Netherlands since the Middle Ages."

6 Stone, "Homicide and Violence," p. 304.
7 Österberg's Swedish evidence, for example, shows that theft offenses have only risen consistently since the 1950s, as theft rates in the early 1900s were at the same level she reports for Stockholm in the late fifteenth century. See her "Criminality, Social Control, and the Early Modern State," pp. 79–80. J. A. Sharpe has argued this point in several essays about the history of English crime. Spierenburg also makes this point in his recent essay on Dutch homicide trends. See notes 1 and 3 above.
8 Richard J. Evans, "Öffentlichkeit und Autorität. Zur Geschichte der Hinrichtungen in Deutschland vom Allgemeinen Landrecht bis zum Dritten Reich," in Heinz Reif, ed., *Räuber, Volk und Obrigkeit. Studien zur Geschichte der Kriminalität in Deutschland seit dem 18. Jahrhundert* (Frankfurt am Main, 1984), p. 245. Helmut Thome, "Gesellschaftliche Modernisierung und Kriminalität. Zum Stand der sozialhistorischen Kriminalitätsforschung," *Zeitschrift für Soziologie* 21 (1992): 226. Spierenburg calculates that Amsterdam's annual homicide rate in the last three years of the 1980s was sixty per million inhabitants compared with five at the beginning of the century. Spierenburg, "Long-Term Trends in Homicide."

empirically the modernization thesis during the period of the industrial revolution, when the change in crime patterns from "violence to theft" should be most dramatic. If the modernization theory were to hold for the German case, one would expect to find an increase in property offenses and a decrease in violent offenses, as Germany moved from a premodern and largely rural, feudal society to a modern, urban, bourgeois-capitalistic society in the course of the nineteenth and early twentieth centuries. Of course there is considerable debate over whether bourgeois values, practices, and power elites ever really triumphed in nineteenth-century Germany.[9] But this debate is primarily about the degree of bourgeois triumph and about whether the checkered struggle of the German bourgeoisie was in reality so different from that of other societies as the exponents of the German *Sonderweg* (separate path of development) thesis have argued. And, as few people on either side of the debate would contest that nineteenth-century Germany became more capitalistic and more bourgeois over time, the more bourgeois capitalistic Germany of the late nineteenth and early twentieth centuries should have had a rise in property crimes and a decline in violence. But this did not occur. Even though some property offenses like fraud and embezzlement either held steady or increased moderately, the most common property offense, simple theft, declined markedly from the late 1850s until the First World War. And violent crimes like assault and battery, homicide, and rape climbed upward throughout the nineteenth century, from at least the mid-1830s, and perhaps even earlier.

At the least, these findings point out the dubious nature of sociological theorems like "modernization theory," which do not take into account the particularities of individual historical experience. Furthermore, they imply that there may be serious reason to question some of the conclusions of those scholars who previously have argued that their evidence supports the modernization theory of crime. Howard Zehr, whose work on nineteenth-century Germany and France is probably the most significant study of modernization and crime in the same period as my own, argued that homicide was on the decline in late nineteenth- and early-twentieth-century France

---

9 The argument that Germany followed a *Sonderweg* (special path) by having a "feudalized" bourgeoisie and becoming only partially modernized is common to much of German historical scholarship. Two prominent uses of this argument are found in Hans-Ulrich Wehler, *Das deutsche Kaiserreich 1871–1918* (Göttingen, 1973); and Ralph Dahrendorf, *Society and Democracy in Germany* (London, 1968). The leaders of the argument against this thesis are the British historians David Blackbourn and Geoff Eley. See their *Mythen deutscher Geschichtsschreibung: Die gescheiterte bürgerliche Revolution von 1848* (Frankfurt, 1980) and, in English, *The Peculiarities of German History* (Oxford, 1984). For an intelligent review of the debate, see Richard J. Evans, "The Myth of Germany's Missing Revolution," in his *Rethinking German History: Nineteenth-Century Germany and the Origins of the Third Reich* (London, 1987), pp. 93–122.

and Germany.[10] But this was possible because he looked only at court records, which reflected only a softening trend in criminal prosecution and not a real decline in the actual incidence of homicide.

Related to the modernization theory, and equally as questionable, are theories based on the supposed unsettling processes of urbanization and industrialization encountered by societies undergoing modernization. These range from nearly hysterical notions held by clerics and ideologues about the infernal attributes of noisome modern cities to classical conceptions of the anomie and dislocations engendered by urban and industrial change, and the mental pressures imposed by the population density and anonymity of the metropolis. Again the German evidence does not fit. Neither dynamic factors such as population growth, urban growth, or industrial growth nor static measures of population density or the size of cities had anything to do with explaining the crime trends. Violence was always just as prevalent, and often more so, in the countryside as it was in the city, and big cities were no more violent than smaller ones. Theft offenses may have been more numerous in the city than in the village, and this may help to support a structural theory which posits that city populations are more concerned with property and cities have more to steal, so they may provide better breeding grounds for property offenses than the less materialistic countryside. But the decline in the rate of theft offenses in both city and countryside in Imperial Germany makes it doubtful that cities promote more property offenses. Furthermore, the German evidence shows that the perceived surplus of theft offenses in cities may have become more noticeable over time due to the particular economic and ethnic problems that many urban centers encountered around the turn of the century and to increasing efforts on the part of the German authorities to punish their socialist and other urban political adversaries.

The arguments that fit best with the German evidence hinge on hardship, ethnicity, and values. Economic difficulties were significant in explaining both time-series trends in property offenses and the variation of both property and personal offenses in German communities – small and large, growing and declining, industrial and pastoral – at different points in time. Economic hardship was also instrumental in explaining the differential impact of ethnicity, particularly when it accompanied social stigmatization and political repression. Communities with significant Polish and Lithuanian minorities, or in some cases majorities, had much higher than average crime rates.

---

10 Zehr, *Crime and the Development of Modern Society: Patterns of Crime in Nineteenth Century Germany and France* (London, 1976).

But they also had serious economic difficulties, and their Slavic minorities often suffered from severe discrimination. The other ethnic minorities of the Reich – Danes, Dutch, French, Belgians, Wends, and Italians – appeared to have crime rates that were no higher than, and often lower than, the German ethnic majority population. But this was related to their solvent economic status and their greater acceptance by German society. Hence ethnicity did make a major difference, but only insofar as it was tied to economic hardship, social stigmatization, and political repression.

These findings jibe closely with Lane's American observations. He found that the perceived rise in post–World War II American homicide rates in Philadelphia was directly associated with the increasing size and poverty of the black community in Philadelphia. Almost all other ethnic groups in Philadelphia had no increase in their homicide rates at all, as the overall white rate held absolutely steady from the mid-nineteenth century to the mid-1970s.[11] Being "ethnic" is not important; being a poor and discriminated-against person is very important.

What society thinks and what it values or does not value may hold the other key to explaining criminal trends. Although Ted Robert Gurr argues that a shift in cultural values does more than anything else to account for the decline in violence in Great Britain from the fourteenth through the nineteenth centuries, and Lawrence Stone and others nod in at least partial agreement,[12] it is very difficult to obtain a precise measure of feelings and mentalities. As V. A. C. Gatrell has stated in regard to the decline of violence in Britain: "We are forced . . . to explain the decline in terms of heavy generalizations about the 'civilizing' effects of religion, education and environmental reform."[13] Our task is made all the more difficult in that violence in Germany did not decrease, despite the great changes and reforms of the nineteenth century. Indeed, the increasing incidence of interpersonal violence in Imperial Germany reflected a society that was trying desperately to hold on to aristocratic tradition, power, and privilege while at the same time being threatened by domestic reform from within and foreign pressure from without. The German press and popular magazines appeared to become increasingly concerned with violent acts; the German nation became increasingly more imperialistic and heavy handed in its foreign policy; strike

---

11 Lane reports that the white rate of homicide in Philadelphia was 2.7 per 100,000 inhabitants per year around the turn of the century, 1.8 in 1948–52, and 2.8 in 1972–4. The black rate in these three periods was 7.5, 24.6, and 64.2. Lane, "Urban Homicide in the Nineteenth Century," p. 164.
12 See Gurr, "Historical Trends in Violent Crime," and Stone, "Homicide and Violence."
13 V. A. C. Gatrell, "The Decline of Theft and Violence in Victorian and Edwardian England," in V. A. C. Gatrell, B. Lenman, and G. Parker, eds., *The Social History of Crime in Western Europe since 1500* (London, 1980), p. 300.

activity increased; the socialist vote multiplied; and women moved into the work force. Many of these things happened in other societies like England and America, but not always, and perhaps not to the same degree.[14]

The threat to the old order represented by the emergence of the women's movement and the growing economic importance of women certainly helped to account for the growing proportion of homicides committed against women and for the increase in rape offenses. Still the importance of gender and age needs far more study, as both factors are always of great significance in the genesis of crime trends. A better understanding of the different ways in which a particular society at a particular point in time values and views women and youth could explain much of the ebb and flow in criminal trends.

The preceding discussion of the importance of values in criminal trends begins to suggest ways in which the study of criminal trends, and of criminal justice in general, sheds light on the history of a particular society. The preoccupation of all segments of German society with honor and *Rechtsstaatlichkeit* (vaguely defined as correctness or lawfulness), demonstrated so clearly in the press and in popular literature, provides additional insight. Germany was a lawful, honorable, and obedient society, to be sure, but sometimes to a fault. The desire to prove oneself honorable perhaps led many to demonstrate this by showing others to be dishonorable, and this can get a person, and a society, in trouble. German intellectuals must shoulder some responsibility for not educating the public about the real roots of disorder and criminality, which lay on German soil. And many of them, and large segments of the popular media, did the society a disservice by constantly pointing the finger of blame at foreigners and supposed enemies both outside of and inside Germany. Furthermore, the constant casting of accusations by political groups at their political enemies, common practice for both the Left and the Right in the ideological spectrum, as being responsible for

---

14 In a study that argues that tension between men and women may have decreased in late-nineteenth-century Britain as working-class women came to accept more the bourgeois ideal of staying in the home, see Nancy Tomes, "A 'Torrent of Abuse': Crimes of Violence between Working Class Men and Women in London, 1840–1875," *Journal of Social History* 11 (1978): 328–45. For the German women's movement, see Richard J. Evans, "Liberalism and Society: The Feminist Movement and Social Change," in his *Rethinking German History*, pp. 221–47; and Evans, *The Feminist Movement in Germany 1894–1933* (London, 1976). On tensions in industry, see Klaus Saul, *Staat, Industrie, Arbeiterbewegung im Kaiserreich* (Düsseldorf, 1974). On the strike movement, see Charles Tilly, Louise Tilly, and Richard Tilly, *The Rebellious Century 1830–1930* (Cambridge, Mass., 1975); and Klaus Tenfelde and Heinrich Volkmann, eds., *Streik: Zur Geschichte des Arbeitskampfes in Deutschland während der Industrialisierung* (Munich, 1981). And for an excellent review of the broad literature on labor and social history in Germany, see Geoff Eley, "Labor History, Social History, *Alltagsgeschichte*: Experience, Culture, and the Politics of the Everyday – A New Direction for German Social History?" *The Journal of Modern History* 61 (1989): 297–343.

illegal activities, not only served to fractionalize German politics, it also served to make Germans uncritical of themselves and prevented them from confronting the real problems of their own making. But the frantic desire of each political constellation to prove itself to be the most upright suggests how nearly all Germans shared in accepting the narrow and overlegalistic interpretation of what was right and wrong in Imperial Germany. Karl Dietrich Bracher, among others, has illustrated how such narrow legalistic thinking was later transmogrified into one of Hitler's greatest weapons, which he used so skillfully in his "legal revolution."[15]

Another way in which the study of criminal justice and criminal activity can heighten the understanding of history can be found by employing one of the leading concepts of radical criminology. Its practitioners argue that recorded rates of crime often reveal more about the values and power relationships of a society than they do about criminality and its causes. But if one believes that more than just the ruling elite should be responsible for the acts of a society, a society's laws and criminal justice activities may be seen to be a reflection of more than just the power elite. A more moderate stand, which still uses the tools of radical criminology, would be to consider the recorded crime rates as measures of the values of society in general. Hence, the lack of a city–crime relationship suggests that Germans valued their cities more highly than have many other societies. The high rates of crime in Polish and Lithuanian and the low rates of crime in Danish, Dutch, Belgian, and French areas in Germany underscore the deep biases against Eastern European countries and peoples that lurked in German society. The high crime rates in political but not in normal criminal offenses of working-class people point to a society severely rent by dissension over its fundamental goals. The increasing victimization of urban and single women reflects a society that was fundamentally threatened by any breaks with tradition.

In sum, under the veneer of public orderliness and safety in the late nineteenth and early twentieth centuries lay a troubled and divided society with an irritable and potentially violent spirit. Controlling individual acts of crime committed "against" German society would later prove to be far easier for Germany than controlling greater acts of crime committed "by" German society. It is easy for a police state to control crime. But who controls *it*? Imperial Germany was not quite a police state, but its police had exceptional numbers and powers. Its judges, appointed by an authoritarian elite, often dispensed conservative, discriminatory justice, especially to the

---

15 Karl Dietrich Bracher, *The German Dictatorship: The Origins, Structure, and Effects of National Socialism* (New York, 1970), pp. 191–8.

detriment of stigmatized ethnic minorities and socialist workers. Most citizens dutifully accepted non–popularly derived regulations infringing on their personal freedom. The press built a tradition of selective, ideological reporting of even mundane individual behavior. Critics and nonconformists were frequently silenced by the use of extensive libel laws made possible by an overdetermined concern for honor. *Ruhe und Ordnung* (silence and order) were defining characteristics of German society.

Index

Aachen, 151, 171
abortion, 28
administration, 17, 74, 143
 higher, 21
 of justice, 21
 local, 20–1
acquittals, 72, 83, 122
 in murder and manslaughter cases, 130
 table of rates, 123
adultery, 28
age, 107, 191–8
Allgemeine Zeitung, 86, 86n
Allgemeines Landrecht, 24
Alsace-Lorraine, 31n
America. *See* United States of America
Amtsgericht (county court), 42
Anhalt-Dessen, 24n
Anklageschrift. See indictment
Annales, 10
Amsterdam, 1, 17, 114, 115
Arnsberg, 151
arson, 24n, 28, 98, 134
Aschaffenburg, Gustav, 51, 159, 173, 193–5, 198–9, 205–6, 208
assault and battery, 72, 73, 80, 86, 117, 168, 233
 regional distribution of, 151, 156
 roots in countryside, 180
attitudes. *See* popular opinion and crime
attorneys, 18, 21, 22, 39–48
Austria, 22, 30, 120

Bade, Klaus, 157
Baker, Ray Stannard, 15–17, 160
Balzac, Honore de, 54
bankruptcy, 204
Barmen, 170, 178

Bavaria, 24, 31n, 61, 117, 119, 149, 151, 156, 206
Bavarian code, 24
Bebel, August, 17, 30
Beethoven, Ludwig van, 57
Belgians, 158, 174, 235, 237
Berliner Tageblatt, 51, 58, 62–74, 78, 83–8, 90
Berlin, 1, 4, 5, 15n, 31, 33, 34, 35, 37, 58, 75
 in crime novels, 99, 103, 105–6
 crime rates, 164–6
 lack of poverty in, 161
 means of homicide in, 226–7
 murder rate in, 230
 newspapers, 56–7, 61–75
 rate of violent crime in, 134
 size of police force, 35n
 women's homicide rates in, 220
Berlin, Lucie, 78, 95
Bernstein, Eduard, 142
Bismarck, Otto von, 2, 5, 17, 26, 27n, 48, 57, 120, 121, 142, 143
Blackbourn, David, 4, 7, 111
Blacks, 97, 146, 235
Blasius, Dirk, 7, 31n, 117, 119, 125, 143, 163
 study of women's crime rates, 188–9
 table of statistics generated by, 118
Bochum, 135
Bonn, 170
bourgeoisie. *See* liberals
Bracher, Karl Dietrich, 237
Bremen, 76, 171
Breslau, 149, 156, 171
Bromberg, 149, 151
Bücher, Karl, 159

239

Carolina (Constitutio Criminalis Carolina), 23
Catholics, 19, 30, 171
  Center Party, 56. See also *Kreuzzeitung*
  crime rates of, 201–6
  and homicide, 222–3
censorship, 3
census data, 5, 6, 174
Chemnitz, 171
Chevalier, Louis, 54, 96, 107
"Chicago School," 9–10
children, 28
churches, 8, 26
cities
  bias of conservatives against, 8, 79, 83
  as centers of vice, 159
  "Chicago School" study of, 9–10
  crime correlations with socioeconomic variables in, 169–70
  crime statistics in major cities, 154–5, 165, 170
  foreign visitors' observations on, 15–16, 160–1
  Germany's comparatively low crime rates in, 16, 134, 160, 171
  growth of, 4. See also urbanization
  and incorporation of surrounding territories, 176–8
  lack of a dominant metropolis, 5
  as a literary theme, 54, 95, 102, 105–6, 107
  Marxist views of, 9
  police reporting in, 58
  Ruhr cities' crime rates, 135
  theft rates higher than violence rates, 166, 171
  and theories of crime causation, 8–13
  violence levels today, 1
  violence relatively absent, 171, 229–30, 231
Classen, Walter, 159
Coburg, 24n
Code Penal, 24, 25
Colmar, 170, 171
Cologne, 1, 4, 31n, 134n, 151, 156, 165, 171, 220
  reasons for rise in crime rate in, 176–8
communists, 2, 4, 26. See also Social Democratic Party
conservatives, 8, 21, 143
  and arguments concerning the causation of crime, 146

Conservative Party, 21, 56, 61–74. See also *Kreuzzeitung*
  crime reporting in conservative press, 78–83
  literary treatment of crime and justice by, 96–9
  stigmatization of cities, 158–9
constitution, 20
courts, 7, 18, 37, 39–45
  cartoons of, 92–3
  criminal procedure used in. See criminal procedure
  district court (*Amtsgericht*), 41
  hierarchy of, 41–2
  rights of defendants, 40
  superior court (*Landgericht*), 42
  superior court of appeals (*Oberlandesgericht*), 42
Code of Criminal Procedure, 41, 42
Code of Judicial Organization, 41
crime rates
  and attitudes, 137
  and industrial work force, 211
  long-term decline in Europe, 162
  and death rates, 175–6
  and ethnicity, 171–81, 221, 234–5
  and hardship, 171–81, 234
  and food prices and economic conditions, 138–41, 195–6
  geography of. See regions
  Germany's comparatively low level of, 133–4
  maps of, 149–50
  and occupations, 206–12
  and poverty, 137–8, 164, 171–2, 234. See also crime rates: and hardship
  and political factors, 22, 141–3, 146
  problems in the concept of, 162
  and regions, 148–58
  and religion, 201–6
  in Ruhr cities, 135, 155
  in rural areas, 145, 148, 163, 166
  of women, 151, 156, 188–91
  yearly trends
    prior to 1871, 116–20
    after 1871, 120–6, 137–43
    in property crime, 134–7, 138
    in violent crime, 126–34, 143
  of youth, 121, 151, 191–2
criminal code, 6, 18, 22–30, 39
  Bavarian Code of 1813, 24

French Code Penal, 24
Prussian Code of 1851, 24, 25
criminal intent, 29
criminal negligence, 29
criminal procedure, 6, 18, 39–45
criminal statistics, 6, 53, 109, 117n, 120–2. *See also* crime rates
   coroners, 130, 130n, 131–4, 179
   of courts, 121, 179
   "dark figure" in, 118
   organization of German statistics, 148
   of police, 121
Crites, Laura, 185
Czechs, 101

Dahrendorf, Ralph, 111, 143
Danes, 56, 158, 174, 178, 179, 235, 237
Darkehmen, 148
Danzig, 149, 171
Darmstadt, 170
Dawson, William, 173
death rate, 168t, 169t, 175–6
defendants, 37, 40, 42, 43–5, 48, 71, 86
Delbrück, Hans, 38n
Denmark, 149
Dessau, 171
Detroit, 1, 114
Die Gartenlaube, 89, 100
Dickens, Charles, 54, 57, 95, 99
Diederiks, Herman, 231
divorce, 72, 198–201, 227
Dostoevsky, Fyodor, 95
Dresden, 31n, 58, 160
dueling, 143
Duisburg, 135
Düsseldorf, 31n, 134n, 135, 151, 156, 171, 220
Durkheim, Emile, 9, 10, 113, 133, 142, 157, 159, 206, 216–17, 229
Dutch, 158, 174, 178, 179, 235, 237. *See also* Holland

East Prussia, 136
Elberfeld, 171
Eley, Geoff, 4, 111
Elias, Norbert, 11–13, 114–15, 231, 232
embezzlement, 73, 82, 137, 198, 233
Engelsing, Rolf, 55, 75
England, 23, 26, 35, 37, 39, 49, 54, 95, 145, 161, 229, 236. *See also* Great Britain

crime reporting in, 58
female victims in, 226
crime patterns over the long term, 232
Essex (county in England), 115
Evans, Richard J., 7, 23, 49, 55, 124, 232
executions, 23, 27, 48. *See also* punishment: capital
extortion, 24n

First World War. *See* World War One
Fischer, Fritz, 7, 17
Fliegende Blätter, 90
Fontane, Theodor, 55, 57, 95, 99–102
Fosdick, Raymond, 29, 58, 160
Foucault, Michel, 6, 11–13, 23, 49, 114–15, 115n, 135, 231, 232
France, 5, 6, 23, 26, 39, 49, 54, 96, 110, 120
   code of criminal procedure used in, 42
   crime rates along French border, 149
   crime reporting on, 87, 88
   crime studies on, 161
   newspaper reporting in, 56
Franco-Prussian War, 142
Frankfurt am Main, 1, 170
Frankfurt Parliament of 1848, 47–8
fraud, 73, 86, 137, 198, 204, 233
French, 158, 174, 179, 235, 237. *See also* France
Freud, Sigmund, 184
Friedrich II, 57
Fuld, Ludwig, 202–3, 204, 205

Gatrell, V. A. C., 235
Gelsenkirchen, 170
gender. *See* women
Gendarmerie, 32
Gestapo, 27, 40
Giessen, 170
Gotha, 24n
Great Britain, 5, 6, 35, 110, 146. *See also* England
Greece, 88
Guelphs, 56
Gumbinnen, 148, 149, 151
Gurr, Ted Robert, 113, 231

Hall, Alex, 49, 59
Hamburg, 4, 7, 35n, 55, 89, 124, 157, 171
   decline of crime rate, 176
Hannover, 151

Hauptmann, Gerhart, 55, 95, 96, 102–6
Hentig, Hans von, 213, 214, 216–17
Herne, 173
Heydekrug, 148
Hitler, Adolf, 2, 11, 17, 27, 39, 158, 237
Hochstadt, Steve, 157
Hohenzollern, 75
Holland, 6, 133, 149
　murder rates in, 229–30, 232
Holmes, Sherlock, 145, 164
homicide. *See* murder
honor, 8, 12, 61, 72, 87, 111, 133, 143, 238
　and decline of violent crime, 232
　and Jews, 204
　as a literary theme, 97, 98, 99, 102, 107
　in modernization theory, 115, 232
Hugo, Victor, 95

Ignatieff, Michael, 49
illegitimacy, 28, 196
illiteracy, 196
incest, 28
indictment, 43, 59
infanticide, 28, 130, 223–4
infant mortality, 161
intellectuals, 236
International Association for the History of Crime and Criminal Justice (IAHCCJ), 13n, 114, 231
Italians, 179, 235
Italy, 89, 97, 133

Jackson, James, 157
Jarausch, Konrad H., 7, 48
Jena, 82
Jews, 2, 4, 8, 77, 79, 81, 82, 82n, 83, 158, 180
　crime rates, 201–5
　and homicide, 222
　and honor, 204
　lack of literary crime treatments of, 95
　murder rates, 204–5
Jones, Gareth Stedman, 10
judges, 3, 18, 22, 24, 27, 28, 39–45, 48, 50
　literary treatments of, 98–9, 101, 102, 103, 105
　Simplicissimus cartoons, 92–4
　social background of, 47
　training of, 46
Junkers, 8, 20, 47, 90, 105

Simplicissimus cartoon, 94
juries, 18, 45
juvenile delinquency. *See* youth

Kampfhoefner, Walter, 157
Karlsruhe, 171
Kater, Michael, 7
Kladderadatsch, 90
Klassenjustiz ("class-based justice"), 26, 76, 96, 104, 214
Klein, Doris, 184–5
Koblenz, 151
Königsberg, 149, 151, 156, 171
Konstanz, 149
Krefeld, 170
Kreistag (county assembly), 20
Kretzer, Max, 55, 95, 102–3
Kocka, Jürgen, 7, 111, 143
Kreuzzeitung, 57, 62–74, 78–83, 188
Krimininalstatistik (governmental criminal statistics), 6, 53, 121n

Landflucht, 157
Langbehn, Julius, 159
Landgericht (superior court), 42
Landkreise, 166, 169, 175–6
Landrat, 20–1, 32, 33
Lane, Roger, 113, 230, 235
law, 3, 4, 16, 17, 53, 112
　criminal, 22–30
　legal positivism, 3, 237
　regulating workers and work practices, 30, 124–6
　Roman, 18
lawyers. *See* attorneys
Leipzig, 75, 76, 157, 171, 176
Lees, Andrew, 159
libel, 3, 26, 27, 29, 39, 59, 61, 87, 133, 143, 204, 238
liberals, 8, 19, 21, 56, 61. *See also Berliner Tageblatt; Vossische Zeitung*
　crime reporting in the liberal press, 83–8
　degree of bourgeois triumph in Germany, 233
　treatment of crime and justice issues in literature by, 99–106
Liebknecht, Karl, 76
Lippe, 75
Liszt, Friedrich von, 193–5
Lithuania, 149
Lithuanians, 2, 71, 81

crime rates of, 178–9, 234, 237
  in literary treatments, 95, 98
  poverty of, 179–80
  stigmatization of, 110, 158, 173, 174
Liverpool, 160
Lombroso, Cesare, 184–5
London, 114, 161
"Long Depression," 166
Los Angeles, 114
Lübeck, 170
Lüdtke, Alf, 30
Lutherans, 61, 83
Luxembourg, 149

magazines, 56, 235
  crime reporting in, 88–95
Manchester, 38n
Mannheim, 171
Mannheim, Hermann, 185–6, 200, 206
manslaughter (*Totschlag*), 128–34
Marienwerder, 149
marriage, 198–201
Masurians, 179
May, Karl, 95, 97, 99, 102
Mayr, Georg von, 117, 117n, 119–20, 143
  table of statistics generated by, 118
McHale, Vincent, 195
media. *See* newspapers
Meldewesensystem (local registration system), 35–6
Mexicans, 97
migration, 156, 157–8
military, 21, 30, 32, 143
Minden, 151
modernization, 2, 8, 11, 12
  of German society, 111–12, 133, 143
  and juvenile delinquency, 194–5
  as theory for explaining crime patterns, 109–16, 134, 137, 143, 230, 232, 233
moral offenses, 28
Moore, Barrington, 111
Morrison, William D., 193
Münster, 151, 170
Müller, Ingo, 48
Mülheim-am-Rhein, 135
Mulhausen, 170, 171
Munich, 4, 31n, 78, 86, 157
murder, 6, 24, 27, 72, 83, 85, 86, 156, 204
  and age, 223–4
  comparison of Germany with other societies, 230

  decline over long term since Middle Ages, 232
  and ethnic homogeneity, 221
  and manslaughter, 24n, 73, 80, 81
  and marriage, 225–6
  in novels, 101
  roots in countryside, 180
  and religion, 222–3
  trends in prior to 1871, 120
  trends in Imperial Germany, 127–34, 233
  women's rates, 189
  and urbanization, 217–21

National Liberal Party, 56
Native Americans, 97
Nazi Germany, 3, 7, 17, 23, 27, 39, 40, 48, 111, 229, 232
  biases against cities, 159
  "legal revolution," 237
newspapers, 55–88, 235, 238
  circulation figures, 56–7
  regulations of, 59
New York City, 89
Niederbayern, 149

Oberbayern, 149
Oberhausen, 135
Oberlandesgericht (superior court of appeals), 42
occupations,
  and crime, 206–11
  women in workforce, 210
Oder River, 100
Österberg, Eva, 230, 231
Oldenburg, 151
Old Shatterhand, 97
Oppeln, 149, 151
Osnabrück, 151

Paris, 114
perjury, 24n, 204
Pfalz, 149
Philadelphia, 216, 230, 235
poaching, 73, 101, 104
Poland, 22, 149, 171
Poles, 2, 19, 21, 30, 38, 51, 57, 63, 71, 79, 81, 83, 87
  crime rates of, 178–9, 234, 237
  in crime literature, 95, 101, 105
  and "Germanization," 142, 174
  police surveillance of, 36–7, 82

Poles (cont.)
  Polish newspapers, 56
  poverty of, 179–80
  stigmatization of, 110, 158, 172, 173–4
police, 3, 7, 16, 18, 21, 22, 29, 30–8, 63, 78, 163
  Berlin police commissioners, 33
  brutality of, 30, 31n, 77, 87n
  militaristic nature of, 31–2
  ordinances, 26, 29, 37
  portrayed in crime novels, 101, 102, 104
  powers of surveillance, 35–6
  rural, 32
  Simplicissimus cartoon, 91
  statistics, 117n, 121, 124
politics
  constitution, 20
  crime as a political theme. See popular opinion and crime
  fractionalization of, 237
  political power in Germany, 19
  rural. See *Landrat*
  use of criminal law to enforce comformity, 29
Pollack, Otto, 185
popular opinion and crime,
  and conservative politics, 8
  in conservative press, 78–83
  in liberal press, 83–8
  in literature, 95–107
  in middle-class magazines, 88–95, 235
  in newspapers generally, 55–61, 235
  problems in measuring, 53–4
  in socialist press, 75–8
population growth, 156, 157
ports,
  as centers of crime, 171
Posen, 31n, 75, 136, 149, 151, 156, 171
poverty, 171–81, 234. See also crime rates
  as correlate of death, 175
  of Slavic minority population, 174
press. See newspapers
Preussische Statistik, 6
prisons and prisoners, 49–51, 83
Progressive Party, 56. See also *Berliner Tageblatt*
prosecutors, 18, 40, 43, 59
prostitution, 159
Protestants, 171
  crime rates of, 202–6
  and homicide, 222–3
Prussia, 20, 31, 119, 120, 131
  crime rates in Prussian northeast, 151, 155, 156, 171
  homicide rates in, 133–4
  House of Deputies, 21
  Slavs in, 173, 203, 206, 235
punishment, 24, 27, 29, 48–51
  capital, 24, 24n, 25, 130, 141. See also executions
  corporal, 24, 49
Puttkamer, Robert von, 20

Rabbe, Wilhelm, 55, 95, 99–100
radical criminology, 237
rape, 28, 139, 156, 233, 236
Rechtsstaat, 76
regions, 147–58
  changes in regional bases of, 157–8
  generation of criminal statistics on, 148
  maps used in analyzing crime trends, 148–50
  women's and youths' regional crime rates, 151, 156
Reichsgericht (supreme court), 42
Reichjustizamt (Reich Bureau of Justice), 121
Reichkriminalamt (Imperial Criminal Bureau), 202–3
Reichstag, 21
Reichstag Fire Decrees, 2
religion, 107, 124, 143
  and crime rates, 201–6
  and homicide, 222–3
resisting arrest, 28
Revolution of 1848, 112
Riehl, Wilhelm Heinrich, 158
robbery, 24n, 136
Roesner, E., 213, 214
Rostock, 171
Rothmann, David, 49
Royal Statistical Bureau, 148
Rugge, Christian, 158
Ruhr cities, 4, 135
Russia, 18, 71, 149, 171

Saul, Klaus, 124
Saxony, 31n
Saxony-Meiningen, 24n
Saxony-Weimar, 24n
Scandinavia, 6
Schenda, Rudolf, 96, 97
Schleswig, 149, 151, 178
Schöffengericht, 42

Schwarzburg-Rudolfstadt, 24n
Schwerin, 170
Schwurgericht (jury court), 43
Second International, 17
Sharpe, J. A., 231
Silesia, 100, 103, 104
Simplicissimus, 90–4
Slavs. *See* Lithuanians; Poles
socialists, 2, 3, 4, 8, 19, 21, 26, 30, 51, 143, 236
  antisocialist legislation, 2, 26, 26n, 75, 124
  lack of literary crime treatments of, 95
  police surveillance of, 36, 37
Social Democratic Party, 9, 17, 82
  publications of, 21n, 56, 57, 59, 61–78. *See also Vorwärts*
Social Science History Association, 13
sodomy, 28
Sondergerichte (Nazi "Special Courts"), 27, 27n, 40
Sonderweg thesis, 31n, 112, 233
Spain, 95, 97, 133
Spierenburg, Pieter, 230, 231
Sue, Eugene, 54
Starke, Wilhelm, 117, 119–20, 143, 211
  study of women's crime rates, 188–9
  table of statistics generated by, 118
Statistik des Deutschen Reichs, 6, 121n, 202
Stettin, 171
Stinchcombe, Arthur, 163
Stockholm, 1, 114, 115
Stone, Lawrence, 231, 232
"structural theory of crime," 163–4, 166
Stuttgart, 37, 76
Sudermann, Hermann, 54, 95, 97–9, 101, 102
Sundin, Jan, 231
Sweden, 161, 229–30, 232
swindling, 73, 82, 86, 137
Switzerland, 22, 149

Thackeray, William, 54, 99
theft, 73, 86, 163, 168
  decline of, 166, 233
  regional distribution of, 151, 156
  trends in after unification, 134–7
  trends in prior to unification, 118–20
  and women, 198
  of wood, 28, 29, 104, 163
Third Reich. *See* Nazi Germany
Thome, Helmut, 112, 232

Thuringia, 24n
Tilly, Charles, 113, 163
Tobias, J. J., 54, 96, 107
Tolstoy, Leo, 95, 100
Tomes, Nancy, 226
Tönnies, Ferdinand, 9, 113, 157, 159
torture, 23, 24
treason, 24, 24n
Trier, 151
Trollope, Anthony, 99
Trivialliteratur, 96–7
Turkey, 18

Übertretungen (minor infractions), 25, 25n, 37, 124–5
Ulk, 90
United States of America, 6, 10, 19, 23, 26, 35, 39, 49, 89, 95, 111, 146, 147, 161, 229, 235, 236
  criminal procedure in, 43
  criminal reporting in, 58
  divorce in, 227
  social theorists, 113–14
urbanization
  growth of German cities, 4
  and homicide, 217–21
  in late nineteenth century, 157
  as theory for explaining crime trends, 109, 110, 113–14, 143, 146, 158–71, 233

values
  and causation of crime, 234–7
Van Abbe, Derek, 90
victims, 102
  age of, 223–5
  in Berlin, 220
  and changing status of women, 212, 220
  and ethnicity, 221
  and marriage, 223, 225
  means of death, 226–7
  men, 217–19
  and religion, 222–3
  and urbanization, 217–20
  typology of, 213–14
  in Victorian England, 226
  women. *See* women
violence. *See* assault and battery; murder
Vizetelly, Henry, 15n, 161, 173
Volksgericht (Nazi supreme court), 40
Vom Fels zum Meer, 89

Voruntersuchung (preliminary judicial investigation), 43–4
Vorwärts, 56, 61–78
Vossische Zeitung, 57, 62–73, 83–8, 100

Waldeck, 75
Walker, Samuel, 19
war, 7, 142
Washington, D.C., 1, 114
Weber, Adolf, 159
Wehler, Hans-Ulrich, 7, 17, 111, 143
Weidlich, Karl, 30
Weimar, 170
Weimar Republic, 22, 23, 41, 138
  crime rates in, 126, 127t, 137
  criminal statistics in, 121n
  ministry of justice, 125
Wends, 179, 235
witnesses, 18
Westphalia, 136, 173
West Prussia, 136
Wilhelm II, 143
women, 3, 110, 142, 183–91, 236
  as agricultural workers, 210
  assault and battery rates, 189
  biases of criminology toward, 184–5
  and crime in America, 185
  crime rates in Weimar, 190–1
  crime statistics on, 121, 151, 156, 188–91
  economic activity of, 186–7, 210
  lack of literary crime treatments of, 95, 107
  murder rates, 189
  ratio of women's to men's homicide rates, 217–19
  regional patterns in crime, 151
  reporting of crime about, 89
  theft rates, 189
  as victims, 212–17, 226
  and violence, 191
Wolfgang, Marvin, 206
World War One, 29, 78, 122, 142
workers, 8, 51, 79. *See also* socialists; Social Democratic Party
  discriminatory laws against, 125. *See also Klassenjustiz*
  wages, 5
  policing of, 30
Worms, 171
Württemberg, 31n

youth, 28, 191–8
  crime statistics on, 121, 192, 194–8
  impact of urbanization and industrialization on, 192–5
  regional patterns in crime, 151

Zahn, Margaret, 216–17
Zehr, Howard, 11, 113, 116, 117, 118, 120, 126, 127, 134–5, 140, 142, 233
Zola, Emile, 54, 57, 95

Printed in the United States
5521